Exile Economics

Also by Ben Chu

Chinese Whispers: Why Everything You've
Heard About China is Wrong

Exile Economics

What Happens if Globalisation Fails

BEN CHU

BASIC BOOKS

LONDON

First published in Great Britain in 2025 by Basic Books UK
An imprint of John Murray Press

1

Text and figures copyright © Ben Chu 2025

The right of Ben Chu to be identified as the Author of the
Work has been asserted by him in accordance
with the Copyright, Designs and Patents Act 1988.

All rights reserved. No part of this publication may be reproduced, stored in a retrieval system, or transmitted, in any form or by any means without the prior written permission of the publisher, nor be otherwise circulated in any form of binding or cover other than that in which it is published and without a similar condition being imposed on the subsequent purchaser.

A CIP catalogue record for this title is available from the British Library

Hardback ISBN 9781399817165
Trade Paperback ISBN 9781399817172
ebook ISBN 9781399817189

Typeset in Janson Text LT Std by
Palimpsest Book Production Ltd, Falkirk, Stirlingshire

Printed and bound in Great Britain by Clays Ltd, Elcograf S.p.A.

John Murray Press policy is to use papers that are natural, renewable and recyclable products and made from wood grown in sustainable forests. The logging and manufacturing processes are expected to conform to the environmental regulations of the country of origin.

Carmelite House
50 Victoria Embankment
London EC4Y 0DZ

www.basicbooks.uk

John Murray Press, part of Hodder & Stoughton Limited
An Hachette UK company

The authorised representative in the EEA is Hachette Ireland,
8 Castlecourt Centre, Dublin 15, D15 XTP3, Ireland
(email: info@hbgi.ie)

For Hattie

Contents

Introduction	1
1. The Creed	9
2. Origins	35
3. Food	57
4. Energy	83
5. Silicon	117
6. People	139
7. Steel	163
8. Medicine	189
9. The Future	211
Acknowledgements	227
Notes	229
Index	295

Introduction

Nations are turning inwards. Barriers to international trade have been rising for years – and more are cropping up almost every day. The president of the United States has promised 'protection' for American workers through taxes on imports known as tariffs. He wants a clampdown on immigration and the mass 'repatriation' of Mexicans and 'criminal aliens'.[1] He has confidently predicted this will all lead to domestic 'employment and prosperity'.[2] 'There never has been a time in the history of the United States when tariff protection was more essential to the welfare of the American people than at present,' the president declares.[3]

Dozens of nations have petitioned Washington to change course and not to put up taxes on imports from their countries. More than 1,000 eminent American economists have written to the president, imploring him to think again.[4] But the opinions of the rest of the world have been ignored; the experts have been sidelined. He has imposed tariffs anyway.

And now a second wave of import taxes is crashing onto the traumatised shores of the global economy. Countries are lurching further into protectionism. The French government makes it clear to the US ambassador in Paris that they are prepared to wage 'economic war' against Washington if they have to.[5] The British prime minister is in 'despair' at the absence of cooperation from the White House.[6] But the man in the Oval Office is unmoved and describes European leaders as a 'bunch of bastards'.[7]

New tariffs are being imposed almost everywhere – from Canada, to Britain, to Germany, to France, to Japan, to Mexico, to Switzerland, to Italy, to Spain, to India, to China, to Australia, to Argentina, to

Brazil, to South Africa and New Zealand. 'There has been a veritable panic, which has piled new tariffs on old. There has never before been such a wholesale and widespread retreat from international economic co-operation,' laments the world's central multilateral organisation.[8]

There are rampant fears of surplus manufacturing goods being dumped on other countries at prices below the cost of production, suffocating local firms with unfair competition. Corporations are lobbying for further protection. Cross-border investment is dwindling too. Some nations are trading more within new discrete geopolitical blocs, though more in anticipation of a potential future conflict rather than any great spirit of solidarity. A delegation of economic experts warns that 'a world-wide adoption of ideals of national self-sufficiency' seems to be in train, something that will surely crush everyone's living standards.[9]

International summits to negotiate an end to the trade wars have failed. There is a vacuum of global leadership, as America eschews its natural role. Fear and insecurity are rife. It feels like it's every nation for itself. There is confusion and demoralisation. A leading British intellectual changes his mind and suggests tariffs and national economic isolation might actually be more conducive to peace than globalisation.[10] The far right in Europe is pleased to see attempts at international coordination flounder, sensing an opportunity to seize power amid the crumbling of multilateralism. Democracy is perceived to be under threat. Authoritarian regimes in Asia are flexing their muscles.

The year? 1933. We have been here before.

The echoes of the 1930s in our own era are not, of course, exact. We are not dealing with mass unemployment, or monetary breakdown, or the collapse of banks, as the populations and governments in Europe and America were in the interwar period. We are not in the midst of a Great Depression, with slumping prices. Indeed, the great complaint today is that prices – and the overall cost of living – are too high. The rising authoritarian power in the East is not Japan but China. And one of the most pressing global challenges today but unknown in 1930 is the risk of runaway global warming. But the resonances are nevertheless unmistakable.

The vast new curtain of protective tariffs drawn around America by the US Congress in June 1930 – named after the senator Reed Smoot from Utah and congressman Willis Hawley from Oregon – provoked opposition from just about every professional economist in America, just as Donald Trump's 2024 campaign pledge to put tariffs of 20 per cent on every import into America did. 'We are convinced that increased protective duties would be a mistake. They would operate, in general, to increase the prices which domestic consumers would have to pay,' intoned a letter signed by more than 1,000 US economists in May 1930. Eighty-eight years later, 1,000 economists sent a similar letter to Donald Trump. And, in that, they literally reprinted the arguments from 1930 to underline that the economic case against tariffs had not changed in the intervening period.[11]

Smoot-Hawley was signed into law by the Republican president Herbert Hoover despite the pleas of America's trading partners in Europe. And most of those countries hiked their own tariffs in response – not necessarily because they thought it would bring them much benefit, but because they felt they simply had no choice if they wanted to prevent their own producers being swamped by a flood of goods newly excluded from other countries and to retain any international negotiating leverage in a protectionist world. It was this dynamic that prompted the British economist Joan Robinson to coin the phrase 'beggar-thy-neighbour' in the context of international trade, drawing an analogy with the card game in which the way to win is by imposing losses on the other player.

The British finance minister, Neville Chamberlain, articulated this zero-sum logic in a speech to Parliament in June 1933.

> Most of us, I am sure, regret the economic warfare which has arisen between us and other countries. Still we must maintain that warfare so long as it is the other countries who have taken the aggressive [action] and are unwilling to make any sort of

reparation or restitution for the wrongs they have done to us. We have tried the experiment of leaving ourselves completely open to the importation of foreign goods while others built up walls against us. The result very nearly landed us in disaster.[12]

This is the same cage in which leaders find themselves in 2025. Turning the other cheek in a tariff war, while it might theoretically be economically wise, is easier said than done for elected politicians faced with aggrieved domestic industrial lobbying groups and furious workers who fear losing their jobs.

A World Economic Conference, held in the Geological Museum in London in 1933, was a belated attempt to cooperate and coordinate, to reach an agreement to stabilise currencies and establish a truce in the escalating tariff conflict. But the conference failed because national governments were too distrustful of one another, too consumed by narrow perceived self-interest and, most of all, because of the failure of the Democratic president Franklin Roosevelt, who had succeeded Hoover in 1933, to accept the responsibility of international leadership. Roosevelt, preoccupied with the economic slump at home, failed to use America's dominant financial and geopolitical position to grip the international economic crisis in the way that was needed.

As the economic historian Charles Kindleberger summed it up: 'When every country turned to protect its national private interest, the world public interest went down the drain, and with it the private interests of all.'[13] Economic nationalism and populism were in the ascendancy, both fuelling the retreat from international trade and feeding on its effects. This was, then, the original era of exile economics.

Exile economics is a programme that holds that many of the modern connections between nations, mainly in trade but also in investment and certainly in the migration of people, ought to be reduced, if not severed. It's an inclination to isolationism, a rejection of multilateralism, a downgrading of cooperation, a striving for greater national self-sufficiency. Its cheerleaders argue that this new order, or rather the dismantling of the old one, will be economically beneficial. 'Protection will lead to great prosperity and strength,' as Donald Trump enthused in his first inaugural address as president in January 2017.

Others argue that a retreat from global integration, while accepting that it will be economically costly, is simply inevitable – a movement with clear popular appeal whose time has come and can only be managed, not resisted. Like the captain of a raft about to be sucked down into some horrendous whitewater rapids, the limit of the ambition of these pilots is to guide the vessel safely through the trial and prevent it from being smashed to pieces on the rocks.

Yet there are profound dangers lurking in this strategy of managed retreat from globalisation. Modern supply and value chains are often just too big and complex for a single person to grasp. But it is worth trying to get a sense how complicated they are, if only to understand how difficult it will be to unpick them without inflicting grave economic damage. In the pages of this book we will delve into some of the key supply chains of the deeply integrated globalised economy to look at what we risk by breaking them.

We will explore the importance of soybeans – first cultivated in Asia, now predominantly grown in the Americas – and how they have become the most globalised of agricultural products, vital to the livelihoods of both American farmers and the modern Chinese diet, playing havoc with Beijing's aspirations to food self-sufficiency. We will trace how critical minerals, spread unevenly across the territories of the world, are transformed into clean technologies, from batteries to solar panels and wind turbines. Nations want to industrialise and also control their own supplies of these minerals, but geography means that that is an impossible aspiration for most.

We will examine how silicon chips are made, how their production processes span continents, drawing in materials from around the globe, requiring the irreplaceable expertise of some of the most advanced industrial companies in history. Self-sufficiency in semiconductors is a non-starter for most states but the quest to achieve it threatens to be costly. We will analyse the importance of the trade in human capital and talent, also known as migration, in propelling economic success – and how uncontrolled nativism could sabotage the engine. We will follow the transformation of iron ore into steel, the most ubiquitous industrial material, now seen as the litmus test of national manufacturing strength and sovereignty. Many countries are vying to produce more steel, but a global surplus of production of the metal has become a toxic accelerant of geopolitical tensions. Finally, we will explore the intensely globalised supply chains of medicines and medical equipment and the lessons of the traumas of the coronavirus pandemic – and bust the myth that countries would have been better off alone in the face of that plague.

A central argument of the proponents of exile economics is that there exists a trade-off between profit and security when it comes to global trade, meaning that choosing one automatically means less of the other. In the age of globalisation, it is claimed, governments have leaned too far in the direction of profit, thereby neglecting security. Yet that claimed idea of a trade-off between money and security is largely a false one. As we will discover, the evidence suggests globalisation of trade made the world *more* resilient to the shocks of the pandemic and the energy crisis, rather than less. We will explore how, in the twenty-first-century economy, a heavy reliance on domestic production can serve to create *greater* insecurity, not reduce it, as Ukraine found when it was invaded in 2022 and proved unable to harvest its copious grain.

Arguably a better way for governments to deal with risks to national security that result from globalisation is: first, to invest in mapping supply chains, generating vital data on potential chokepoints, bottlenecks and vulnerabilities; second, to invest in stockpiling important materials and components, rather than attempting reshoring, or onshoring, or even friendshoring; and third, to commit to more cooperation and coordination among nations to pool strategic reserves for common use in times of crisis and to cultivate a greater diversity of trading partners, rather than going it alone. So, in this respect, *more* globalisation rather than less.

INTRODUCTION

This is an age of digital insecurity – with microchips in seemingly everything – making the threat of cyberattacks, hacking and state spying loom ever greater. But rather than brutally severing merchandise trade links, governments might do better to address specific vulnerabilities potentially arising from the digital connectivity of critical infrastructure, or from the unauthorised transfer of data across borders, at source through strict regulation of the technological hardware embedded in imports, assiduous monitoring and firewalls. Is it sensible to deal with the risk of infection by cutting off the limb?

The election of Donald Trump in 2024 on a platform of massive protectionism and rampant economic nationalism is the most profound challenge to the post-1945 global economic order imaginable. The direct economic effects of a new fortress of American trade barriers would be deeply damaging for the US and the world. But the indirect effects – the likelihood of tariff retaliation by other states in Asia, Europe, Latin America and Africa – would greatly compound that damage. And the negative impact of the linchpin of the post-Second World War trade system disintegrating is hard to fathom. At the time of writing, in the immediate wake of Trump's re-election, it is impossible to know for sure where his second presidency will lead and just how deep it will plunge into exile economics. But there is no reason to believe that he will not attempt to pick up where he left off in his first term and deliver what he promised on the 2024 campaign trail. And there is surely no reason to think that the prescient warning of that legion of experts to President Herbert Hoover in 1930 that 'a tariff war does not furnish good soil for the growth of world peace' is any less relevant in 2025.

In the wake of the Second World War the great St Lucian economist Sir Arthur Lewis looked back on the confusion and policy failure of the 1920s and 1930s and came to a stark conclusion: 'Without international cooperation we are lost . . . Nations cannot prosper in isolation.' He went on: 'Each generation looks contemptuously on the failures of its predecessors; it is for ours to show that it can learn also from their mistakes.'[14] It is a challenge for our generation too. The fundamental question that we all should be asking – and we all have a stake in the outcome – is: what really maximises the chances of us achieving long-term security and prosperity? Is it a groping for self-sufficiency or rather an embrace of interdependence?

I

The Creed

A curtain of mist slowly descended, caressing the jade-green bushes of the hills. Thin horizontal pathways inlaid the verdant slopes like the contour lines of an enchanted map. Dew glistened on the tea leaves and a yellow-eared bulbul trilled out its call. There's something ineffably beautiful about a Sri Lankan tea plantation at dawn, in the pause between waking and the beginning of the day's picking. I was staying in Nuwara Eliya, the highest town on this teardrop-shaped island in the Indian Ocean. But I was not there to admire the view, but to hear testimony of pain and hunger.

Amurthavalli, a forty-four-year-old ethnic Tamil wearing a striped woollen cardigan, was soon moving along one of the paths, squeezing her slight frame between the waist-high tea bushes. As she went, she plucked ripe leaves from the tops of the plants with a practised motion, depositing the tips over her shoulder into a large plastic sack carried on her back and attached by a band to her head. 'Rice, sugar and everything else is expensive,' she sighed. 'Even bus fares are expensive. Everything is a problem now. I can't say we have enough food. I am afraid for my child's future.'

A younger Tamil picker in the team at Hayleys Plantations, working a short distance down the line, voiced the same anguish. 'The cost of living is high and my children's education is suffering,' said Sakunthala Devi, her eyes widening beneath a white horizontal stripe of sacred ash on her forehead. 'Books are expensive and pencils that used to cost 10 rupees now cost 60. An eraser is 50 rupees. This is making life hard. It's difficult to manage and it's difficult for my kids to study.'

At the time of my visit, in January 2023, more than 6 million people – around a third of Sri Lanka's population – were estimated to be food insecure by the United Nations. And around 19,000 tea plantation workers, including Amurthavalli and Sakunthala, were deemed to be in the most severe trouble.[1] Sri Lanka was at the heart of a cost-of-living emergency of global dimensions. The country's government had recently defaulted on its international loans. The state was bankrupt and unable to pay for fuel imports, locking up the island's economy. As we travelled around we passed kilometre after kilometre of lines of cars, scooters and tuk-tuks, queuing up just in case the island's petrol stations received a delivery. I was sent by the BBC to report what it was like on the ground – to show what it was like to exist under such conditions.

There were multiple reasons for Sri Lanka's plight, ranging from corrupt local politicians and the impact of the Russian invasion of Ukraine on global energy prices to the intransigence of the Chinese state over restructuring its official loans to the country. But the struggles of the tea pickers I spoke to in Nuwara Eliya had a more specific cause.[2] In April 2021 the government of Gotabaya Rajapaksa had imposed a ban on all chemical fertiliser imports into the country – fertilisers that were used by the country's tea plantations. The consequences for Sri Lankan farmers and the tea industry in particular were calamitous. The ban was soon reversed after loud rural complaints but even a brief hiatus in supplies at a key moment in the farming calendar was enough to guarantee highly destructive effects.

Without the fertiliser, the country's tea production yields collapsed by around a sixth over the following year, cratering the revenues of the plantations and pushing some to the brink of insolvency.[3] 'It's a tragedy because last year was a good year for tea prices,' Roshan Rajadurai, the managing director of Haleys Plantations, explained. 'Had we had that crop, it was ours for the taking and we lost it.'

But the biggest loss was borne not by the plantation's owners, but by tea pickers like Amurthavalli and Sakunthala, who earned a day rate of around 1,000 rupees, a little less than US$3. Because of the chaos in Sri Lanka's agriculture unleashed by the country's political leaders, they were not only losing food from their tables and education for their children – they felt they were losing hope itself.

Self-Sufficiency

Over the past decade and in most countries around the world, including the United States, China, India, Russia, the UK, Germany, France and many more, there has been a surge of potent political forces: economic nationalism, isolationism, protectionism, nativism. The word 'self' has been propelled into our political language, in the form of calls for greater national 'self-sufficiency' and economic and technological 'self-reliance'. An awareness of national boundaries and borders has grown in intensity, with an avalanche of new subsidies aimed at incentivising the 'onshoring', 'reshoring', 'near-shoring' and 'friendshoring' of the production of goods and materials. State pressure and financial incentives have also been brought to bear on firms to buy from local producers, rather than from overseas. At the same time, governments have been more prepared to introduce unilateral bans on certain exports – surgical masks in the pandemic, wheat in the energy crisis, microchips in the new Cold War between the US and China – than at any time in the past half-century.

After the Second World War there was a trend for trade barriers between nations to be removed, driven by government policies and facilitated by technological innovations such as the container ship of the 1950s. That tendency accelerated from the late 1970s with the emergence of China into global trading networks, and sped up even more after the fall of the Soviet Union in 1991, which enabled a host of new nations in Eastern Europe and Central Asia to integrate. And then we had the internet and virtually costless digital communications, which gave another boost to our ability to connect across the planet.

Yet in recent years we seem to have been living through a reversal of the great global liberalising and integrating trend. Global trade growth has slowed down dramatically as a result, coming close to stalling. In the decade to 2009, the average growth in goods and service trade volumes every year was 5.1 per cent. In the decade to 2019 that decelerated to 4.5 per cent. In 2023 it collapsed to just 0.1 per cent, and only a partial recovery to 2.5 per cent was forecast by the World Bank for 2024. Indeed, the World Bank projects that the five years to 2024 will register the weakest half-decade of global trade growth since the 1990s.[4] And this was all *before* the election of Donald Trump in the most recent US presidential election. Trump has described 'tariff' as the most beautiful word in the dictionary and campaigned in 2024 on a promise to implement the most protectionist trade measures seen from America since the Second World War.[5]

How to define all of this? 'Deglobalisation' is a common label. Yet that makes the suite of policies sound like a reaction to what came before – the effort to progressively liberalise the movement of goods, services, technology, money, ideas and people between nations. But the movement that we are seeing rise today purports to build something fairer, something more secure, something better, rather than just dismantle its predecessor. It's not, for most, a manifesto for pure autarky – zero trade. But it is a programme that generally holds that the links between nations – in trade, commerce, investment and the migration of people – ought to be less extensive and that a reduction will be beneficial. It's argued that this inward turn is not just practical, but morally right too. 'Globalists' and 'citizens of nowhere' are presented as enemies of the people. Let's call this movement 'exile economics'.

The Sri Lankan government's prohibition of fertiliser imports in April 2021 was an example of exile economics – not just in terms of its effects, but in how it was justified. The stated rationale for the ban was to protect the environment and promote a nationwide transition to organic farming. 'Lives are more valuable to me than a high yield,' President Gotabaya Rajapaksa asserted, citing the polluting impact of fertilisers on Sri Lanka's lakes and groundwater.[6]

The main reason, however, was probably that the Rajapaksa administration, which was desperately mismanaging the economy, wanted to conserve the nation's scarce supplies of foreign currency.

What's striking is that the ban was sustained initially by an argument that severing imports in a specific product would ultimately make the country's economy stronger, not weaker, and an apparent conviction that whatever disruption ensued would be tolerable for the sake of a higher strategic goal. What I saw in Nuwara Eliya on the faces of Amurthavalli and Sakunthala, though, told a different story.

The Hound That Didn't Sound

When the Wall Street bank Lehman Brothers filed for bankruptcy in September 2008, unleashing chaos in global financial markets and threatening a general economic breakdown, it briefly felt like everything was up for grabs. The globalised financial system – along with three decades of free-market dogma – had manifestly failed and governments were being forced to bail out multinational banks (and their bonus-rich employees), loading taxpayers across the world with massive financial liabilities in the process. Meanwhile, world trade volumes were collapsing, economic activity was sinking just as fast, ordinary businesses were failing and unemployment was soaring.

It was in this febrile atmosphere of economic emergency, when unorthodox policy levers were being pulled (including large-scale money printing by central banks), that suggestions arose that perhaps it was time to impose restrictions on imports, or to insert 'buy local' clauses into economic stimulus policies, to help local firms weather the storm.

I was working for the *Independent* newspaper at the time and vividly remember the day the subject was brought up for consideration in a morning meeting at our offices in a rather barren extremity of London's Docklands. It was a notion that I felt duty bound – as someone who had studied the economic history of the 1930s at university – to caution against. I pointed out that the last time such protectionist measures had been widely implemented, in the wake of the 1929 Wall Street Crash, the results for humanity had been terrible, balkanising the world economy, prolonging the Great Depression and fuelling global animosities between states that eventually culminated in the Second World War.[7] To turn to protectionism at such a point would be to repeat the mistakes of history.

World trade collapsed in the interwar period

World exports and imports, divided by world GDP

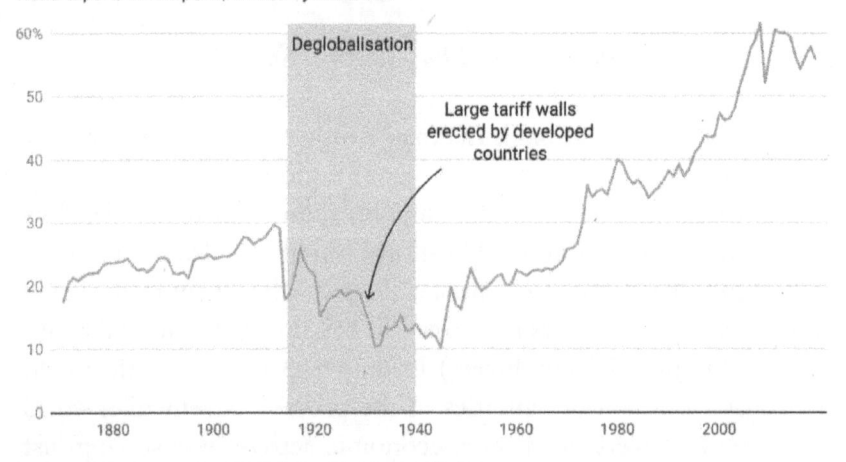

[Chart showing world trade as % of GDP from 1880 to 2000s, with a shaded "Deglobalisation" period around 1920-1940, and an annotation "Large tariff walls erected by developed countries". Y-axis ranges from 0% to 60%.]

Klasing and Milionis series for 1800-1949, Penn World Table 1950-2019
Chart: Ben Chu · Source: Our World In Data · Created with Datawrapper

Figure 1

The *Independent* did not, in the end, advocate restricting trade. I've got little doubt, though, that the result would have been the same had I not been in the meeting room that day. There was no real appetite for it among my colleagues. Protectionism was still well beyond the intellectual pale in the offices of that publication and elsewhere.

As I was making my editorial representations, preparations were being made down the road at the sprawling ExCeL conference venue, situated in a renovated East London dock, for the UK government to host a meeting of the leaders of the recently established G20 group of nations, the most populous and powerful collective in the world. Gordon Brown, the UK's prime minister, who was setting the agenda for the G20 meeting, was determined to vanquish any hint of economic nationalism. He was successful.

The summit's communiqué on 2 April 2009 resoundingly stated: 'We will not repeat the historic mistakes of protectionism of previous eras ... [and will] refrain from raising new barriers to investment or to trade in goods and services.' Protectionism was, in a sense, the hound that didn't sound in the global financial crisis. But this turned out to be a stay of execution, not a reprieve.

Fast-forward nine years to Buenos Aires in December 2018. The host of the G20 meeting is now the Argentinian president Mauricio Macri. Donald Trump is the US president. Trump has earlier that year launched a barrage of trade tariffs not only against China but also, bafflingly, against America's allies in Europe, Canada, Mexico, Turkey and South Korea, citing 'national security' concerns, and plunging the world into a trade war. He has also used America's state power to effectively hamstring the World Trade Organization, the adjudicator on global trade disputes and one of the guardians of the post-Second World War order.

Only a last-minute watering-down of the proposed G20 communiqué's wording on trade ensured that Trump would sign it at all on behalf of the US. 'International trade and investment are important engines of growth ... We recognize the contribution that the multilateral trading system has made to that end,' the document limply conceded, before adding: 'The system is currently falling short of its objectives and there is room for improvement.'[8] Just nine years separated the London and Buenos Aires summits – but it felt like many decades. Everything had changed.

End of an Era

The reasons the united spirit of the London G20 communiqué on trade had evaporated by 2018 – and today, with the re-election of Donald Trump, seems to belong to another era entirely – are vigorously debated. Economic nationalists and populists on both the left and the right argue it's because globalisation simply failed to deliver what its adherents claimed. They say that the system of liberalised cross-border trade profited multinational corporations and the wealthy but left most ordinary people in Western countries behind. The slowdown in the growth in living standards in many developed countries that followed the 2008 financial crisis confirmed, they say, that it could not deliver and had lost popular consent. The 2009 G20, under this reading, was a last hurrah for a system that was already economically and politically moribund.

This is echoed by some on the left who have long presented globalisation as something that was hijacked to further the interests of a narrow social and economic elite rather than the broad mass of the world's population and as a force that has widened inequality.[9] Layered over this is a growing popular conviction that globalisation has contributed to the deindustrialisation of the West, with factories shuttered in the US and Europe and production increasingly offshored to Asia and Latin America, where wages are lower and regulations less onerous. In 2004 China's share of global manufacturing was less than a tenth. By 2021 this had risen to almost a third, while the shares of America and Europe had declined substantially. Was this not the bitter fruit of globalisation?

Authoritative economic empirical analysis in 2014 suggested a major and lasting 'China shock' had been imparted to the employment and prosperity of some manufacturing communities in the US industrial heartlands as a result of China's entry into the global trading system, costing up to 2.4 million jobs in the decade after its admission to the World Trade Organization in 2001.[10]

To the economic nationalist this is not only a disaster for the communities that used to work in these industries, such as steel production, but a source of deep national weakness. Donald Trump's first inaugural speech on the steps of the west front of the US Capitol building in Washington on 20 January 2017 encapsulated this sentiment. 'We've made other countries rich while the wealth, strength, and confidence of our country has disappeared over the horizon,' he declared. 'One by one, the factories shuttered and left our shores, with not even a thought about the millions upon millions of American workers left behind. The wealth of our middle class has been ripped from their homes and then redistributed across the entire world.'[11] The same anger and sense of betrayal at being left behind and forgotten can be heard in many of the faded industrial belts of Europe, from the North of England to the Nord-Pas-de-Calais and to the Ruhr. Strikingly, Gordon Brown, who had coordinated that international repudiation of protectionism as UK prime minister and G20 host in 2009, was, by 2016, lamenting the 'hollowing out of our industrial towns as a result of the collapse of manufacturing in the face of Asian competition'.[12]

The global economic traumas inflicted by the 2020 pandemic and the 2022 Russian invasion of Ukraine have compounded this sense that the system has not only failed but needs to be torn down – that globalisation is not only failing to deliver what was promised, but has turned into a source of harm and vulnerability. In the summer of 2024, 59 per cent of the sample of Americans approached told pollsters that the US had lost more than it had gained from trade with other nations.[13] Polling done in China also showed a marked decline of public support for international trade between 2019 and 2021.[14]

The US figures, no doubt, have a lot to do with the degree of political polarisation in America – anti-trade sentiment was much stronger among Republicans than Democrats. Yet a poll in 2021 suggested the souring of public opinion on trade has been a global phenomenon, not one confined to the postwar hegemonic power of the US and the rising power of China.[15] The average proportion of people across twenty-five countries who agreed with the statement that 'overall globalisation is a good thing for my country' was 48 per cent, down from 58 per cent in 2019. There were steep declines in agreement in countries including Mexico, South Korea, Australia, the UK and Germany.

The popularity of globalisation has declined

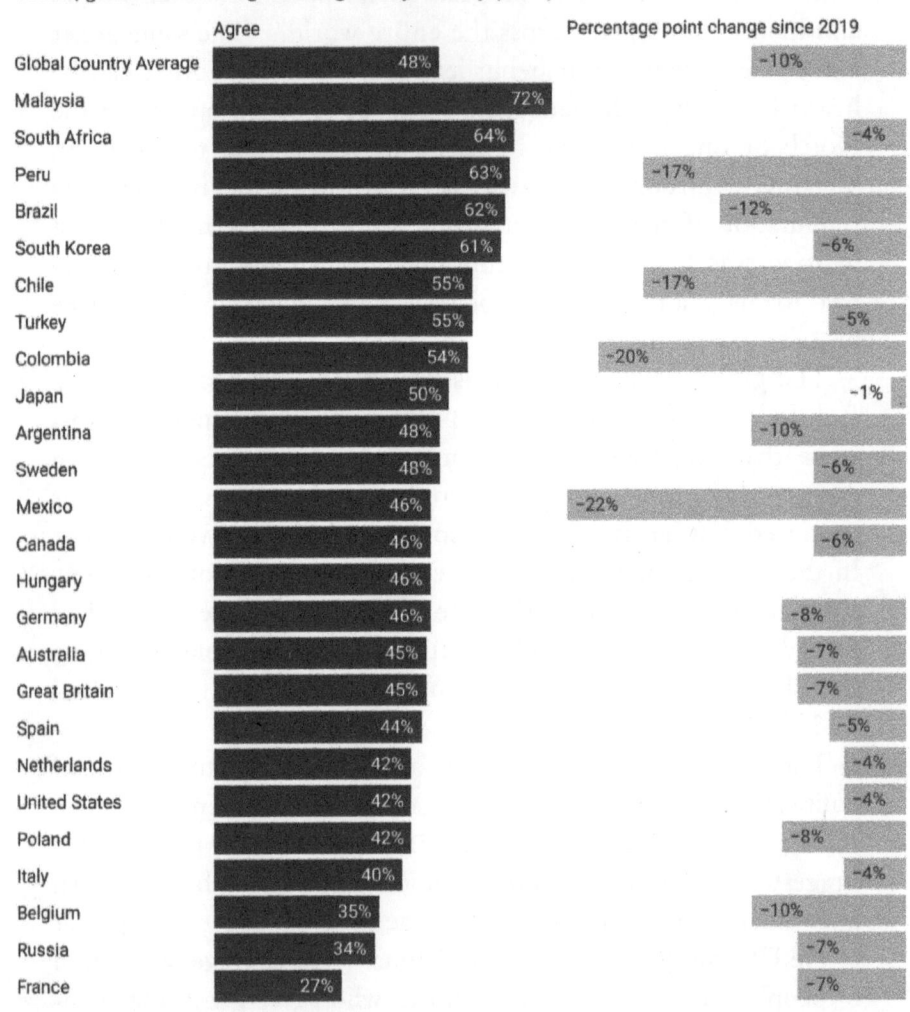

Overall, globalisation is a good thing for my country (2021)

Country	Agree	Percentage point change since 2019
Global Country Average	48%	-10%
Malaysia	72%	
South Africa	64%	-4%
Peru	63%	-17%
Brazil	62%	-12%
South Korea	61%	-6%
Chile	55%	-17%
Turkey	55%	-5%
Colombia	54%	-20%
Japan	50%	-1%
Argentina	48%	-10%
Sweden	48%	-6%
Mexico	46%	-22%
Canada	46%	-6%
Hungary	46%	
Germany	46%	-8%
Australia	45%	-7%
Great Britain	45%	-7%
Spain	44%	-5%
Netherlands	42%	-4%
United States	42%	-4%
Poland	42%	-8%
Italy	40%	-4%
Belgium	35%	-10%
Russia	34%	-7%
France	27%	-7%

Global Country Average reflects the average result for all the countries where the survey was conducted - not adjusted for population size

Chart: Ben Chu • Source: Ipsos • Created with Datawrapper

Figure 2

And across the same group of countries, the share of people who agreed in 2021 with the proposal that 'there should be more trade barriers to limit imports of foreign goods and services' was 37 per cent, considerably more than the 27 per cent who disagreed. The polling lead of those who wanted less trade was high in countries such as Turkey, Malaysia, the US, Belgium and Brazil. But any narrative of the faltering of globalisation that does not have great-power rivalry – between the US and a rising China – at its centre is glaringly incomplete.

Donald Trump might have always been hostile to globalisation, but the vast majority of Republican senators and members of Congress had agreed with his predecessor but one as president, George W. Bush, when he said in 2000 that 'trade with China serves our own national interest'.[16] Most Democrats likewise agreed with Bill Clinton when he argued in the same year that allowing China into the World Trade Organization would 'advance our own economic interests'.[17] What made globalisation newly unacceptable in the eyes of many American politicians over the following two decades is not so much its impact on the country's ordinary workers but that it seemed possible the system would enable China to begin to rival the US in economic, military and technological might. In the 2010s Beijing came to be seen not as a competitor economy operating in a common framework of global rules but rather as an enemy in a new Cold War.

China's steady descent under Xi Jinping since 2013 into authoritarianism, repression and personalised rule gave those who wanted to argue for the maintenance of the old liberal trade order little to work with. This was a world in which a gain for China was perceived as a loss for the US and vice versa. Once that zero-sum strategic framing was in place, the logic of globalisation that US presidents from Bill Clinton to Barack Obama had embraced, a system that would enable both the US and China to grow and prosper, appeared to fall away.

A large share of people in many countries seem to favour less trade

There should be more trade barriers to limit imports of foreign goods and services (2021)

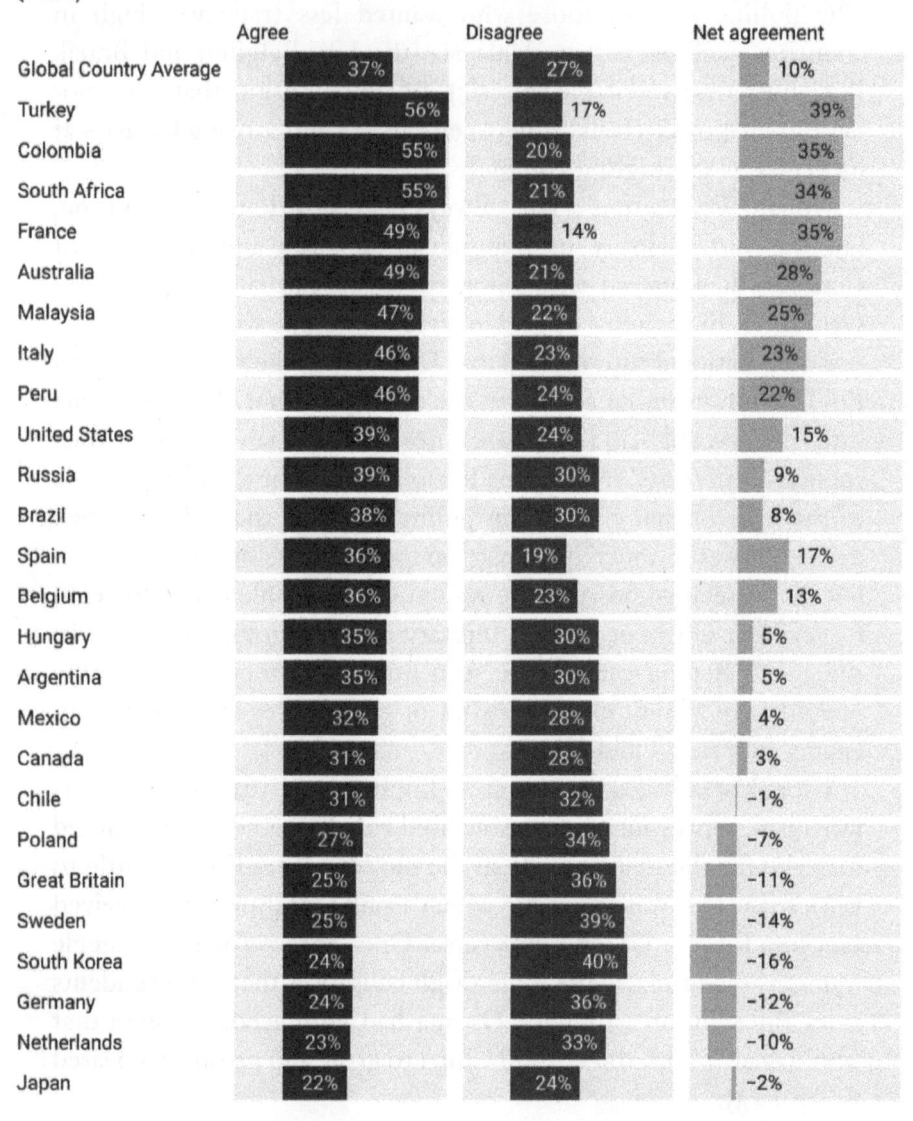

	Agree	Disagree	Net agreement
Global Country Average	37%	27%	10%
Turkey	56%	17%	39%
Colombia	55%	20%	35%
South Africa	55%	21%	34%
France	49%	14%	35%
Australia	49%	21%	28%
Malaysia	47%	22%	25%
Italy	46%	23%	23%
Peru	46%	24%	22%
United States	39%	24%	15%
Russia	39%	30%	9%
Brazil	38%	30%	8%
Spain	36%	19%	17%
Belgium	36%	23%	13%
Hungary	35%	30%	5%
Argentina	35%	30%	5%
Mexico	32%	28%	4%
Canada	31%	28%	3%
Chile	31%	32%	-1%
Poland	27%	34%	-7%
Great Britain	25%	36%	-11%
Sweden	25%	39%	-14%
South Korea	24%	40%	-16%
Germany	24%	36%	-12%
Netherlands	23%	33%	-10%
Japan	22%	24%	-2%

Chart: "Global Country Average" reflects the average result for all the countries where the survey was conducted - not adjusted to the population size of each country • Source: IPSOS • Created with Datawrapper

Figure 3

It's this framing through which one has to understand Donald Trump's explicit aspirations of an economic 'decoupling' from China.[18] This was subsequently reframed as 'de-risking' by the Joe Biden administration, although the actual policies were hard to distinguish from one another.[19] Indeed, in some respects Biden went considerably further, notably in shutting off China's access to cutting-edge microchips made in Taiwan in 2022.

The Biden administration initially promised a 'small yard' and a 'high fence' in its efforts to reconfigure America's economic relationship with China, meaning a limited number of very strict controls in areas defined as of critical importance for national security, a formulation intended to reassure multinational businesses and provide some stability. Yet since restrictions were introduced on advanced microchips, the American yard of control has steadily widened to the proportions of a football field. It now encompasses electric vehicle imports, the Chinese-owned social media site TikTok and the China-founded fast-fashion retailer Shein. American politics now resembles a bidding war for who can offer the most powerful economic repudiation of Beijing. Donald Trump campaigned in 2024 on a pledge to impose a universal tariff on goods from the rest of the world of 10 to 20 per cent – but with a special 60 per cent rate reserved for everything coming from China.

But let's be clear: America is not the only driver of this fracturing. It takes two to have a Cold War. 'One hand cannot clap', as a Chinese saying has it. Growing belligerence over the past decade from the Chinese government towards its neighbours in the South China Sea, from the Philippines to Malaysia, and especially towards Taiwan further to the east, has added fuel to the bonfire of anxieties about supply chains. It's the prospect of a forced 'reunification' of Taiwan with China – something Xi Jinping has described as 'historically inevitable' – that provides a great deal of the momentum and energy behind exile economics.

The 130-km-wide Taiwan Strait is one of the world's busiest shipping lanes. Military action by Beijing to invade or blockade the island would likely sever a global sea transport artery that is vital for the international flow of medicines, pharmaceutical ingredients, oil, soybeans, semiconductors, critical minerals and much else. If Western sanctions on China in response to a Taiwan incursion were anything like those imposed on Russia after the invasion of Ukraine in 2022 the impact would be catastrophic for global supply chains.

If such an eventuality is perceived as considerably more likely than it was previously – even if the overall risk is still regarded as modest – which responsible Western political or business leader would not be seeking to reduce the length of their supply chains and generally to lessen their exposure to international trade? Which Chinese, or Indian, or Brazilian, or Japanese political or business leader would not also be considering the same? And so a heightened perception of risk drives policy pre-emption, which itself further increases a perception of risk as it looks like the old economic order is crumbling. And the ratchet tightens. Such is the logic of exile economics.

The Perfect Storm

It's difficult to see what could break this cycle. One of the very few subjects that can command bipartisan support in Washington today is the need to isolate and weaken China, economically and militarily. And China seems unavoidably set on a course to provoke further hostility from the US as its economic model of chronic overinvestment and low household consumption results in a surplus of industrial production which it will try to sell abroad in what is already being billed as a second impending China shock. Beijing, under Xi Jinping, seems both unwilling and politically incapable of enacting the reforms that would be necessary to rebalance the Chinese economy and reduce the tension – even though such reforms would very much be in China's own economic interests, as some wiser domestic advisors have been recommending, in vain, for more than a decade.[20]

Indeed, as the Chinese economy stumbles amid a heavy burden of private-sector debt linked to a bust domestic property sector, the

Communist Party leadership appears to be hoping that a surge of export-driven growth will put it back on its feet again. So a perfect storm could be coming where industrial 'dumping' of merchandise by China provokes further protectionism from the US.

Many European countries seem paralysed by indecision, struggling to choose between their defence interests in following America's anti-China lead and their economic interests in standing up for open trade. Before the re-election of Donald Trump a widely predicted outcome was the separation of the world trading system into two broad blocs, one centred on the US and its military allies in Europe, East Asia and Australasia and the other bloc centred on China and involving states like Russia, Iran and Venezuela. How key regional powers such as Brazil, India, Indonesia and Turkey might align is unclear. And what would happen to smaller states is anyone's guess. But with no hegemonic power, in the form of the US, willing to bolster and defend the institutions and accepted rules of global free trade, embodied by the World Trade Organization, many countries will be tempted to disregard them and go their own way. Moreover, with Trump back in the White House – a man who verbally attacks allies like Taiwan and Europe more readily than adversaries such as Russia on the grounds that these allies have allegedly taken economic advantage of America – even a unified US-orientated trade bloc cannot be taken for granted.[21]

Again, make no mistake, there are problems in relation to global trade flows that are crying out to be addressed. Grievances about Chinese industrial overproduction and the dumping of the surplus overseas at a price that is below the cost of production, unfairly undercutting domestic firms, are legitimate. Yet there are strong grounds for suspecting unfocused trade protectionism would make the situation worse rather than better.

Economists estimate that Donald Trump's 2024 trade election manifesto would take America's national rate of tariff protection back to heights last seen in the 1930s.[22] But building a great tariff wall around the US would be most unlikely to deliver Trump's promised reindustrialisation of America's heartlands. In the short term it would, as Trump's tariff hikes in his first term in office did, automatically weaken other currencies against the US dollar, which would substantially cancel out any benefit for protected domestic American firms as the effective price of imports would fall. In 2018, when Trump slapped 25 per cent tariffs on almost half of all imported Chinese goods, the value of the Chinese currency, the renminbi, fell by around 10 per cent against the dollar, largely offsetting the impact of the tariff on America's overall terms of trade with China.[23]

The mental image many people have of trade is the exchange of finished goods: shoes, solar panels, furniture etc. Yet the reality is that around half of all international trade in value terms is made up of so-called 'intermediate goods': components, parts or materials that go into making other goods, which themselves can today be traded across borders multiple times over.[24] Around 48 per cent of America's imported goods by value in 2020 were intermediates.[25] A blanket tariff on all imports would harm those US companies, including most manufacturers, which rely on these imported components. It would also put US manufacturers that export at a competitive disadvantage. To be a successful exporter today a country needs to be open to imports.

And in the longer term, erecting a tariff barrier around American firms would likely sap the productivity growth of US industry in general by reducing its exposure to global competitive pressures, which would ultimately hold back US workers' wages. The evidence shows that firms that export, whether based in developing countries or rich ones, tend to be more productive.[26]

A general barrage of tariffs could also open the door to greater corruption of the public sphere in America. The importance of political donations and lobbying in influencing the fortunes of private firms in the US is long-standing and well chronicled, and a surge in protectionism would likely enhance that influence. Evidence from Trump's first term suggests that firms led by people who had made contributions to his campaign were favoured when it came to discretionary tariff exemptions, while the companies associated with people who had supported his political opponent, Hillary Clinton, were deliberately penalised in the setting of trade policy.[27]

Trump insisted at rallies on the 2024 campaign trail that his proposed wave of tariffs would not be a cost to ordinary Americans but rather 'a cost to another country'.[28] Yet a host of detailed studies of the impact of his first-term tariffs suggest most of the cost fell on US consumers in the form of higher prices.[29] There is no reason to believe another, far bigger wave will not now crash onto the same people. Researchers at the Peterson Institute for International Economics in Washington estimate Trump's new proposed tariffs would lower the incomes of Americans, with the impact ranging from around 4 per cent for the poorest fifth to around 2 per cent for the wealthiest fifth. A typical household in the middle of the US income distribution, the thinktank estimates, would lose around $1,700 each year.[30]

It is true that globalisation creates relative winners and losers in any country, but claims that it has undermined the average living standards of people in America or Europe or anywhere else in the developed world are grossly exaggerated. The China shock on the number of people employed in US manufacturing was real, but factory automation also had an impact. The contributions of each to that decline are hard to disentangle.[31] Some researchers have estimated that the China shock was a relatively minor component of the overall decline in employment.[32] And those estimated US national job losses of up to 2.4 million resulting from Chinese import competition need to be put in the context of three key facts. First, that the overall American labour market in 2011 was made up of 133 million workers. Second, that it's a market subject to immense churn all the time – between 2013 and 2023 (excluding the pandemic year of 2020 when churn was even greater) an average of 5 million workers left their jobs and 5 million workers filled new jobs every single month.[33] Third, that globalisation, including trade with China, has had a positive impact on job creation in the US services sector, which might plausibly have entirely offset the China shock on manufacturing.[34]

On top of this, while a larger share of the financial gains of globalisation might have gone to the more highly skilled in rich countries, globalisation has also kept consumer prices down for households across the board. Indeed, the lower consumer prices likely benefited lower-income families in rich countries more because a larger share of their spending is on imported goods than among wealthier groups.[35] Deglobalisation would have the opposite effect on the cost of living.

While the biggest relative beneficiaries of globalisation have been people in poorer nations, the proposition that Western countries would have been more prosperous if they had never opened up to more trade is not very credible. Indeed, one study found that in 2022 the US economy was around 10 per cent bigger than it otherwise would have been due to the nation's engagement in world trade since 1950, equivalent to a benefit of just under $20,000 per household.[36] Nor is there any compelling evidence that globalisation has been a major driver of rising inequality within richer countries, certainly relative to factors such as technological advances and tax and spending decisions by governments.[37]

Kicking Away the Ladder

The dangers of exile economics, as we've seen in the case of Sri Lanka, are greatest for smaller nations, who have the most to gain from an open global trading system and the ability to export to the widest range of countries. Globalisation, since 1980, is reckoned by most economists to have played a major role in helping to lift hundreds of millions of people out of poverty by enabling poor countries to join the international trading system and access foreign technology and investment.

What allowed states such as Taiwan, South Korea, China, Malaysia, Mauritius and Vietnam to drive up the incomes of their populations was building up their domestic manufacturing sectors, usually starting with a focus on textiles for exports. A base in textile manufacturing then enabled them to push into higher value-added manufacturing, such as assembling electronics. These are countries that 'learned by doing'. Each step up the industrial ladder delivered higher incomes.[38] Textiles – making T-shirts from its own cotton crop – is precisely the bottom rung of the industrialisation ladder that a state like Benin in West Africa is groping for today.[39] Some argue that the ability of poorer states to follow that particular development path would be attenuated in future in any case because of the rise of automation in manufacturing and the growing importance of services in trade.[40] Trade will nevertheless remain vitally important in enabling such countries to grow. Tearing down globalisation would be to kick the ladder away which other countries could and should be able to use to climb to better lives.

Since 2020, decades of declines in the global poverty rate – the share of people living below $2.15 per day – have levelled off.[41] That's primarily the impact of the global economic shocks emanating from the Covid pandemic and the global energy crisis, but it also likely reflects the slowdown in global trade growth. One study by the World Bank has estimated that an additional 52 million people globally, most of them in Sub-Saharan Africa, would be below this international poverty line in 2030 if there were a global rush to national reshoring of industrial production.[42] Lower incomes mean hunger in many countries. Since 2020 the number of people on the planet who are undernourished – Amurthavalli and Sakunthala among them – has also risen by tens of millions. The trade slowdown has contributed to that.[43]

But those dangers face all of us, not just those on the planet in the direst poverty. Exile economics, taken to its extreme, risks a severe slowdown in the growth of living standards everywhere. Lower trade in goods and services will mean lower growth in the productivity of businesses, less innovation and investment, which spells a weaker expansion of our wages and incomes.

Researchers at the International Monetary Fund suggest that a major fragmentation of global trade – where the US and EU break off trade with China and the rest of the world has to choose between trading with a Western or an Eastern geopolitical bloc – could result in a global economy that is up to 7 per cent smaller than it otherwise would have been. That's equivalent to a loss of around $7 trillion today – a chunk of activity equivalent to the total national income of Britain, France and Spain put together.[44]

Economists at the Organisation for Economic Co-operation and Development (OECD), an association of mainly rich nations, used a different scenario to model the economic impact. They assumed that tariffs on all merchandise goods traded between countries shot up to 25 per cent – effectively undoing seventy years of liberalisation in advanced countries – and that each country spent an additional 1 per cent of GDP subsidising local production. This extreme localisation model suggested that global GDP would be around 5.5 per cent smaller, with higher losses for the US, South Korea and Australia. In such a scenario the UK and Canada, which rely more heavily than most on importing inputs for industrial production, could suffer a loss of more than 10 per cent of their GDP.[45]

There is, of course, inherent uncertainty about the scale of these impacts – and the damage would depend on the pattern and extent of the fragmentation – but there are no credible scenarios in which the economic impact is positive. On top of that, exile economics could very plausibly lower our resilience to future shocks like pandemics, reduce our collective ability to tackle planetary threats like climate change and end up ratcheting up geopolitical and military tensions even further. In other words, the total cost could end up being greater still.

Bark and Bite

There are two likely objections to such warnings. First, that this is an unwarrantedly alarmist picture about where the planet is heading, that globalisation is not likely to collapse and that the exile economics rhetoric of 'self-sufficiency' coming from political leaders should be taken with a large pinch of salt. When Joe Biden said the future would be 'made in America' he was not advocating US autarky but simply seeking to bring back a decent portion of manufacturing to US shores in some key sectors.[46] Similarly, when the president of the European Commission, Ursula von der Leyen, demands European prosperity be 'made in Europe', or when

Narendra Modi launches a 'Make In India' initiative, isn't this as much about political style as substance?[47] Even Donald Trump, some still claim, has been using the threat of massive tariffs as a bargaining chip to get trade concessions from other countries and greater access for US firms and producers to foreign markets. 'Some of this is "Art of the Deal",' his economics advisor Stephen Moore has said, a reference to Trump's 1987 book.[48] 'My general view is that at the end of the day, he's a free trader,' Scott Bessant, another of Trump's advisors, has said. 'It's escalate to de-escalate.'[49] In other words, the bark will be worse than the bite.

The UK's chief finance minister, Rachel Reeves, talks of 'securonomics', which on the face of it sounds like a relation of exile economics. 'There must be red lines – things for which we should not rely on states whose interests conflict with our own,' she has insisted. Yet Reeves has also said Britain should increase its exports and imports, and not retreat into 'fortress Britain'.[50] The French president, Emmanuel Macron, says Europe must 'put an end to our strategic dependencies in key sectors, from semiconductors to critical raw materials'. Yet he also accepts that 'we need to continue importing and exporting'.[51]

And it is just possible that the world can travel down a narrow corridor that pairs a step back from 'hyper-globalisation' with continued openness, an approach that marries greater productivity-boosting investment in strategically important domestic industries with enhanced cooperation and economic interconnection with allies. We will in due course discuss what that world might look like. Yet today the bigger risks are of a dangerous unravelling. Donald Trump promised a trade war in his inaugural speech in January 2017 – and delivered one. Despite softening the rhetoric, the Biden administration did little to end it. Actions speak louder than words.

It is true that the value of global trade as a share of the world economy has stagnated rather than collapsed, prompting some to suggest that talk of deglobalisation, like the death of Mark Twain, is exaggerated. And cross-border permanent migration is running at record highs. Yet an objective evaluation of the direction of travel on goods is not encouraging. In 2015 states imposed around 700 new restrictions on trade, a mixture of subsidies, tariffs and other measures. By 2023 the equivalent number of new trade restrictions imposed had soared to 3,500, with around 2,500 of those relating to trade in goods. Since 2020 governments across the world are estimated to have imposed more than 7,000 policy interventions impeding global trade in essential items, including medicines, food, fuel and raw materials. More than half of those interventions remain in place.[52]

This is not simply a reflection of the Western sanctions imposed on Russia in 2022. The share of G20 nations' imports affected by trade restrictive measures was around 2 per cent in 2011. By 2021 – before Putin's invasion of Ukraine – it was already close to 12 per cent. And we should not underestimate the fragility of the wider geopolitical climate or fail to recognise just how broadly exile economics is gaining ground. Putin immolated almost all of Russia's commercial ties with the West with his military adventurism. But China and India are just as prone to the politics of self-sufficiency as America or any state in Europe. The Indian prime minister, Narendra Modi, has adopted a slogan of *atmanirbhar bharat*, or 'self-reliant India', which he insists will deliver 'economic strength and prosperity for every Indian'. Xi Jinping has for many years been advocating *zili gengsheng*, which translates as 'self-reliance', and has made it a national mission to dramatically scale-up domestic Chinese production of everything from food to microchips. We are already starting to see the global economy being reconfigured along political lines. Countries are trading less with perceived geopolitical rivals, defined by their voting records at the United Nations.[53]

The second objection to the warnings laid out here will be that this essentially amounts to a call for the maintenance of the status quo. Some will dismiss them as a reflection of a politically rejected free-trade orthodoxy. Others will see them as a failure to recognise how the national security picture has been transformed in recent years by Russia's willingness to use its gas and food exports as economic weapons and, most of all, by China's dominance of key twenty-first-century supply chains with military applications, such as batteries, and Beijing's ability and increasing willingness to leverage this position in a hostile way. In October 2024 China sanctioned Skydio, America's largest drone maker, meaning it was unable to source batteries from China. 'This is a clarifying moment for the drone industry,' its chief executive said. 'If there was ever any doubt, this action makes clear that the Chinese government will use supply chains as a weapon to advance their interests over ours.'[54]

And such vulnerabilities have been further underscored by accidents and natural disasters. When the mighty *Ever Given* container ship wedged its 220,000-tonne bulk into the sand on the banks of the Suez Canal in March 2021, halting the flow of container ships for six days through the waterway that carries 12 per cent of global trade, the world was alerted to the transport chokepoints of global supply chains. Another reminder was the severe 2024 drought which prevented containers passing through the Panama Canal, which handles a further 6 per cent of global trade. How many warnings, some ask, do we need that the logistics of global trade, on which we have become reliant, are perilously fragile?

But governments do not have to do nothing in the face of such dangers, whether from states or from nature. An alternative is for political leaders to think more clearly about the meaning of national security in a twenty-first-century globalised economy – and how this concept differs from narrow national self-sufficiency. Policymakers could separate security goals from considerations of domestic industrial policy and job creation, important though those undoubtedly are. Governments could invest in supply chain resilience and diversification rather than trying to bring as much industrial production home as possible.

As for the political orthodoxy arguments, there are without doubt inequalities that arise from globalisation within most countries and these have too often been neglected in recent decades. But these inequalities could be addressed by social safety net and state investment policies, which compensate individuals and communities adversely affected and provide them with training in new opportunities, rather than by cutting off trade. These are the recommendations made by multilateral organisations ranging from the OECD and International Monetary Fund to the World Trade Organization. Yet they are suggestions that have mostly been disregarded in recent years.

Defusing the Powder Keg

The overproduction problem is by far the most difficult challenge. The problem stems from the unbalanced way countries such as China – but also, importantly, Germany, Japan and South Korea – have run their domestic economies, with those governments effectively holding down the consumption power of households for the sake of building a larger domestic manufacturing and export sector than would otherwise exist.[55] It is these policies that generate the risk of dumping and harm to the manufacturing sectors of other countries.

These harms are real and those who want to preserve an open global economy would do well to address them, rather than dismiss them. Yet these imbalances can be addressed multilaterally or bilaterally. In the early 1980s, in somewhat similar circumstances of anxiety about the future of the US car manufacturing industry, the administration of Ronald Reagan was able to negotiate a Voluntary Export Restraint agreement with Japan.[56] China is, of course, far from being a US ally in the way that Japan was, and the only lasting solution is Chinese domestic rebalancing. But it would be better to attempt negotiations to that end and, if they fail, impose capital controls.

If China were prevented, through externally imposed financial controls or punitive taxes on capital flows from investing its financial surpluses from trade in the government debt and currencies of other large nations with open financial systems such as the US, France or the UK, it would have no choice but to absorb that money domestically, which would compel a national economic rebalancing.[57] The challenges of achieving rebalancing through financial controls should not be underestimated – nor the potential and highly unpredictable side effects for the global financial system and the role of the US dollar in global trade invoicing.[58] It would be, in the words of the economic historian Adam Tooze, 'a bold leap of macroeconomic faith'.[59]

Yet, as demonstrated by the 2008 global financial crisis, which was partly created and greatly exacerbated by cross-border risk-taking by Western banks, international financial integration has not been an unalloyed good. If there is one aspect of globalisation that would arguably be safer to roll back than others it is the globalisation of finance. This would create a globalisation more akin to what occurred in the aftermath of the Second World War, when capital flows between nations were controlled but restrictions on merchandise were progressively loosened. For the US and others in the West, going down the route of financial controls to deal with Chinese overproduction would be far less distortive and damaging than attempting to tackle the threat through a proliferation of merchandise tariffs and bans on the imports of goods.

And for China's Xi Jinping, if he genuinely wants, as he still sometimes claims, to maintain the existing global trading system and if he desires to avoid a tariff or capital control backlash from the West (and also from developing countries such as Brazil, India, Mexico and South Africa which are increasingly alarmed by Chinese overproduction), figuring out a way to reduce China's internal imbalances might be his best means of achieving that. The Chinese president has just as much agency as Donald Trump when it comes to defusing the powder keg of exile economics.

Trump once claimed that trade wars are 'easy to win'.[60] They can certainly easily get out of control. States that feel they have to react in response to the protectionism of others, or in anticipation of their actions, especially in the context of weaker growth which creates greater domestic discontent and pressure to act, could lead to an unravelling faster than any government either anticipates or truly wants. The lesson of history is that new tariffs beget new tariffs, even when other countries realise they are only harming themselves in imposing them. To fail to respond is to relatively disadvantage one's own producers and to risk the fury of domestic workers and employers for one's passivity. This is, as we have seen, what happened in the 1930s, but also what happened when Trump imposed tariffs on imports of steel and aluminium from America's trading partners in 2018. It wasn't only China that retaliated with tariffs on the US, but Canada, Mexico and the European Union too. When we consider the scale of what Trump has threatened, a potential total fracturing of global trade of the sort seen in the 1930s – when country after country raised tall tariff barriers against the outside world to try to protect their domestic industries at the expense of others, amid a grand game of beggar-thy-neighbour – cannot be ruled out. 'A vicious downward spiral' is the scenario painted by the managing director of the International Monetary Fund.[61] 'A free-for-all, which would upend the stability and predictability of trade', is how the head of the World Trade Organization describes it.[62] The return of Trump to the White House unquestionably makes those risks greater, not smaller.

But before we get too deep into the details of the havoc that an uncontrolled fragmentation of our globalised economy would wreak and before we explore how a safer path through this perilous moment might be navigated, it's important to take a step back. We have been here before – and not just once but many times. Let's first try to understand the gravitational historical pull of the creed of exile economics.

2

Origins

There were no ivory towers for the ancient philosophers. The fourth-century BCE Greek philosopher Diogenes lived in a barrel and barked at people like a dog in the marketplace to demonstrate his scorn for social conventions and what he saw as the artificiality of civilisation. When Alexander the Great paid Diogenes a visit in the city of Corinth, the conqueror of worlds asked the ragged ascetic, who was enjoying a siesta at the time, what he wanted, with the implication that he would provide it for him. What would the request be: property, money, power, status, sex? The answer, or so the story goes, came back from Diogenes: 'Stand a little out of my sun.' Alexander was impressed by this modest request, even if it might have been considered rather rude. 'But verily, if I were not Alexander, I would be Diogenes,' the chuckling ruler told his retinue, according to Plutarch.[1]

Whether this encounter between the king and the philosopher, a founder of the school of thought of Cynicism (from the Greek *kynikos* or 'dog-like'), actually took place is questionable. But there's no doubting the influence of the story and of the idea it encapsulated. The tale of Diogenes' extreme indifference to the most powerful ruler in the ancient world has been in circulation for almost 2,000 years as perhaps the supreme example of the virtue of moral and intellectual self-sufficiency.

For ancient Greek philosophers, self-sufficiency, or autarky – from *auto* (self) and *arkeo* (power) – was first and foremost a personal moral virtue. To be reliant on others was to compromise one's ability to pursue wisdom. And if self-sufficiency meant sheltering in a barrel, barking like a dog and running the risk of offending a mighty king, then so be it. The moral virtue of self-sufficiency became a political goal as well as a personal one. According to Diogenes' contemporary Aristotle, the ideal city-state in the ancient world was a self-sufficient one, by which he meant that those inside the polity would have everything they needed to pursue a good philosophical life, unlike those outside it.[2] Autarky also had a geopolitical dimension. The classical scholar Mary Beard argues the idealisation of Athenian self-sufficiency was bolstered by its experience during the Peloponnesian Wars when the entrepôt's Black Sea grain imports, on which its citizens relied, were cut off by its enemies.[3] 'The aim of autarkeia was survival,' argues the classicist Peter Jones. 'Such a mindset was essential in the ancient world, where the threat of starvation, disease or disaster was permanent, and death everywhere.'[4] As the centuries passed, these virtuous connotations of self-sufficiency endured and were elaborated and modified by Christian thought.

The Dumb Ox

Thomas Aquinas, a thickset scholar born on the island of Sicily in 1225, so underwhelmed his University of Naples classmates that they nicknamed him the 'dumb ox'. But the dumb ox did more than perhaps any other medieval thinker to build the philosophical underpinnings of the Catholic faith. Drawing on Aristotle, Aquinas talked of the 'self-sufficiency' of God, in the context of the argument that all existence ultimately flowed from the creator and that the deity wasn't reliant on anything exterior to himself. That was the seminal scholastic argument of the age, but intriguingly Aquinas came down on the side of economic autarky too in one of his more worldly treatises. He noted in 1265 that there were two ways a city could feed itself: by growing food in its own surrounding fields or through trade. 'It is quite clear that the first means is better,' Aquinas concluded. 'The more dignified a thing is, the more self-sufficient it is, since whatever needs another's help is by that fact proven to be deficient.'[5] And in an echo of Greek thought he suggested that self-sufficiency was safer too since '[t]he import of supplies and the access of merchants can easily be prevented whether owing to wars or to the many hazards of the sea, and thus the city may be overcome through lack of food.' For good measure Aquinas threw in a classical moral argument: 'Greed is awakened in the hearts of the citizens through the pursuit of trade.'

There is a romantic, as well as religious, strain to autarkic thinking too. In Daniel Defoe's *Robinson Crusoe* (1719), the hero is shipwrecked on a desert island and has to learn to survive entirely isolated from the rest of humanity, making his own clothes, growing his food, living off the land. Defoe had been inspired by the case of Alexander Selkirk, a Scottish mariner who had been marooned on an island off the Peruvian coast and was ultimately rescued after spending years in isolation. But in its details – such as the goatskin umbrella Crusoe fashions to shield himself from the burning sun – Defoe's novel was a stunning work of imagination.

Crusoe begins by lamenting his plight. But soon he starts to look on the bright side:

> My condition began now to be, though not less miserable as to my way of living, yet much easier to my mind: and my thoughts being directed, by a constant reading the Scripture and praying to God, to things of a higher nature, I had a great deal of comfort within.[6]

To be more self-sufficient is to be closer to God; Aquinas would have approved. The reader is also encouraged to admire Crusoe's resourcefulness and also to envy the simplicity of his life of self-sufficiency, not least his idyllic and secluded 'country house', deep in the island's jungle interior, with its store of raisins. The popularity of the tale over the centuries – which lives on in TV reality shows like *Survivor* – owes a good deal to this romantic idealisation of self-reliance.

The philosophical father of the Romantic movement, Jean-Jacques Rousseau, embraced self-sufficiency from what he felt was an anthropological perspective. In the work that propelled him to fame in 1755, his *Discourse on the Origin and Basis of Inequality among Men*, Rousseau conjectured that primitive man had been naturally 'solitary', coming together with others only for mating purposes, and had been much happier for this isolationist tendency. It was a radical challenge to the view that human existence before modern civilisation had been 'poor, nasty, brutish and short', in the formulation of Thomas Hobbes, the political philosopher who published his treatise *Leviathan* (1651) shortly after the conclusion of the English Civil War. By contrast, Rousseau's mind's eye saw an early man:

> wandering up and down the forests, without industry, without speech, and without home, an equal stranger to war and to all ties, neither standing in need of his fellow-creatures nor having any desire to hurt them, and perhaps even not distinguishing them one from another.[7]

Like Aquinas before him, Rousseau made the leap from extolling the general virtuousness of self-sufficiency to recommending it as a trade policy at state level for Corsica and Poland. The Poles, Rousseau advised, should 'pay little attention to foreign countries, give little heed to commerce, but multiply as far as possible your domestic production and consumption of foodstuffs'.[8] Meanwhile, since Corsica was, in Rousseau's view, 'capable of self-sufficiency' it should close herself off to foreign trade.[9]

Dr Gaspar Rodriguez de Francia, the first ruler of Paraguay, after the South American colony achieved independence from Spain and then Argentina in 1811, claimed to have been influenced by Rousseau. Under the authoritarian rule of 'El Supremo', the country broke with the Catholic Church and foreign commerce was significantly choked off. The Scottish essayist Thomas Caryle admired the 'tawny-visaged, lean, inexorable Dr Francia' and described, in lyrical terms, in 1840 how: 'For twenty or near thirty years [he would] stretch out his rod over the foreign commerce of Paraguay, saying to it, Cease! The ships lay high and dry, their pitchless seams all yawning on the claybanks of the Parana.'[10] Some historians question the extent to which the 'Perpetual Dictator of Paraguay', brutal and capricious as he undoubtedly was, genuinely sought, or achieved, autarky.[11] But Francia's rule, whatever else it managed, did not yield economic success, not least perhaps because, despite Carlyle's poetic imaginings, he saw fit to direct considerable resources to building up the navy in the landlocked country.[12]

Around the time Francia was conducting his national economic experiment, a French cotton mill owner and provincial politician, Auguste Mimerel, was recommending something similar to the post-1830 French monarchy on the grounds that bans on imports would prevent the wages of French industrial workers from being undercut by the more efficient British. Blocking textile imports from across the Channel would, of course, also have helped to protect the profits of the likes of Mimerel. This was the first sighting in the wild of the argument, heard many times since, not least from Donald Trump, that economic self-sufficiency is about protecting the economic interests of the working class.

Support for economic self-sufficiency came from a less worldly source in this era too. One of the paragons of German Idealist philosophy, Johann Fichte, produced a work in 1800 called *The Closed Commercial State*. Fichte conceived of the treatise as a project that built on the work of Rousseau and his intellectual hero, the 'Sage of Königsberg', Immanuel Kant, who had conceived of a model for 'perpetual peace' between states.

The orthodoxy of the time was that trade tended to engender good relations between nations. 'Peace is the natural effect of trade,' as the French aristocrat Montesquieu had put it half a century earlier, in 1748. 'Two nations who traffic with each other become reciprocally dependent; for if one has an interest in buying, the other has an interest in selling; and thus their union is founded on their mutual necessities.'[13] And Kant had also written about the power of the 'commercial spirit' to incline nations to cooperation.[14] But for Fichte, on the contrary, commerce among rivalrous European states had served to corrupt relations, and economic life had to be disentangled for peace to have a chance.

In his rigorous autarkic manifesto, Fichte articulated some arguments for self-sufficiency that stress the remoralising benefits: 'In a nation which has closed . . . whose members live only among themselves and very little with foreigners . . . a higher degree of national honour and a sharply determined national character will develop very quickly.'[15] 'It seems to me,' he added, with a nationalist flourish, 'that through our striving to be everything, and to be at home everywhere, we have become nothing, and find ourselves at home nowhere.'[16] The very same thought was uttered by British prime minister Theresa May in 2016 when she raised the hackles of liberals in the wake of the contentious and narrow vote for Britain to leave the European Union by asserting: 'If you believe you're a citizen of the world, you're a citizen of nowhere.'[17]

Fichte's treatise feels familiar in other ways. He argued that free trade inherently benefits richer states and harms poorer ones – a foreshadowing of the central argument of the modern anti-globalisation activist movements. Yet Fichte was far from a conservative reactionary. He envisaged ideas and culture, if not goods, continuing to cross borders. And his novel arguments that closed states should guarantee a right to work and be prepared to intervene extensively in economic life have led some scholars to see him as an intellectual progenitor of socialism.[18]

Closed Country

It was by no means only Europeans and their colonial descendants in Latin America who were attracted to the dream of self-sufficiency. The great naval expeditions of the fifteenth-century Chinese admiral Zheng He – who was, in a fact that rather belies our historical stereotypes of China, a Muslim eunuch – were remarkable not only for the incredible distances his giant diplomatic 'treasure ships' sailed but also for the abruptness with which the voyages stopped.

Zheng He's expeditions had demonstrated that Chinese maritime shipbuilding and navigation were superior to anything that contemporary Europeans could muster. The great Spanish Armada of 1588 consisted of 132 vessels. Zheng He had more than 300 ships in his fleet, which transported 28,000 men. And the largest ones, 120 m long and 50 m wide, would likely have literally towered over contemporary European vessels.[19] Zheng He's fleet reached Malindi in East

Africa, modern-day Kenya, and brought home a giraffe for the Chinese emperor. This was almost seven decades before Portugal's Vasco da Gama rounded the Cape of Good Hope and arrived at the same kingdom, en route to India and its valuable spices.

This was a moment that could have represented the first step towards Chinese pre-eminence in global commercial and military power projection. Instead, a new faction came to power at the Ming Dynasty court, and such voyages and even the construction of oceangoing ships were banned. And so it was European explorers from Portugal, Spain, the Netherlands and then Britain who first mapped, and then came to dominate, the world.

The reasons for such a Chinese turn inward at a crucial juncture in global history are debated by historians. There may have been an economic motivation – the treasure ships were not cheap to construct and there were other competing demands on the imperial treasury. One influence seems to have been a hostility among some Confucian-trained officials to trade and contact with foreigners on principle.[20] Like Aquinas, these philosophical bureaucrats feared the moral consequences of such contacts. Unlike Aquinas, they were in a position to determine national trade policy directly.

As they were in Japan. The policy of *sakoku* or 'closed country' was imposed on the islands of Japan from 1635 by the Tokugawa shogunate, a form of feudal military dictatorship.[21] Western Christian missionaries were banned and those who were already in the country were persecuted, as vividly portrayed in Martin Scorsese's 2016 film *Silence*. Emigration was forbidden. So determined were the shoguns to eradicate all foreign influence that even Japanese natives who had migrated abroad were forbidden from returning to their homeland. Foreign trade was curtailed almost to nothing, with the exception of a small concession for the Dutch, who were allowed to operate on an artificial island off Nagasaki. The Japanese, via Dutch texts, did study Western developments in fields such as medicine and cannon manufacture, but the shoguns' policy of quarantining their people from European influence (although not, importantly, from Chinese cultural influence) was remarkably effective for the best part of two centuries.[22] It wasn't until a US naval commander, William Perry, under orders to intimidate the Japanese into opening up to trade, sailed four military steamships into Tokyo harbour in 1853 that the policy of *sakoku* finally crumbled.

Perry used the stick in East Asia, but there were carrots too. In 1793 a royal diplomatic mission from Great Britain, led by one Lord Macartney – famous for describing the British empire as one on which 'the sun never sets' – arrived in Beijing to propose an increase in trade between the two empires through new trading concessions on the Chinese mainland. The Macartney mission carried with it wind-up clocks and a model steam engine, the fruits of Britain's nascent Industrial Revolution, to show the Chinese court the sort of goods that could be theirs through liberalised trade. Yet the Chinese declined. The Qing Dynasty emperor wrote directly to King George III: 'We possess all things. I set no value on objects strange or ingenious, and have no use for your country's manufactures.'[23] The imperial Chinese elite not only saw self-sufficiency as desirable – but apparently believed they had achieved it.

Or did they? It's clear that, despite the rhetoric of the letter, the Chinese court was actually very interested in Western technologies and arts, from cannon manufacture and map-making to portraiture and architecture. Unlike the Japanese, they were welcoming to missionaries, appointing Jesuit priests to powerful court positions, in part because of their astronomy skills. And the Chinese had a tendency to disguise grubby trade with barbarians under the banner of gift and tribute ('our emperor will gift you this silk and porcelain as a sign of his generosity and magnificence and you will pay him tribute in the form of your spices, etc, but we won't call it an exchange'). So some historians have interpreted the formal rebuff to the Macartney embassy more as a warning to an imperial rival to back off, rather than as the deluded assertion of self-sufficiency that it seems on the face of it.[24] Whatever the truth, the dream of self-sufficiency has quite often been a response to the external pressure of a great empire.

Tiny Gardens of Eden

Mahatma Gandhi's vision of an India independent of British rule consisted of a network of economically autonomous villages, 'tiny gardens of Eden',[25] growing their own crops and spinning their own cotton for clothing. 'Every village has to be self-sustained and capable of managing its affairs even to the extent of defending itself against the whole world,' he wrote.[26] This is why the image of the spinning wheel sits at the heart of the tricolour Indian flag. Though, importantly, self-sufficiency did not mean there would be no trade, but rather trade only in the things that the village could not realistically produce itself. 'Self-sufficiency,' Gandhi stressed, 'does not mean narrowness. To be self-sufficient is not to be altogether self contained.'[27] But at other times he struck a much more insular, even xenophobic tone, insisting that 'it is our right and duty to discard everything foreign that is superfluous and even everything foreign that is necessary if we can produce or manufacture it in our country'.[28] So how to reconcile such statements? Gandhi's self-sufficiency movement – *swadeshi* in Hindi – has to be understood as self-sufficiency for India in relation to Britain, the imperial overlord.[29] The movement was first announced in 1905 in Bengal alongside a boycott of British goods.

Swadeshi was Gandhi's antidote to what he saw as the predatory imperial capitalism of the British. In the view of Indian independence campaigners, Britain effectively forced its textile exports on to the giant Indian market in the eighteenth and nineteenth centuries.[30] In the early eighteenth century India had been a major exporter of textiles – known as 'calico' – to Britain. But under imperialism Britain imposed tariffs on those imports into the mother country, while ensuring that there were no Indian tariffs on the imports of the fruits of the newly mechanised looms of Lancashire. This destroyed India's existing domestic industry and held back its broader national economic development. Whether it was a direct result of imperialist trade policy or something that would have happened anyway due to the far higher productivity of British manufacturing, the statistical record shows that India did indeed undergo a profound deindustrialisation during the British Raj. In 1750 India had been producing around 25 per cent of global manufacturing output. By 1900 this had declined to just 2 per cent.[31] Fairly or not, Britain was blamed and self-sufficiency was seen as the answer.[32] In the years after Indian independence in 1947 the country's exports as a share of its national income fell as low as 3 per cent, less than half the average level seen under the decades of British rule.

It was a similar story in post-independence Tanzania, where President Julius Nyerere's Ujamaa (Swahili for 'familyhood') movement in the 1960s and 1970s was founded on the belief that European colonialism and urbanisation had perverted African economic life and that the answer was a return to self-sufficient, rural living using ploughs instead of tractors. In some ways arguments for a drive to economic self-sufficiency were a natural outgrowth of the 'dependency discourse' of writers and activists in the 1960s and 1970s, which argued that colonial territories had been held back by the foreign, extractive capitalist institutions – financial, legal, educational, administrative – that had been imposed on them.[33] The exhortation was for former colonies like Tanzania to 'de-link' from an extractive Western economic system.[34] 'Independence means self-reliance,' stated Nyerere's 1967 Arusha Declaration.[35] His was a strikingly technologically pessimistic vision:

> We must stop dreaming of developing Tanzania through the establishment of large, modern industries. For such things we have neither the money nor the skilled man-power required to make them efficient and economic. We would even be making a mistake if we think in terms of covering Tanzania with mechanised farms, using tractors and combine-harvesters.[36]

Though Nyerere later added an important caveat, similar to Gandhi's: 'The doctrine of self-reliance does not mean isolationism. For us, self-reliance is a positive affirmation that for our own development, we shall depend upon our own resources.'[37]

One of the most famous ripostes attributed to John Maynard Keynes was his response to the charge of inconsistency: 'When the facts change I change my mind. What do you do, sir?' Keynes is unlikely to have said those precise words but the father of modern macroeconomics certainly changed his mind over self-sufficiency. In a 1933 essay, written close to the climax of the global retreat into tariffs and protectionism following the traumas of the Great Depression, he renounced his former attachment to free trade and, in a famous passage, declared: 'let goods be homespun whenever it is reasonably and conveniently possible'.[38] In that same essay Keynes echoed some of the moral arguments for self-sufficiency that have bounced around since ancient times. 'Decadent international but individualistic capitalism,' he complained, 'is not intelligent, it is not beautiful, it is not just, it is not virtuous.' What is more, amid swelling European militarism, Keynes suggested: 'A greater measure of national self-sufficiency and economic isolation between countries, than existed in 1914, may tend to serve the cause of peace rather than otherwise.'

But, like Gandhi and Nyerere, Keynes, the great lover of the arts and pillar of the Bloomsbury Group of London intellectuals, left a window open for the trade in the intangibles of culture: 'Ideas, knowledge, science, hospitality, travel – these are the things which should of their nature be international.' The argument that aiming for self-sufficiency, despite appearances, does not mean a repudiation of openness to the world is made by many economic self-sufficiency advocates today. Nyerere and Gandhi were figures on the left, as was Keynes (though he was more of a liberal). Leftist thinking has a strong self-sufficiency pedigree.

The Phalanstery

Portraits of Charles Fourier, the son of a cloth merchant from Besançon near the French border with Switzerland, show an austere-looking individual with a thin mouth with sharply downturned corners. Yet Fourier was one of the most eccentric of the utopian socialists of the early nineteenth century, speculating that the world's seas would one day turn into lemonade and that humans would develop tails.[39] Fourier's most lasting contribution, though, was his vision of how humans could and should live. He envisioned self-sufficient rural communities, which he called 'phalansteries', derived from the words 'phalanx' (a military formation) and 'monastery'. A group of 1,620 people, large enough to accommodate all the different personality types he had categorised and the three social classes, would live together on a specially designed estate – 'a multitude of colonnades and domes' – with music rooms, workshops, dining rooms, an opera house and living apartments.

The members would grow their own food and share sexual partners through an institution he called the 'Court of Love', responsible for the efficient organisation of orgies in which all could participate, although without compulsion.[40] Parts of Fourier's prospectus were bizarre, such as deciding when the children of the phalanstery were to graduate from the status of 'urchins' to 'cherubs' based on whether they could wash a sufficient amount of dishes without crockery breakages.[41] The dirty job of cleaning the phalanstery's toilets would fall to those congenitally unruly prepubescent children who, according to Fourier, were naturally attracted to filth: 'They gallop frenetically to labour, which is executed as a work of piety, an act of charity towards the Phalanx, the service of God and of unity.'[42]

Part of Fourier's vision was strikingly modern. He outlined a 'unitary education' for all children in the phalanstery, regardless of family wealth, and a 'social minimum', which was effectively a guaranteed minimum annual income. In a very contemporary twist, he said that children's genders would be chosen by them, rather than prescribed. Fourier was clearly enchanted by his own vision:

> At sunrise on a spring morning one can see thirty groups with their distinctive banners and emblems passing out through the gates of the palace. These various squadrons take their places in the fields and gardens . . . singing hymns in chorus as they march along.[43]

Some idealistic Fourierists tried to make his vision a reality in the United States, in Ohio and Texas, but failed after a few months for want of the necessary farming skills among the community.[44] Self-sufficiency is easier in theory than in practice.

Yet the influence of the phalanstery on 1960s hippie communal living and 'free love' is evident. The kibbutzim of Israel – agricultural communes with communal dining and no private property, established from 1910 by Jewish migrants to British-mandate Palestine – also echoed many elements of his ideas. Some see the British cooperative movement – common ownership of shops by their customers – as a more practical manifestation of those utopian Fourierist fantasies. The modern 'degrowth' and environmentalist movements have strong elements of self-sufficient thinking (they also make morality-infused calls to reduce our wasteful and destructive 'wants') in ways that Diogenes might have appreciated. 'A better answer than economic globalisation is a shift in the direction of revitalised, local, diversified and at least partially self-sufficient smaller economies,' asserted ecologists Edward Goldsmith and Jerry Mander in 2001.[45] Environmental sustainability more broadly can perhaps be seen in a self-sufficiency framework, with exhortations for us to 'live within our planetary means'. But self-sufficiency is by no means exclusively a leftist impulse.

Autarchism

Robert Lefevre, like Fourier, was an odd figure. Born in Idaho in 1911, he began his career as a self-confessed 'fly-by-night' door-to-door salesman, graduating to promoting a New Age cult in the 1930s called the 'I Am' movement as a radio broadcaster.[46] Lefevre, though, found his true calling as a populariser of libertarian economic ideas in the 1960s. Thanks to his cultist radio training, he had a knack for making some very right-wing ideas sound like folksy common sense. At his 'Freedom School' in Colorado Springs, Lefevre's theory of 'autarchism' was an attempt to clarify his philosophy and distinguish his radical anti-government beliefs from 'anarchism'. As he put it:

> Autarchy will signify total self-rule. It will presume a system or social arrangement in which each person assumes full responsibility for himself, proceeds to control himself, exercises authority over himself ... and does not in any way seek to impose his will by force upon any other persons whatsoever.[47]

This was essentially a strain of libertarianism reaching back to the Greek philosophical roots of autarky, rather than the modern economic concept. Lefevre was by no means opposed to trade and was an evangelist for free markets. His school was an implacable opponent of any kind of government intervention or economic redistribution. Franklin Delano Roosevelt's collectivist New Deal policies of the 1930s were anathema, seen as, at best, a wrong turn for America and at worst a form of crypto-Communism.

The future billionaire chemicals and fossil fuels industrial magnate Charles Koch was one of the students of Lefevre's Freedom School in the 1960s and was profoundly influenced by the experience. It was, Koch recalled, at 'Bob LeFevre's Freedom School where I began developing a passionate commitment to liberty as the form of social organisation most in harmony with reality and man's nature'.[48]

Koch went on to pour huge amounts of his family's money into libertarian thinktanks, arguing for major tax cuts, drastic reductions in government welfare spending and radical deregulation – and also funding various climate-change-denying outfits. Yet some elements of the modern US libertarian movement do seem, perhaps paradoxically, amenable to the communitarian vision, even if they abhor collectivism. The New Hampshire Free State Project, established in 2001, is trying to create a libertarian community in the US by encouraging like-minded folk to move, en masse, to the state of New Hampshire. 'By concentrating our efforts in one small state with a pre-existing pro-liberty culture, we are turning the tide against big government, and we're experiencing the benefits of expanded personal and economic freedoms,' its website states.[49]

One of its members, Carla Gericke, a cheery South African-born corporate lawyer, described life in the community to me for a BBC radio documentary:

Friends of mine have an off-the-grid farm, and they raise pigs and cows and sheep, and I tend to source almost primarily all my meat directly from them. We do actually believe in free trade and all of that, but we're also building a community, so we do tend to try and sort of interact within our community.[50]

The goal of community-based, self-sufficient living, provided it is freely chosen, is not inherently left-wing or collectivist. But the Free State Project's members number only around 7,000, despite initial hopes of attracting at least 20,000. Today around 125,000 Israelis live on 270 kibbutzim; just under a quarter are still communal cooperatives, and those that are still primarily agricultural mostly rely on Thai immigrant workers.[51] There are estimated to be between 10,000 and 30,000 communes, or 'intentional communities', around the world, including religious communities such as monasteries and temples.[52] It remains an alternative lifestyle, appealing to a very small minority of the global population. The fact is that big modern economic self-sufficiency movements have been state-directed, not bottom-up. And the big driver has been war, or the threat of it.

Totalitarian Autarky

As he sat in a Bavarian prison in 1925 after a failed coup attempt against the Weimar Republic, Adolf Hitler wrote out his conclusions in *Mein Kampf*: 'If this earth has sufficient room for all, then we ought to have that share of the soil which is absolutely necessary for our existence. Of course people will not voluntarily make that accommodation. At this point the right of self-preservation comes into effect.'[53] Hitler's autarkism was a response to Germany's experience in the First World War, when the country had been starved by the British navy's blockade.

In an unpublished second book, penned shortly afterwards, Hitler dismissed the idea that Germany could feed itself through increases in agricultural productivity and lamented that 'the German people is today even less in a position than in the years of peace to feed itself from its own land and territory'.[54] The road to national self-preservation for the former corporal turned paramilitary agitator would have to run through national self-sufficiency. Germany's salvation lay in conquering and exploiting the rural bounty of lands to the east.

In a speech in 1936, when he had ascended to the German chancellorship and crushed all internal opposition, Hitler made his territorial intentions plain: 'If I had the Ural Mountains with their incalculable store of treasures in raw materials, Siberia with its vast forests, and the Ukraine with its tremendous wheat fields, Germany and the National Socialist leadership, would swim in plenty!'[55]

Ironically Hitler's nemesis, Joseph Stalin, despite having those fecund lands under his direct control, also felt the pinch of national insecurity and in those same years. The trauma and economic dislocation of the Great Depression had prompted a furore in Western economies over the supposed dumping of cheap Soviet grain exports on them, undermining the livelihood of farmers, and Stalin was worried about the impact of an economic blockade led by France, and possibly joined by other European powers, against the Soviet Union. Stalin decided to get his retaliation in first, by pursuing a policy of self-sufficiency for the Soviet Union, deliberately curbing exports and seeking to establish Soviet economic independence from the 'capitalist world'.[56] The impact can be seen in the official figures, with Soviet exports and imports almost halving in the 1930s. And as a share of the Soviet economy the value of exports fell to virtually zero. In Germany exports collapsed from 17 per cent of the economy in 1933, when Hitler took power, to 6 per cent by 1939.[57]

Similar self-reliance national security justifications were used in Communist China during Mao Zedong's Great Leap Forward of the 1950s. *Zili gengsheng*, regeneration through one's efforts, was the slogan. In the so-called Great Leap Forward Mao argued that agrarian China could exceed Britain in steel production within fifteen years and catch up with the United States in fifty – all without external trade and foreign technical know-how. Mao's orders, commanding farmers to neglect their fields and to melt down their pots and pans to make steel in backyard furnaces, had all-too-predictably awful results, with tens of millions dying in the ensuing famines.

This go-it-alone idea could be traced to the formative years of the Communist movement in China. 'We stand for self-reliance,' Mao had told party cadres in the remote northern Ningxia border region in 1945, while the civil war between Mao's Communists and the nationalist Kuomintang was raging. 'We depend on our own efforts, on the creative power of the whole army and the entire people.'[58]

He contrasted the reliance of the Kuomintang on financial and military aid from the United States and went on to praise (in a familiar propaganda technique) what he said was the superhuman ability of some army units to operate entirely independently and to require supplies of neither grain, clothing nor bedding from the centre. And now the slogan of *zili gengsheng* is back, found on the lips of the man who has sought to erect a Mao-style personality cult around himself: Xi Jinping.

But probably the most assiduous modern autarkists lie in the hermit kingdom to the east of China. In the 1950s Kim Il Sung, the North Korean Communist leader and anti-Japanese guerrilla fighter, made national self-sufficiency not just an important objective, but the lodestar of his new regime. And he called it *juche*. 'To us juche is the Korean revolution . . . The Korean revolution cannot be made by foreigners for us; it must be made by us Koreans on our own responsibility,' Kim instructed officials in 1956 as he sought to build up his regime's strength in the wake of the Korean War, which had sucked in not only the United States but China.[59] Historians suggest that Kim's *juche* was motivated, in large part, by a desire to resist the overlordship of Moscow, which wanted to pressure Pyongyang into falling into line with its own economic strategy. It was thus seen as a defence against Soviet imperialism, as much as against pressure from the West.

Regardless of the motivation, the North Korean regime has hardly achieved such self-reliance in practice. Today it relies heavily on food and energy imports from China, extorted with the help of nuclear blackmail. But the rhetoric of self-sufficiency lives on in the mouth of Kim's portly grandson, Kim Jong Un. Indeed, some have argued that the ideology of *juche*, given how central it is to the regime's constitution and the Kim family personality cult, effectively traps North Korea in its hermit state, since to open up the population to any foreign influence at all now would risk unravelling the ideological underpinning of the regime.[60]

One might also argue that Communist dictators like the Kims, Mao and Stalin are in their comfort zone with autarkic policies, cutting their populations off from outside influence through foreign trade, appealing to their instincts for control and also driving militarisation. Yet it would be a mistake to assume that economic policies of self-reliance are limited to poor countries emerging from colonial rule or totalitarian dictatorships.

Infant Industries

In January 1790 George Washington, America's first president, rose to deliver his first address to the US Congress: 'A free people ought not only to be armed but disciplined,' he declared, '. . . And their safety and interest require that they should promote such manufactories as tend to render them independent of others for essential, particularly for military supplies.'[61]

The context was the lowering menace of Great Britain, which had been cast out in the War of Independence but which was still a profound military threat to the nascent republic. And this Britain was a free-trading, industrialising superpower. Washington and his treasury secretary, Alexander Hamilton, believed that they urgently needed to build up America's industrial base to enable the republic to defend itself.[62] This meant a high tariff wall to prevent the 'infant' factories of America from being asphyxiated by cheaper imported products from a more productive Britain. Hamilton's industrial tariffs don't get a mention in Lin-Manuel Miranda's hip-hop musical, but they were arguably, along with the act of consolidating the debts of US states, one of his most impactful, indeed world-changing, economic policies.

The 'American system', as it became known, inspired a German émigré to Pennsylvania called Friedrich List. List, who had fled the Kingdom of Württemberg after being jailed for having the temerity to advocate civil service reforms, wrote an influential book in 1841 recommending what he called a 'national system of political economy', which rejected the classical arguments of the likes of Adam Smith and David Ricardo on the rationality of nations pursuing free-trade policies. Instead, List said that countries with great unrealised industrial potential that were trying to catch up with the productivity frontier leader – in this case Britain – should act to protect their immature factories from competition with the leader by means of powerful import restrictions until they were strong enough to compete.[63]

Some in Britain tend to conceptualise the nineteenth century as the high point of global free trade, the age of political figures such as Richard Cobden and John Bright and their Anti-Corn Law League. And it might have been for Britain, with its commanding lead in manufacturing and wave-ruling naval supremacy.[64] But it certainly was not for America. Washington maintained high tariffs throughout most of the century, nurturing its baby factories into strapping giants.[65] The clearly-articulated goal was self-sufficiency.

There's a conspicuous wrinkle in the idea that Britain was unwaveringly committed to the cause of laissez-faire free trade in this era. A monocle-wearing businessman and municipal government pioneer from the industrial city of Birmingham, Joseph Chamberlain, spearheaded a national campaign for 'imperial preference' in the early twentieth century. This would have meant Britain levying new tariffs on food imports from outside the empire, but not on supplies from within its Canadian, Australian and New Zealand colonies. It has been described as a form of 'imperial autarky'.[66]

Chamberlain promoted this idea on the basis that 'tariff reform' was a rational economic response to the protectionism practised by Britain's strengthening industrial rivals in America and Germany – and also that it would benefit the British working man by raising money for new forms of social spending. The working man felt differently. The British electorate overwhelmingly rejected Chamberlain's protectionist manifesto, adopted by the Conservatives, in the 1906 general election, with the Liberal Party managing to convince voters it would push up bread prices. But it is clear that, even at the height of Britain's free-trading pomp, there were doubts and contrary viewpoints, especially among the grassroots of the Conservative Party.[67]

Those alternative points of view on trade, even if defeated, never truly die, but seem to have an endless capacity for resurrection. It's striking to compare George Washington's first address to Congress with the seminal speech given by Jake Sullivan, Joe Biden's national security advisor, in April 2023. In this, Sullivan essentially read the funeral rites of the neoliberal, free-trading vision that had animated Democratic administrations for the past forty years. 'A modern American industrial strategy identifies specific sectors that are foundational to economic growth, strategic from a national security perspective,' he informed the Brookings Institution, a venerable liberal thinktank located in the US capital. 'In today's world, trade policy needs to be about more than tariff reduction, and trade policy needs to be fully integrated into our economic strategy, at home and abroad.'[68] By explicitly linking economic and trade policy to national self-reliance and defence capabilities, he wasn't just tearing up the orthodoxy, he was – for good or ill – resurrecting ideas as old as the American republic itself.

Neo-Sakoku

Others have been excavating old ideas from further afield. Mencius Moldbug is the blogging name for the American computer programmer Curtis Yarvin, who is a kind of tech-authoritarian theoriser, influential in the milieu of some Donald Trump-aligned politicians and wealthy supporters.[69] As international travel collapsed at the onset of the coronavirus pandemic in 2020, Yarvin saw his chance, not just for tolerating isolationism 'but promoting it'.

'This state of absolute isolation is not generally ideal. But if we need one relationship that clearly combines unconditional independence with unconditional peace, absolute isolation is always available,' he wrote. 'Any country, at any time, can or should be free and able to isolate itself completely from the world.' This, he said, would enhance the prospects of peace between states. In a world of isolated nations, he conjectured,

> neither hostility nor adoration toward any foreign country has any remaining meaning. Both the nation and its citizens are so far from their old international crushes and beefs that it contemplates them with no emotion but vague regret, like a college senior thinking about high school.[70]

Yarvin drew on some historic Asian autarkic regimes by way of justification for his ideas:

> Had the Western powers honoured the wishes of the Qing Dynasty and Tokugawa shogunate and not only complied with these policies, but cooperated in enforcing isolation against their own citizens, the historical treasures – human and physical – of these ancient civilizations would still exist. What internationalist can stand up and call it good that we destroyed these societies?

His policy recommendation for twenty-first-century America? 'Neo-*sakoku*.' The autarkic urge makes for some strange ideological bedfellows.

Does it go against, or with, the grain of world history? There's a view among anthropologists that economic trade between groups of humans likely extends back hundreds of thousands of years. In Kenya's Olorgesailie basin they have found hand-worked axes made of obsidian, a naturally occurring volcanic glass. The obsidian is not from the area, suggesting that these Stone Age humans who lived some 320,000 years ago were trading with other groups.[71] Part of what defines our species – making us distinct from other apes – seems to be Homo sapiens's cooperative and social nature and, specifically, our capability for 'cultural learning'.[72] Rousseau was mistaken to believe that primitive man was a self-sufficient loner.

The German sociologist Andre Gunder Frank argued that a 'world system' of trade began as early as the third millennium BCE, when there was evidence of market integration of the Sumer civilisation of southern Mesopotamia and the Indus civilisation of north-west India.[73] Yet the impulse to self-sufficiency – to economic unsociability – also reaches back very deep into our history.

What's most striking about autarky is its adaptability as a programme. Exile economics is a school of thought that, as we have seen, can appeal impressively across political, social and ideological lines. It's been adopted at various times by political movements on the left and the right, by libertarians and collectivists, by conservatives and radicals, by believers and atheists, by nationalists and cosmopolitans, by Fascists and Communists, by rich states and poor states, by imperial powers and the colonised, by environmentalists and industrialists.

It can be justified by the objective of peace or of war. Any unit, from the individual to the household, the village to the city, and the nation even up to empires, can apparently aspire to self-sufficiency. It can be born of a backward-looking nostalgia – a desire to turn the clock back or preserve the status quo – or a belief that it is a progressive and necessary programme to build the future. Like a historical El Niño climate pattern, the drive for self-sufficiency keeps coming back, unpredictably but also, seemingly, inevitably. Its tide seems to be flowing in again. But would exile economics deliver the benefits that its adherents claim? It's time to get specific. Let's begin by examining perhaps the most fundamental commodity of all for our species: the food we eat.

3

Food

Between the two great global conflicts of the twentieth century, Ukraine, with its rich black soil and huge tracts of arable land, became known as the 'breadbasket of Europe'. It's still one of the top global exporters of wheat. But in the wake of the Russian invasion in February 2022 Ukraine's wheat exports, as well as its usual shipments of corn and oil, were abruptly cut off as Russian warships blockaded its ports on the Black Sea.

This was widely seen as an attempt by the Russian president, Vladimir Putin, to 'weaponise' the country's food exports, a way of hitting back at the rest of the world after the unprecedented suite of Western financial and economic sanctions imposed on Russia for invading its neighbour. The primary victims, though, were set to be those living in Africa and the Middle East. Egypt, Yemen, Syria, Libya, Lebanon, Sudan, Tanzania and Uganda all relied heavily on Ukrainian wheat and faced a hunger crisis without it.

The response of some countries to the Russian grain blockade compounded the threat. Amid an atmosphere of panic over food supplies, some twenty-three other countries around the world – including Argentina, India, Hungary and Serbia – resorted to food and fertiliser export restrictions, apparently to guarantee their own domestic provisions. Among the commodities affected were wheat, corn, palm oil, vegetable oil and poultry. The result was that the share of globally traded calories for food affected by export restrictions leapt from 5 per cent to 16 per cent.[1] The international price of wheat skyrocketed to a record high of $450 per tonne. Emergency supplies from the United Nations' World Food Programme (WFP), distributed to more than 100 million people, were also imperilled, as the agency was sourcing half of its wheat from Ukraine. The director of the WFP, David Beasley, warned that the war and the international reaction had left millions 'marching to starvation'.[2]

Ultimately, global wheat prices came back down to earth after a deal was brokered by Turkey and the United Nations in July 2022 to allow commodities to be safely shipped from Ukrainian ports. But was this episode of food weaponisation evidence of a dangerously fragile global food system? Many argued so and claimed action was required to mend it. Eliza Manningham-Buller led the UK's domestic intelligence services, known as MI5, between 2002 and 2007. Since retiring and being awarded a seat in the House of Lords, Baroness Manningham-Buller has run a small sheep farm in Wales. But in 2022 she took a break from her fields and returned to the public spotlight to give a lecture articulating the national security argument for greater domestic food production in Britain. 'The more we can be self-sufficient, the better resilience we will have against these global shocks,' she claimed, citing climate change and the Russian invasion of Ukraine.[3] The French president Emmanuel Macron was even blunter. 'Who would be foolish enough to outsource their food?' he thundered in a speech given at the Sorbonne University in Paris in April 2024. 'We have no right to allow food dependencies to develop.'[4] National food security has become one of the central planks of exile economics. But does it make sense?

Feeding a Nation

The most natural way to measure a country's degree of food self-sufficiency might seem to be to compare the volume of its national agricultural production to its national consumption. So, if a country grows 100 tonnes of food a year within its borders and its population consumes 100 tonnes, we could call it 100 per cent self-sufficient. But where do imports and exports fit in? Again, it might seem natural to say that, if a country that consumes 100 tonnes of food grows 90 tonnes at home and imports 10 tonnes from other countries to fill the gap, its self-sufficiency rate is only

90 per cent. Conversely, if a country consumes 100 tonnes of food and grows 110 tonnes at home, of which it exports 10 tonnes, its self-sufficiency rate would be 110 per cent. Rather than volume, we could use the value of the food or the number of calories embodied in it and get slightly different results but a similar overall picture. That might all seem straightforward enough. But on closer inspection things get more complicated.

Some countries might export a lot of food commodities while also importing a lot of food. Are they self-sufficient or not? Perhaps the solution is to break down self-sufficiency rates by certain key food staples. The United Nations' Food and Agriculture Organization (FAO) does this for each country based on cereals – wheat, rice, maize (also known as corn) – and produces a cereal import dependency ratio, which is calculated by comparing the value of imports of cereals to the value of domestic production and exports.[5] Countries that export a lot of wheat and maize like the US and Ukraine have a large negative dependency ratio while a country like Malta, which doesn't produce wheat and imports it all, has a dependency ratio of 100 per cent. Given that cereals are the largest part of most people's diets in most regions of the world and account for most of the calories grown by the planet's farmers, this might seem to give us the information we really need about national food self-sufficiency.

Other measures, such as one produced by the International Food Policy Research Institute, use a wider range of staple crops – including potatoes and sugar – to generate a global ranking of countries based on their ability to supply consumption from their own territory.[6] On this measure the most food import-dependent states are countries in the Middle East such as Oman, Bahrain and Yemen and also island nations such as the Maldives and the Seychelles. And the least dependent are large agricultural producers such as Argentina, Russia and Ukraine. Yet cereal or staple crop self-sufficiency measures taken in isolation can be misleading. The share of staples in a country's diet, in terms of total calories consumed, tends to decline as they grow richer and national tastes expand and change. The Democratic Republic of the Congo's share

Some countries are large exporters of food - others are large importers

Cereal import dependency ratio, 2023

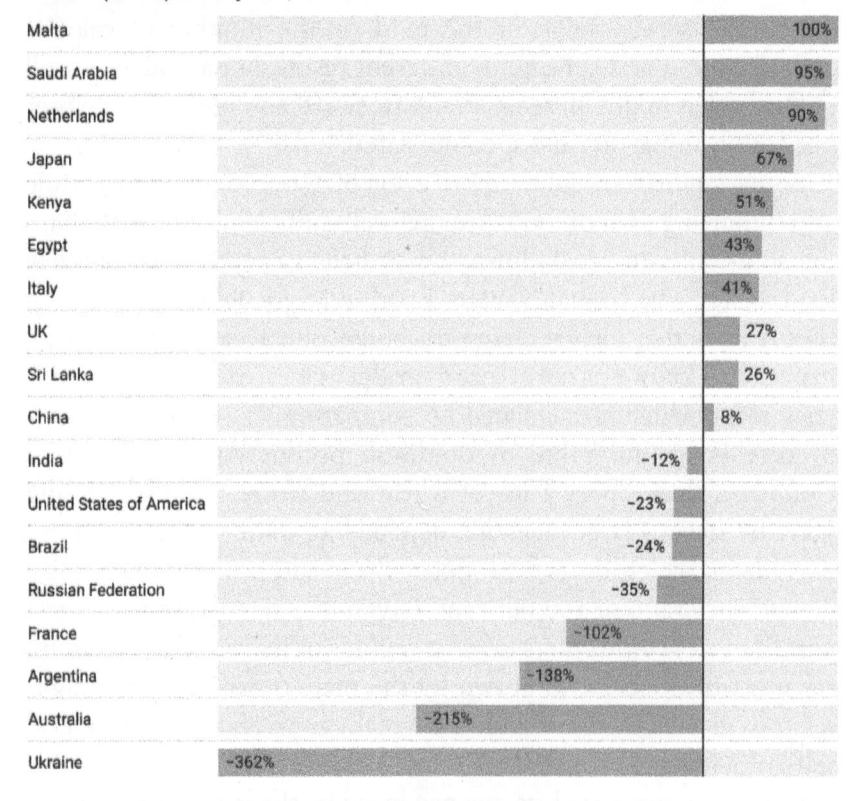

Malta	100%
Saudi Arabia	95%
Netherlands	90%
Japan	67%
Kenya	51%
Egypt	43%
Italy	41%
UK	27%
Sri Lanka	26%
China	8%
India	−12%
United States of America	−23%
Brazil	−24%
Russian Federation	−35%
France	−102%
Argentina	−138%
Australia	−215%
Ukraine	−362%

Import dependency ratio (IDR) is defined as: IDR = imports x 100/(production + imports - exports)
Chart: Ben Chu • Source: FAO • Created with Datawrapper

Figure 4

of those fifteen staple foods in its national diet is 94 per cent. But in the UK and the US it's only around 52 per cent, and just 47 per cent in Germany.

And consider the case of Japan. Japan is pretty much self-sufficient in rice, having prioritised national production of the staple through high import tariff barriers and domestic farming subsidies since the end of the Second World War. Yet the typical Japanese diet now contains far more meat and wheat than in the past. On the basis of the value of domestic food production relative to consumption,

Japan's self-sufficiency ratio is 63 per cent, down from 86 per cent in 1965. And based on the number of total calories consumed and produced in the country, its overall food self-sufficiency rate is today just 40 per cent, one of the lowest in the world, and down from above 70 per cent in 1965.[7] Why has it fallen so low? Because successive governments in Tokyo decided to meet the growing demand for foods (other than rice) from global markets, which was far cheaper than attempting to grow it all domestically on a cluster of severely land-constrained East Asian islands. The cheaper food costs meant higher living standards for the population. Japan's post-Second World War economic miracle, when the country grew into a manufacturing superpower, was fuelled by cheap food imports. Perhaps that seems irresponsible, but it was precisely the same logic that another island nation followed a century earlier. In 1846 the government of Robert Peel repealed the Corn Laws, which had imposed high tariffs on imports of wheat and other cereals, in the name of free trade and cheaper food for the burgeoning population of industrialising Britain. The legacy of that decision is still with us. Britain's overall food self-sufficiency ratio, defined in terms of the value of domestic production as a share of consumption, was around 60 per cent in 2022.[8]

Today the global production and export of cereal crops is highly geographically concentrated. Just four nations – China, India, Russia and the US – produce around half of the world's wheat. Just three countries – China, the US and Brazil – produce well over half of the planet's corn. And two states – China and India – produce more than half of all the rice grown.[9] Endowments of arable land, water sources and the right climate are responsible for turning these nations into food-producing giants. A stark example of this is the fact that the US has sixteen times more arable land per capita than Japan: 0.48 versus 0.03 hectares per person. Australia has sixty-one times more agricultural land per capita than Malta. Geography means some favoured nations can have cheap staples and high domestic production. But geography also means some will, probably inevitably, have to trade off one against another: cheap bread versus domestically produced wheat.

These facts of geography are inescapable. A study in 2020 looked at what proportion of the global population could hypothetically feed itself on cereals, rice and pulses that are currently grown within 100 km of where they live. The researchers found the answer was only around 25 per cent. The average minimum distance required to feed each person on the planet was estimated at 2,200 km. That implies a lot of cross-border trade in food.[10]

And that is what we see. Some states are big food exporters. America and Argentina are responsible for two-thirds of corn exports. America, France and Russia account for half of wheat exports. Thailand and Vietnam are responsible for almost half of rice exports.[11] Other states are big food importers. North African and Arab nations, small island states and some countries in South America such as Venezuela, Chile and Suriname are the most dependent on imported foods. But the reality is that trade in food is how a growing share of the entire planet feeds itself. About a quarter of the food produced for human consumption is traded internationally.[12] Approximately one in every six people in the world consumes food that is internationally traded to meet their basic consumption needs.[13] And the role of trade in feeding people has been growing in recent years, as population growth in food-importing nations has been faster than in food-exporting ones. It is a trend that is projected to continue over the next decade.[14] Without this trade, food prices in import-dependent countries would be considerably higher, meaning lower living standards or even hunger. But our dependence on food imports as a planet extends a lot further, as the remarkable and underappreciated story of soybeans shows.

Magic Beans

Lift a salty green edamame pod to your lips in a Japanese restaurant and you're sucking on a miracle. That's a soybean popping satisfyingly into your mouth. The soybean is a kind of legume, related to peas and lentils. The hairy pods grow on the stem of a plant that rises up to around thigh level. Within each pod there are two or three round seeds, with a diameter of about a fingernail's width. The seeds can be yellow or black or green or brown, and have a 'hilum' or eye, where they were connected to the pod. The whole beans themselves are the edamame, meaning 'stem beans' in Japanese. But edamame are immature soybeans, harvested before they're ripe.

When the beans of the soy plant are actually fully grown they're pretty hard to digest. They're more palatable when watered until the roots of the beans grow long. Then you have a bean sprout, which you can add to a stir fry or salad. Or soak the soybeans in water overnight, boil them, then grind to a paste and add water to create a soy 'milk'. But that's not the end of it. Add gypsum rock to coagulate the milk from the soybeans until it turns into a block of curds which is excellent for absorbing flavour. Then you've made tofu. And what flavour should you add for that soft, but rather bland tofu to absorb?

Why not steam the soybeans, add roasted wheat, add lots of salt and some special mould, ferment it and filtrate it? That gives you soy sauce. Why, one might wonder, do we call these beans 'soy' anyway? The English name seems to derive from the Cantonese word for soy sauce – *see yow* or 'bean oil'. We've named the original bean after the sauce. In Indonesia they dry out the beans, crush them and add a fungus for fermentation purposes, producing a very versatile rigid slab of white protein called tempeh. All that Asian cuisine comes from the humble soybean. Yet these seeds shape our diets far beyond the delights of Asian cooking. Each bean is around one-half protein and one-fifth oil. The oil that comes out when you crush them goes into Western foods such as margarine, salad dressing and mayonnaise. Soy is, in fact, the second largest global source of vegetable oil.

There's more. Lecithin is a waxy substance that belongs to the lipid family. One half of its molecule attaches to water and the other attaches to oil, making it an ideal agent for binding otherwise unmixable watery and oily ingredients together into a smooth emulsion. And lecithin can, very handily, also be extracted from soy in copious amounts. Soy lecithin is used in most baked goods, chocolates and other confectionery. But it's not just food in which the magic of the soybean is manifested. The oil from the soybean also has industrial uses, being found in innumerable inks, paints, varnishes, soaps, candles, cosmetics, substitute rubbers and even a biodiesel that you can use to power your car.

Still this only scratches the surface of the uses of the soybean. After the beans have been squeezed for oil, the remaining flakes are ground into a 'cake' and become animal feed for pigs, chickens and fish. Soy is the biggest source of protein for the world's livestock and poultry. It's doubtful whether modern meat-producing agriculture would be possible without soy. So soy doesn't just feed us directly, it feeds the animals we eat. Their versatility is part of what makes soybeans a miracle – they're a miracle of protein delivery. Another dimension of the miracle is how well they grow. Soy thrives in a wider variety of soil and climatic conditions than any other major crop. They grow vigorously in poor soils. That's a trait described as 'weedy', but it's exactly what you want in a cash crop – a crop grown to sell in the market rather than for personal consumption. Their roots, which host a special kind of bacteria, handily deposit nitrogen, which is a vital nutrient, in the soil as they grow. Even the stalks and husks left over from processing can be turned into a cake, rich in nitrogen, which itself makes excellent fertiliser. Soy really is nothing short of a miracle of agricultural productivity.

Since 1960 the total amount of land on the planet used for growing cereals has remained roughly the same at around 700 million hectares, which is around 7 million sq km. The amount of land for soy, though, has risen almost five times, to 130 million hectares, an area roughly the size of South Africa. Total annual production has increased more than thirteen times over that period, to 370 million tonnes. It's those numbers that have earned it the label of the 'crop of the century'.[15]

Made in China

There's debate over precisely when it happened, but botanists tend to agree that soybeans were 'made' in China. A wild species of soy plant can be found across Asia, from Afghanistan to Japan and from southern Siberia to southern China. But they were probably first cultivated by human hands in northern China around 9,000 years ago. In ancient China, though they were designated one of the five 'sacred grains', alongside rice, wheat and two types of millet, they were not particularly favoured. They were seen as weeds that could be eaten if absolutely necessary. They seem to have grown more popular as the centuries passed. A seventeenth-century Spanish missionary to Fujian remarked on their dominant role in the local diet. 'A Chinese person who has tofu, vegetables and rice does not need anything else to work,' he wrote. 'Nor do I think there is anyone who cannot get it because for a quarter [of a silver coin] one can buy 20 ounces or even more.'[16]

In 1910 China and its northern province of Manchuria produced around nine in ten of all the world's soybeans – some 12 million tonnes a year. But there was huge disruption to Chinese soybean production as a result of the civil war that followed the demise of the Qing Dynasty, when warlords fought for control, and thereafter when the Nationalist government of Chiang Kai-shek sought to exterminate the Communists of Mao Zedong. Mao's Communists ultimately prevailed in the civil war in 1949, pushing Chiang Kai-shek's Nationalist forces to take refuge on the island of Taiwan where they, or rather their descendants, have remained ever since: this is unfinished business as far as Mao's successors are concerned. But in the meantime, Mao forced collectivisation on Chinese farms in the 1950s and then a brutally disruptive Cultural Revolution followed in the 1960s. All of that further crushed Chinese soy production. By 1957 China was producing just four in ten of the world's soybeans. In 1980 it was down to under one in ten. And then came the great opening up. In 2021, as China entered the World Trade Organization, Beijing lifted import restrictions and tariffs on soybeans. In 2022 the land where soybeans were first made produced 20 million tonnes – a record high. Yet China today is a massive net importer of the little beans. Where are they coming from?

Going Global

At the dawn of the twentieth century Harbin, a city in the chilly north-east region of modern-day China, was a boom town of ambitious newcomers and pioneers. It was full of Ukrainians, Russians, Poles, Georgians and Tatars attracted by its commercial opportunities. Even the Han Chinese were new to Harbin. Into this cultural and commercial melting pot came Russian Jews, including a merchant called Roman Kabalkin.

The central plain of Manchuria, while undeveloped, had also become a centre for Chinese soybean production. Visiting the markets and seeing the growing exports of soy fertiliser cake to Japan, Kabalkin came away with a vision of soybeans as the 'gold of Manchuria'. So in 1908 he sent a trial shipment of 5 tonnes to the port of Hull in England, via Vladivostok, in order to test the Western market.[17]

Potatoes had spread around the world after the European encounter with the Americas, the so-called 'Columbian exchange', which also included horses, tobacco and infectious diseases. However, soy remained an Asian food, despite the fact that the trade routes to China had existed for centuries longer. But then, at the dawn of the twentieth century, soybeans finally had their global breakout moment in the West. The market was receptive to Kabalkin's 'miracle beans' from Harbin and the orders flooded in.

Europe, especially the relatively late industrialising giant of Germany, was keen on new forms of protein and oils to feed a new mass market, to grease the wheels of industry and to manufacture new consumer goods. Production of dairy products like butter, tallow from beef and lard from swine struggled to keep up with the demand for edible fats. For industrial greases, Britain, Germany and France had up to that point relied on imports of flaxseeds, palm nuts, coconuts, cottonseed and peanuts, all of which could be squeezed for their oils. But Europe badly needed more to meet the burgeoning demand for soaps and paints. And soy, it seems, was better on price grounds. After the First World War expectations for superior diets and new consumer goods were running into the buffers of economic austerity. Soy seemed to provide a solution. The soybeans themselves were coming from the East, but it was the West that exploited the full potential of the bean through the science of industrial chemistry.

In 1922 a Hamburg oil miller called Hermann Bollmann directed the chemists he employed in his lab to tinker with soybeans to see if the use of chemicals could extract higher yields of oil than the existing methods of hydraulic (using fluids) or screw presses were delivering. They were successful and Bollmann became the king of soybean processing.[18]

Out of one tonne (1,000 kg) of soybeans his factory could extract 160 kg of oil and 820 kg of soybean cake fit for feeding animals. But perhaps the best part was a happy accident. As part of the experiments Bollmann's chemists found that adding benzene and alcohol to the soybean processing created a somewhat cloudy oil product. When they extracted and isolated this fluid and studied it, they discovered it was lecithin.

Until that point lecithin, a sought-after emulsifier, had only been extracted in relatively small quantities from eggs. It was named after the ancient Greek for egg yolk. It was also expensive. So soy lecithin, costing a twentieth of lecithin from eggs, was a game changer. The price of margarine, which used lecithin to make it as smooth and spreadable as butter, soon dropped. And the discovery opened up its use in new products like chocolate. Pick up a chocolate bar today and look at the label and you will likely see the words 'soy lecithin'.

Lecithin also began to be used in products such as pasta and pastries, and to create new cosmetic creams and moisturisers. Bollmann filed patents across Europe and America, and within two years his Hamburg factory was churning out 50 tonnes of soybean lecithin per year. The level of production was facilitated by technological progress – a miracle courtesy of a German corporate research laboratory. And the demand was met, largely, by the supply of soybeans. In 1927 Germany became the largest importer of soybeans from China, eclipsing Japan. In 1929 its ports accepted 1 million tonnes. But it was in America that the beans were planted and grown in world-changing volumes.

Good Ol' Soy

Soybeans first arrived in the US in the nineteenth century, although the precise timing is obscure. One account has them being introduced by the US naval officer Matthew Perry, whose 'black ships', belching dark smoke and steam, forced Japan to open up to Western trade in the 1850s. The first US farmers who planted soy generally didn't harvest it, usually letting their livestock graze on the plants directly.

Harvesting started after the First World War as Midwestern corn, cotton and wheat farmers, grappling with various insect blights and the consequences of soil mismanagement during the conflict as they rushed to increase production, discovered the extraordinary ability of the soy crop to rejuvenate their land. And planting of the crop slowly grew as farmers realised that this 'lowly bean', as it was sometimes termed, could be used as a cheap source of feed for their pigs and poultry.

The automotive manufacturing pioneer Henry Ford was a notable proponent. In 1941 he presented an experimental vehicle at the Michigan State Fair whose body was made of plastics derived partially from soybean fibres.[19] Perhaps surprisingly the car was white rather than black. Ford was a devotee of America's 'chemurgic' movement of the period. The objective of chemurgy – an amalgam of 'chemistry' and *ergon*, ancient Greek for 'work' – was to make the country more self-sufficient by cutting down on raw material imports to the US. The belief was that the genius of modern science, industrial entrepreneurship and America's vast agricultural resources would allow the country to grow and manufacture everything that it needed at home, without having to depend on potentially unreliable foreign states.

In 1935 the chemurgic movement's founders – a group of agriculturalists, scientists and industrial leaders – met in the city of Dearborn in Michigan to issue their 'Declaration of Dependence upon the Soil and the Right of Self-Maintenance'. It read: 'When in the course of the life of a Nation, its people become neglectful of the laws of nature . . . necessity impels them to turn to the soil in order to recover the right of self-maintenance.' Ford said he aimed to 'grow automobiles from the soil'.[20]

It was necessity that drove American soy production. Planting really took off during the Great Depression of the 1930s, as the US federal government also began to promote it as a way of restoring American agriculture's fortunes. Droughts in 1934 and 1936, which badly affected cotton, gave another boost to the cultivation of the relatively drought-resistant soy. Disruption to US vegetable oil imports from Asia in the Second World War provided another major official fillip to domestic soy planting, though with the beans mostly used in food rather than, as the chemurgists had advocated, in industry. Without soybeans, it is likely that Americans, like Europeans, would have faced food rationing. During the Second World War the US became the world's largest producer of soybeans, and after the war American-grown soy was a key component of food aid to a shattered and often starving Europe and Asia.

To this day we think of rolling green and yellow cornfields when we think of American agriculture. Yet soybeans have now overtaken corn as the most widely sown crop in America, with plantings covering over 35 million hectares in 2022, an area the size of Germany. America today has as much of a soy belt as a corn belt.

Shipping Soy to China

China was projected to consume around 110 million tonnes of soybean-related products in 2024, equal to almost a third of global production and far more than any other country. Its imports of soy have tripled in the past decade to around 100 million tonnes. That works out at around five cargo vessels arriving in China a day.

Today around a quarter to a third of the soybeans consumed in China hail from the US.

What are they being used for? Most of the soybeans grown in the US are genetically modified. China bans genetically modified soy for human consumption. So no mapo tofu, the chilli-freighted Sichuan staple, is made from American-grown imported beans. Yet there are no such import restrictions on soy for animals. The explosion of soy imports to China in recent decades is mainly to service the need for livestock feed.

Chinese demand for meat has tripled over the past half-century as rising incomes and economic growth have spurred demand for a diet richer in pork, beef and chicken – just as Japanese diets changed when that country grew richer after the Second World War. But China is ten times more populous than Japan, and the sheer scale of the resulting demand moves global agricultural markets like nothing else. In 1961 there were around 80 million pigs in China. In 2022 it was 452 million, more than half of the global swine population.[21] And those swine need a lot of feed.

China first imported soybeans from the US in 1977 when relations between the two countries had improved as President Richard Nixon sought to capitalise on Mao Zedong's estrangement from the Soviet Union during the Cold War. Around that time the American Soybean Association began to identify China's pigs as a potential market for American-grown beans.

So today America fattens China's animals, which feed the increasingly carnivorous Chinese people, who manufacture many of the goods consumed by the US and the world, from televisions and clothes to furniture and toys. In the first Industrial Revolution 'carrying coals to Newcastle' was an idiom expressing an economic irony, with the north-eastern English city being perceived to be so abundant in the fuel. In the era of globalisation, we might use 'shipping soybeans to China' instead. When the historian Niall Ferguson and the economist Moritz Schularik coined the portmanteau term 'Chimerica' in 2007 they were talking about China using its dollars, acquired from selling goods to America, to buy vast quantities of US government debt in an arrangement of financial and economic mutual dependence.[22] But that mutual dependence could be applied to little magic beans too. Yet this trade is Chimericas (plural), rather than Chimerica.

Soybeans were first introduced to Brazil in the 1880s, when they were referred to as 'Chinese beans'. Yet it was the Japanese who built the industry in the South American country. In 1908 around 800 Japanese peasants from Okinawa emigrated to São Paulo on a promise of farmland, though they found themselves treated little better than the recently emancipated slaves on the coffee farms. In a bid for independence these Japanese migrants started to grow soybeans on a small scale. More emigrated in the decades that followed. In 1925 the first successful soybean plantation was established on São Simão, the high plateau around the city of São Paulo. In 1946 serious commercial production began and spread to the savanna region south of the Amazon rainforest known as the Cerrado.

Argentina, Mexico, Paraguay, Uruguay and states across Central America followed Brazil into soy production. The fact that labour costs in the region were considerably lower than in the US, giving their output a price advantage in global markets, made it all the more desirable for farmers to get into soy. Some researchers have referred to these Latin American states as 'the United Soybean Republic', or 'Soylandia'.[23] Brazil overtook Chinese soy production in the mid-1970s, and today it has even eclipsed America. All this has made the Americas the continent of soy, producing almost nine in ten of all the beans grown on the planet.

In the space of a hundred years we have seen a vast trans-Pacific rotation of soybean production from Asia to the Americas. In their oil form, we have seen a globalisation of their consumption. For most of their history soybeans were grown on small plots. Only in the twentieth century were they first produced on a commercial scale as a cash crop. The environmental implications of that shift are vast. Some have suggested the Anthropocene, an era when mankind shapes the natural world, can be seen as a Soyacene, where the cultivation of soy shapes the planet.[24] Soy is certainly a miracle of globalisation, the process under which our planet has become more interconnected. Today soybeans and their derivatives are the most internationally traded agricultural commodity, with around 45 per cent sold across national borders compared with 28 per cent for wheat, 16 per cent for maize and 10 per cent for rice.[25] It is the most globalised crop in its production and consumption.

Closing the circle, soy is also, as we have seen, a product of globalisation. Its success would not have been possible without the great global flux of people, products and technological knowledge of the twentieth century. It is entwined in the story of the great advancement in living standards of humanity. Without soy, the global price of food would certainly be higher – and we would likely lack innumerable consumer goods that we take for granted. 'Invisible yet ubiquitous' is how one historian of the soybean aptly describes it.[26]

There is a dark side. Some argue that soy is a climate-wrecking bean. The main driver of Amazon rainforest deforestation in Brazil, something that is accelerating dangerous global warming, is land cleared for beef cattle grazing. Yet researchers judge the explosion of soy plantations to have had spillover effects, as Cerrado ranchers move into the Amazon.[27] The Brazilian government imposed a soy-planting moratorium in the Amazon in 2006. Some want this moratorium to be extended to the Cerrado. It's clear that to forestall the deforestation that contributes directly to a perilously heating planet we need to find a way to make the cultivation of the miracle bean environmentally sustainable.

Soy Choke

Analysts talk of a 'chip choke' on China – the ability of the United States to stall and even reverse China's economic development by removing its access to cutting-edge silicon microchips, which are mostly manufactured on the island of Taiwan. But a soy choke, given China's reliance on imports of this staple for its domestic food system, could be just as hazardous. And Beijing is beginning to realise it.

The Chinese Communist Party has long linked its legitimacy to its ability to guarantee staple food supplies to the population. As far back as 2013, the country's newly installed leader, Xi Jinping, gave a speech that showed that he was already fretting about national food security. 'The rice bowls of the Chinese people must be firmly in our own hands,' he told party apparatchiks.[28] Donald Trump's trade war on China, beginning in 2018, and the global spasm of protectionism during the Covid pandemic seemed like a grim vindication of Xi Jinping's philosophy. From then on, rhetorically at least, it was action stations.

Government guidelines encouraged domestic manufacturers of animal feed to use alternatives to soy, and China has designated increasing domestic soybean production as 'a major political task to be accomplished'. Xi Jinping has said China must establish a 'strategic baseline' to ensure self-sufficiency in key commodities, including soybeans. So is this the great reversal? Is China heading for soy self-sufficiency? The problem for Beijing is that it will not be as easy as issuing an edict.[29]

China has a lot of land: some 9.5 million sq km, roughly equal to the United States. But only a tenth of China's land is arable, suitable for crops like soybeans.[30] The US has 45 per cent more arable land and only a quarter of China's population. Chinese academics in 2020 estimated that China had a soybean 'self-sufficiency' rate of 16 per cent – meaning, as we've seen, that it domestically produced around a sixth of the beans it consumed. They calculated the maximum self-sufficiency rate in soybeans that the country could feasibly achieve given these land constraints (and the amount of land in China currently used for growing wheat) would be 42 per cent.[31] The bottom line is that even if China tried to become wholly self-sufficient in soybeans it would be unable to – at least without a radical change in the diet of its population.

In 2017 China's Ministry of Health did release dietary guidelines urging a halving of national meat consumption. But a return to 'tofu, vegetables and rice' is something even the Communist Party, with its promise of 'common prosperity', would be loath to impose. Could such a shift be effectively forced on China by geopolitics? When Donald Trump slapped tariffs on Chinese steel imports in 2018, China responded with tariffs on US soybean imports, calculating that this would hit Trump's Republican base in the US farm belt. The value of soybeans exported to China fell by more than three-quarters in the following year. Yet soybean sales to China have nearly rebounded to their pre-trade-war levels since 2018. This doesn't mean no harm was done. Absent the trade war, US soybean exports would probably have grown more. US farmers lost market share to Brazil and this disruption is one of the reasons Brazil has overtaken America in total soy production.

But the crucial point is that, from China's perspective, importing less from one country doesn't automatically lead to more domestic production and greater self-sufficiency. More beans simply get sourced from elsewhere. In other words if China wants to continue consuming the miracle bean at anything like its current levels, the country's leadership is doomed, whether it likes it or not, to engage in global trade. And it's certainly not just China that is constrained when it comes to food self-sufficiency.

Buy British

With his mop of wild grey curls, long sideburns and khaki shorts, Guy Singh-Watson resembles a tall and rather dashing hobbit. Guy is the owner of Riverford Farm, a progressive farming compound a quarter of an hour's drive from the town of Totnes in the bucolic English county of Devon.

At the heart of Riverford, a large solar-powered two-storey hangar houses the staff who run not only the farm but also its pioneering vegetable delivery box business, which sends out 80,000 neat packs of organic veg to households across the UK every week. There's a staff canteen at Riverford that is almost as well appointed as its award-winning organic restaurant, serving locally sourced fare every day. When I visited, tomato-braised pork medallions and leeks from the farm were on the workers' menu.

In the summer of 2024, during the UK general election campaign the Conservative leader, Rishi Sunak, sent out a message on social media: 'We shouldn't be reliant on foreign food. Buy British.'[32] There was no further elaboration of these words from the then prime minister, whose party was lagging badly in the polls, and most assumed it was nothing more than a rather desperate bid for the votes of farmers. But it did raise a question that had been bouncing around in British politics for some time. Can the UK actually be self-sufficient in food? Could British farms, like Riverford, provide enough food to feed the entire nation?

That was the question I'd come to Riverford to ask. As we tramped up the 30-degree gradient of one of Guy's freshly harvested radicchio fields, his dog digging furiously at our feet, throwing up great loamy chunks of soil onto our boots, Guy gave me his answer. It was yes, but with a rather large caveat. 'People have to be prepared, willing, enthusiastic even, to eat what we can grow in this country in season,' he told me.

Back at Riverford's headquarters Guy elaborated, drawing my attention to a special patch of vegetables, a trial crop of a lettuce called Castelfranco. Riverford was trialling it because of the plant's ability to grow in the colder months. If British people want home-grown salad in winter this is what they can expect.

'When the first frosts come it actually gets better, a bit more tender and a bit sweeter,' Guy enthused, tearing off the corner of a purple-speckled pale green leaf and popping it in his mouth.

> It's part of the dandelion/radicchio/endive family, all of which are quite bitter. For people who are just used to eating a little gem or an iceberg, they might struggle with it. I think it's infinitely more interesting. It's certainly better for you, more nutritious. All those bitter flavours are very cleansing, they're good for your kidney, your liver.

So national food self-sufficiency isn't a fantasy? 'It would be very possible, but we wouldn't all be able to eat fillet steak once a week. You might have it once a year,' chuckled Guy. 'It will require a pretty radical change to our diet. We all need to be prepared to eat a lot less animal protein – so less meat, dairy, eggs. There's absolutely no way we can feed our population without eating a lot less meat.'

And therein, perhaps, lies the rub – and not just for Britain, but for the planet.

The Meat of the Issue

In a world food system shaped by geography, soy and changing diet, very few countries are an island. China is self-sufficient in meat. But livestock needs to be fed. China is, as we have seen, reliant on imported soy fodder for its hundreds of millions of animals.

China is by no means alone in this. Around half of the wheat grown in the European Union is fed to cows. In the US a third of the corn crop goes the same way. It's estimated that around 40 per cent of all the cereals grown by farmers on the planet are used to raise livestock rather than feed humans directly.[33] And those livestock, with their demand for grazing land, are literally crowding out any near-term possibility of greater national food self-sufficiency for many countries – which was the point Guy Singh-Watson was making.

Calls for national food self-sufficiency might be growing. Yet it's far from clear that people have weighed up the full implications of trying to achieve it in many countries. The UK government commissioned an independent review of the national food system in 2021.[34] One of the recommendations, taking into account climate change, was an attempt to cut the average Briton's meat consumption by around a third over the next decade. The suggestion was ignored by the government. Whether because of a lack of knowledge or enthusiasm, there was no public outcry at the absence of action. In 2023 Prime Minister Sunak gave a speech declaring that he was comprehensively 'scrapping' any proposals to tax meat, calculating that this would put him on the right side of public opinion.[35]

Some research in 2024 suggests around 16 per cent of British adults follow or have adopted a meat-free diet – vegans, vegetarians and pescatarians – and that this is more common among younger generations.[36] That implies a growing share over time. Plant-based meat substitutes are rising in popularity and there's a buzz around the technology of lab-grown meat. And for some, ironically, more soy is the answer – but to be consumed directly by us all. Three-quarters of the soybeans grown on the planet are used for livestock feed, most of the rest is for industrial purposes. Less than a tenth is currently for direct human consumption. How transformative would it be for the environment, some wonder, if we got our protein directly from the soybean rather than from the flesh and products of animals that feed on it? To create 100 g of protein from tofu requires around 2.2 sq m of land. To create the equivalent amount of protein from pork requires 10.7 sq m, from milk 27 sq m and from beef 164 sq m.[37]

Yet it would be a stretch to argue that the UK – or indeed any nation in the developed world – is anywhere near approaching a tipping point when it comes to coming off meat, let alone moving to a soy-based diet. A global survey of eating trends put the share of vegetarianism (excluding pescatarians) in the UK in 2021/22 at 6.5 per cent of the population, although that was up from 5.5 per cent in 2018–19. There were also modest gains in the share of vegetarianism in Germany, South Korea and the US. However, the share of vegetarianism in China fell by 4.2 percentage points over that period to 5.4 per cent. India still has a high share of vegetarianism, at 26.5 per cent. But like China, which India has now overtaken as the world's most populous nation, its share is falling rapidly as it grows richer.[38] That's another factor pushing towards trade, rather than national self-sufficiency, when it comes to food.

Food Security

Many people talk about food security and self-sufficiency as if their meanings were interchangeable and self-evident. Neither is the case. Food security on an individual or family level isn't just a question of dependence on national imports, it's also about the price of food domestically. Can someone who can't afford to eat, or eat healthily, in a wealthy country be considered food-secure? Some poorer countries are net food exporters, so with high self-sufficiency rates in theory, yet also have high rates of domestic hunger. Some rich countries are large net food importers, with low rates of self-sufficiency, but have successfully eliminated malnutrition. So researchers tend to use composite measures to assess national food security, which take into account not just national production and consumption, but also domestic food retail prices, the food's availability to all and the diversity of sources of supply and their stability. Japan is ranked the sixth most food-secure nation in the world by Economist Impact, part of the Economist Group, despite importing around 60 per cent of the calories it consumes.[39] That's a higher food security ranking than even the US, which nationally produces more food than it consumes. Japan scores highly because of the domestic affordability and availability of food.[40]

Japan has one of the lowest food self-sufficiency ratios on a calorie basis in the world

National food self-sufficiency ratios, 2019

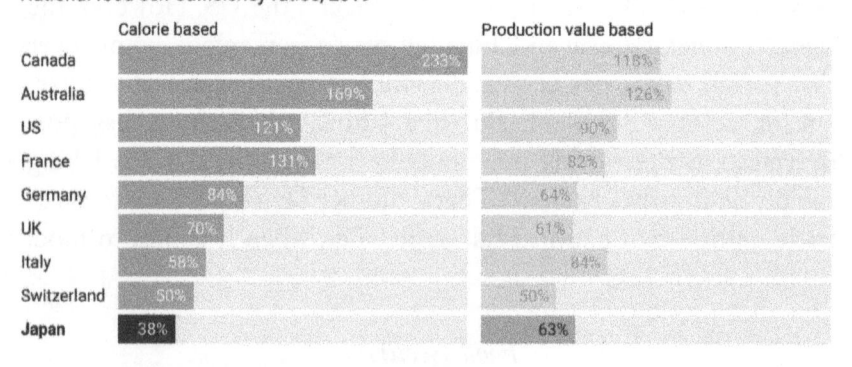

	Calorie based	Production value based
Canada	233%	118%
Australia	169%	126%
US	121%	90%
France	131%	82%
Germany	84%	64%
UK	70%	61%
Italy	58%	84%
Switzerland	50%	50%
Japan	38%	63%

Estimated by Japan's Ministry of Agriculture, Forestry and Fisheries
Source: MAFF · Created with Datawrapper

Figure 5

National agricultural production relative to consumption is certainly only a very crude measure and a potentially fatally misleading one, as the case of soybean imports for Chinese animal feed shows. Another striking reality is the reliance of many giant national agricultural producers on chemical fertiliser imports. The US is self-sufficient in food on most metrics, yet the country is also the world's third largest importer of fertilisers by value – fertilisers needed to grow those crops and achieve high yields.[41] Similarly, Brazil imported $27 billion worth of fertilisers in 2022, including $2.7 billion from China. Global fertiliser trade, particularly in potash and phosphates, makes the world food system one of interdependence.

Food self-sufficiency does not even guarantee national food security in theory. Consider two hypothetical nations. One is capable of fully feeding itself and refuses imports. The other is incapable of fully feeding itself and welcomes exports. Imagine if both nations were struck by an environmental blight, resulting in a failed domestic harvest. What would happen? The country with food autarky would see its food prices shoot up. The food importer would be partially shielded from such inflation by being able to buy supplies from outside. Cross-border food trade is a national agricultural shock absorber. If relying on food imports feels dangerous or reckless, think of the perils of not being able to call on such imports.

Or consider conflict. Ukraine, as a major grain producer, had a food import dependency rate close to zero in 2020. Yet after the Russian invasion in 2022, which saw Ukrainian farms crushed under the tracks of Russian tanks and crops unharvested, the country was forced to rely on World Food Programme assistance to feed 3 million of its 43 million-strong population.[42] A nation's food security clearly depends on a great deal more than the amount of food it produces on its territory.

There are further implications of an exile economics policy on food that would resonate well beyond a country's borders. As we have seen, cereal and fertiliser export restrictions by some states during 2022 increased the famine risk in other food-importing countries in Africa and the Middle East. In seeking to safeguard their own national food security, they reduced the security of others and, in the event, didn't even help themselves because their actions merely pushed up global food prices, which hit their own consumers.

We should think about another dimension of the interdependence of our food system. For a country like Kenya, agricultural produce like green beans, sent to European markets, now makes up a considerable share of its national exports, thanks to tariff-reducing trade deals with Western countries. Agriculture accounts for a fifth of the Kenyan economy, a third of its employment and two-thirds of its exports.[43] Any decline in those agricultural exports – perhaps because countries like the UK attempt to grow more produce at home in industrial greenhouses – will undermine the country's economy and risk increasing food insecurity there. It is already often difficult for developing countries to sell their produce across borders, mainly due to agricultural protectionism by richer states, and food trade liberalisation is regarded as an important lever of development for the least-developed nations.[44] Agricultural subsidies for the production of commodities such as sugar and cotton in rich countries – often justified in the name of self-sufficiency – also lower world prices and have the effect of restricting the export opportunities of some developing countries.

Would such countries be better off if they were themselves self-sufficient in food? The evidence suggests not. According to calculations by the International Food Policy Research Institute, the Sub-Saharan African nation of Zambia has a dependency rate on imports for its food staples of just 7 per cent, which is extremely low by global standards. More than half of its population is employed in agriculture and it is a net exporter of food. Yet the share of Zambia's population in food insecurity, at 70 per cent, is one of the highest in the world.

Figure 6

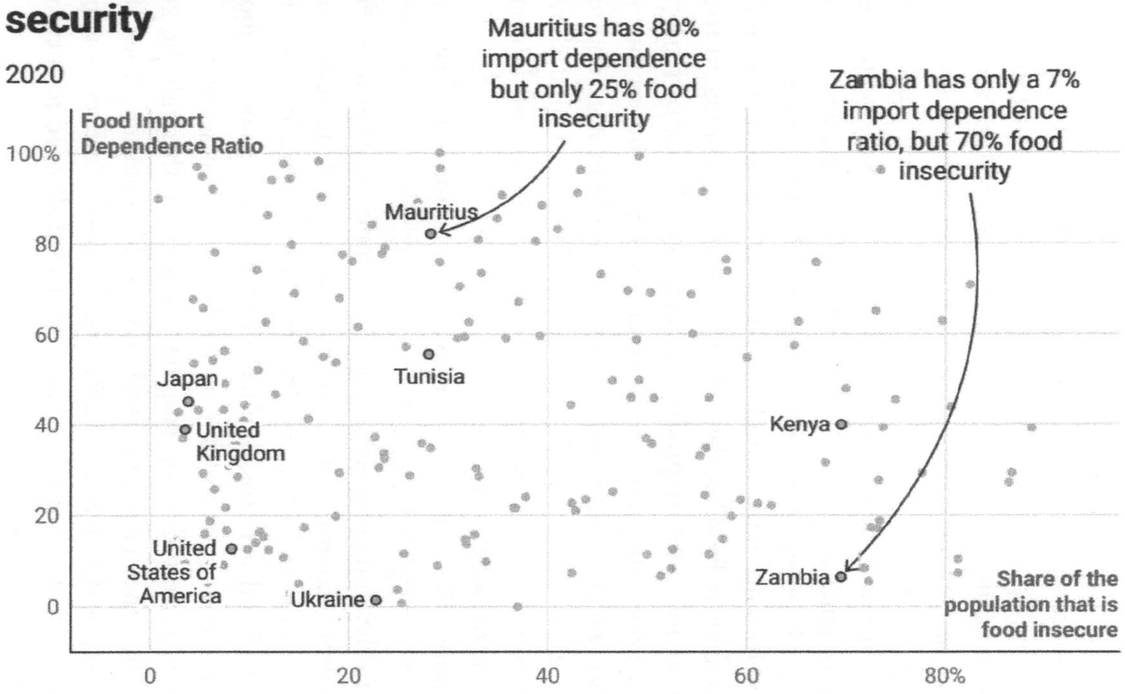

It's instructive to contrast Zambia with Mauritius, an island some 3,000 km to its east in the Indian Ocean. Mauritius has a very high staple import dependency ratio of 82 per cent but food insecurity of just 28 per cent. The difference between Zambia and Mauritius is that Mauritius successfully integrated into global trading networks in the 1970s, moving from being a low-income country producing sugarcane to a middle-income one producing first textiles and today a wide range of services. In 2022 just 5 per cent of Mauritians worked in agriculture and 73 per cent in services, including banking and technology. Mauritius's national income per head is more than $29,000 per year (adjusted for purchasing power), compared to $4,100 in Zambia. What creates food insecurity is not import dependency but poverty.

'Countries with stable societies are invariably those that maintain self-sufficiency in food,' declared China's leader, Xi Jinping, in 2013. 'Those that are unable to produce enough to feed their own people suffer from domestic unrest and foreign pressure.'[45] But as the case of Zambia, which defaulted on its sovereign debt in 2020 and had to apply for a bailout from the International Monetary Fund, shows, a high national food sufficiency rate is no guarantee of domestic stability or geopolitical weight.

For nations like these, the road to greater national food security must pass through plugging into global trading networks and seeking to develop economically in the manner of Mauritius. For most wealthier countries it means focusing on making agriculture more environmentally sustainable, tackling climate change and continued liberalised cross-border trade. When it comes to food, exile economics seems to offer only a false sense of security.

But food is only the first stop on our journey through the key commodities that currently bind our world together. Does the same lesson – that trade is better than self-sufficiency – apply elsewhere? What about other basic things we all need to survive? What about energy?

4
Energy

The letter arrived on 14 July 2022.[1] The recipient was Uniper, an operator of European gas-powered power stations, headquartered in Düsseldorf, Germany. The sender was Gazprom, the Kremlin-controlled operator of Russian gas and oil fields. A large share of Gazprom's business was dispatching natural gas, extracted from its vast Siberian fossil fuel fields, to European generators like Uniper via the mighty Nord Stream pipeline. The 1 m-diameter steel pipe began at the far western Russian port of Vyborg and stretched for 1,000 km under the cold and brackish waters of the Baltic Sea before finally coming ashore at the German coastal resort of Lubmin, near the city of Greifswald.[2]

The year before, 2021, Nord Stream had been a conduit into Europe for some 59 billion cubic metres of Russian natural gas.[3] Nord Stream deliveries alone in that year accounted for around a third of Europe's total Russian gas imports and 40 per cent of those of Germany, the continent's largest economy. And almost half of Europe's total natural gas imports were from Russia.[4] It was Russian natural gas that fed many of the gas-turbine power stations of Germany and many of those elsewhere in Europe too, including in Britain, Sweden and the Netherlands. It was, then, Russian gas that helped keep Europe's lights on and its homes warm in winter. But the letter said a large chunk of those vital gas deliveries were about to stop.

Gazprom informed Uniper it was no longer responsible for delivering gas along Nord Stream because of 'extraordinary circumstances'. So what were these circumstances? Gazprom had been complaining for months about the failure of the German engineering firm Siemens to return a turbine engine, sent for repair in Canada, which the Russian company claimed it needed to operate a compressor station in Vyborg to pump the gas through the pipe to Europe. Uniper and the German authorities scorned this explanation, insisting the turbine in question was ready for shipment and that the problem was that the Russians were refusing to take delivery. Their objections made no difference – the turbine was an excuse. What was really going on here was as transparent as the gas in the Nord Stream pipeline.

Supplies to Europe had already been severely reduced for months by Gazprom because of claimed maintenance works. Russia had been progressively cutting off the flows in Europe's main gas artery in response to the avalanche of Western sanctions that had descended on the country in the wake of Vladimir Putin's invasion of Ukraine on 24 February that year. The letter was merely confirmation that those flows would soon go to zero. The Kremlin was firing its 'energy weapon' at Europe and withholding gas for geopolitical reasons. It was a moment that had been foretold four decades earlier.

In 1981 the Soviet Union had proposed building an enormous pipeline to transport natural gas from the newly developed Urengoy fields of western Siberia into Central Europe via its Ukrainian territories. Europe, especially West Germany, was keen on securing cheap Russian gas supplies after the global energy crisis of the 1970s. But Washington sensed a threat. The new pipeline would triple the Soviet Union's natural gas export capability, and give it a major economic boost and an influx of badly needed foreign currency.[5]

A CIA memo warned the construction of such a direct energy linkage would 'provide the Soviets one additional pressure point they could use as part of a broader diplomatic offensive to persuade the West Europeans to accept their viewpoint' and made reference to Moscow's potential new 'natural gas weapon' against the North Atlantic Treaty Organization (NATO).[6] Ronald Reagan's White House tried to persuade America's NATO allies in Europe to ditch the project. When that failed, the Republican president imposed sanctions, preventing American firms from supplying or collaborating in it.[7] 'They can have their damned pipeline. But not with American equipment and not with American technology,' an exasperated Reagan reportedly exclaimed.[8]

But despite the American anger, the project went ahead, justified by the West German maxim of *Wandel durch Handel*, or 'change through trade'. This was the idea that it would ultimately be more productive for the West to build economic bridges with the Soviet Union rather than erect economic bulwarks against it. The pipeline into West Germany opened in 1984, with the Europeans footing the upfront construction costs and the Soviets paying them back in the form of free gas deliveries. It was the most controversial energy project of the Cold War. A young American wrote a book based on his undergraduate thesis about the episode in 1987 called *Ally versus Ally: America, Europe, and the Siberian Pipeline Crisis*, which concluded that European hopes that 'expanded economic relations will produce positive change in the Kremlin's foreign and domestic policies' were 'wishful thinking'.[9] *Wandel durch Handel*, in other words, was a delusion. By a neat historical irony, that young scholar – Antony Blinken – would be President Biden's secretary of state in 2022 when Vladimir Putin switched off Nord Stream.

On 26 November 2022 Nord Stream (and a second parallel pipeline called Nord Stream 2, which had not yet been put into operation) were mysteriously blown up, causing a massive, bubbling leak of methane into the Baltic. Fingers were pointed, by various sources and with varying levels of credibility, at the security services of Russia, at Ukraine and at the US. As in an Agatha Christie detective story, each had a plausible motive. But there was no compelling evidence for any individual state being behind it.[10] Whoever was responsible, the plain fact was that both Nord Streams were now dead in the water. And the decades of American warnings of Europe's folly in relying on Russia for energy supplies seemed vindicated.

In the summer of that year the wholesale price of traded gas in Europe had spiked to an astonishing ten times its level of a year earlier, driven up by a desperate scramble by European governments to fill gas storage facilities ahead of winter. It was a price that economists were warning was pretty much guaranteed to send the continent into a deep economic recession. Within months German cities were dimming their streetlights at night to conserve energy. Public swimming pools were going unheated.[11] And electricity-powered agricultural greenhouses across northern Europe were either shutting down or drastically scaling back production in the biggest energy crisis since the oil shock of the 1970s.[12]

Independence Day

The speed with which Europe accepted the new reality was impressive. As the gas flows from Nord Stream tapered off, Europe pivoted from a policy of insouciance in the face of external energy dependence to a vigorous dash for self-reliance. The normally sclerotic European Commission, the primary executive arm of the EU, managed to produce a plan in record time, dubbed 'REPowerEU', to reduce the bloc's gas imports from Russia by two-thirds by the end of 2022 and rapidly accelerate the rollout of wind, solar and other forms of renewable energy to fill the gap.[13] The EU had previously been targeting 40 per cent of its total energy coming from renewables by 2030 as part of its 2050 net zero timetable. Overnight that target was raised to 45 per cent.[14] 'Renewables are cheap, they are home-grown, they make us independent,' explained the European Commission president, Ursula von der Leyen, at a Brussels press conference on 27 September 2022. 'Renewables are really our energy insurance for the future.'[15] That sentiment was echoed by Germany's economy minister, Robert Habeck. 'There are no taboos,' Habeck told his country's public service broadcasting network ARD. 'The real path to energy independence is to phase out fossil fuels.'[16] Habeck's ministry proposed that Germany should now aim to generate all of its electricity from renewable sources by 2035 – five years earlier than previously planned.[17]

The same pressures were being felt in Britain, which, despite finally leaving the European Union in 2021, remained connected to wholesale European energy markets and was watching its own domestic gas and electricity prices spike terrifyingly. At around this time I was sent to the Lake District in the picturesque north-west of England to report for the BBC on how small firms there were being affected by the new energy emergency. The manager of a pub called Ye Olde Fleece in the town of Kendal told me that its annual energy bill was set to rise from £44,000 to £124,000, an almost threefold rise. A nearby catering company had already seen its fuel bill rise sevenfold.[18]

That same autumn the newly installed UK prime minister, Liz Truss, informed the *Sun* newspaper that she had 'a clear plan to fix the root cause of this crisis and take back our energy independence', which, as in the EU, also involved ramping up domestic renewables.[19] 'We are accelerating all sources of home-grown energy production,' Truss insisted. The then-opposition Labour leader, Keir Starmer, wanted to go even further. He told his party conference in Liverpool that autumn that he planned to establish a new publicly owned company called Great British Energy to invest in British renewable power and be in a position to rely almost entirely on domestically generated wind, solar and nuclear for all electricity generation by 2030, five years sooner than the government plan. Why? 'Because it is right for jobs, because it is right for growth, because it is right for energy independence.'[20]

The US echoed this European emphasis on national energy self-sufficiency. America had become a net exporter of energy in 2019 for the first time since the 1950s as a result of the extraordinary boom in domestic hydraulic fracturing of natural shale gas.[21] 'Fracking' – which involves firing high-pressure jets of water into shale rock – took off in the mid-2000s in states such as Texas, North Dakota and Oklahoma. The fracking boom helped keep domestic US gas prices more or less under control in the summer of 2022, unlike in Europe.[22] Yet when it comes to energy, no country is a true island. The US market was connected to the rest of the planet via the oil market. In the wake of Russia's invasion of Ukraine, the global oil price hit $110 a barrel, almost double its level twelve months earlier.

That pushed up US gasoline prices for vehicles to a record high of almost $5 per gallon. So Washington too felt the need to recommit to American energy self-sufficiency. 'We'll keep doing everything we can ... to ensure our energy independence and security is available and to lower gas prices here at home and to give folks a little bit of breathing room,' Joe Biden declared at a press conference in the White House's Roosevelt Room on 19 October 2022.[23] The Inflation Reduction Act, signed into law in August 2022, aimed to massively increase US offshore wind production to, in the words of Biden's energy secretary, 'strengthen the nation's energy security'.[24]

India was also moving in the same direction as Europe and America. Speaking from the ramparts of New Delhi's Red Fort on India's seventy-sixth Independence Day in August 2022, the country's prime minister, Narendra Modi, wearing a long turban in the colours of the Indian flag, focused on energy. 'We need to be atmanirbhar [self-reliant] in our energy sector. From solar energy to Mission Hydrogen to the adoption of EVs [electric vehicles], we need to take these initiatives to the next level for energy independence,' he declared.[25] China too was singing from the same hymn sheet – the psalter of energy independence. At the 20th National Communist Party Congress in October 2022 the Chinese government, conscious of the country's heavy reliance on oil and gas imports, pledged to ramp up annual domestic energy production capacity in renewables in response to the spiking global price of fossil fuels.[26] 'We will strengthen our systems for energy production, supply, storage, and marketing to ensure energy security,' proclaimed Xi Jinping.[27]

The global energy shock of the summer of 2022 pushed energy independence to the very top of the policy agenda across the world. It was the same rhetoric from ministries in the West and politburos in the East. Among democracies and authoritarian regimes alike, national energy independence was suddenly seen as essential. Oil and gas are by some distance the most traded commodities in the world, accounting for almost a seventh of the total value of global trade in 2022.[28] The lesson taken from the shock of 2022 was that importing these hydrocarbons was perilous. The safer option was to be self-sufficient in energy generation. And that mainly meant renewables, generating energy from wind turbines and solar panels. 'The sun and the wind simply don't belong to anyone,' as Germany's Robert Habeck put it.[29] It seemed logical. And it connected perfectly with the requirement of the global energy transition, the need to shift away from planet-heating fossil fuels like oil and gas for power. But if this rush into renewables was motivated by a desire for national self-sufficiency, there was a practical problem. Harnessing the sun that shines onto your national territory and the wind that blows across it requires the mass deployment of solar panels and wind turbines. And this requires manufactured components. Can a nation be truly energy independent if it has to rely on others for these?

Solar So Good

Solyndra was a Silicon Valley start-up company, founded in 2005, that had not one but two bright ideas. The first was that it planned to build solar panels, not with the traditional silicon but rather a mixture of copper and three less well-known elements called indium, gallium and selenium. This material base would enable Solyndra's panels to be extremely thin relative to conventional ones. Bright idea number two was that Solyndra's panels would also be cylindrical rather than flat in order to enhance their effective surface area – and therefore the unit's efficiency – in absorbing the sun's rays and turning it into electrical energy. The Solyndra product, with its two dozen rows of cylinders set on a rectangular frame, looked more like a towel radiator than a conventional solar panel. Yet it worked and the company grew, attracting investment from the many venture capital investors of the Valley. But then came the collapse of the US investment bank Lehman Brothers and the 2008 financial crisis, and Solyndra, though it was expanding, found itself running short on cash just as the private investors it needed to cover its losses while it sought to scale up hunkered down to weather the financial storm.[30]

Salvation, though, came in the form of the federal government's cheque-book. In 2009 Barack Obama had just entered the White House and his administration was seeking to help the overall economy recover from the post-Lehman recession and also to support promising new technology firms with government stimulus money. The Obama White House was also looking, specifically, to re-establish American leadership in solar technology. Silicon Valley's Solyndra seemed to fit like a glove.

On 20 March 2009 Obama's energy secretary, Steven Chu (no relation), announced that Solyndra would receive a $535 million federal loan from his department to help it expand. At a groundbreaking ceremony for a new Solyndra manufacturing plant in Fremont, California on 9 September 2009, the Californian governor, Arnold Schwarzenegger, appeared alongside Chu and the company's chief executive, Chris Grone, on a platform in front of some earthmovers. The three men wielded symbolic golden shovels. The then vice-president, Joe Biden, flashed up via video link on a large screen next to the platform. 'Out there at Solyndra, you guys have figured it out,' Biden enthused to the assembled dignitaries and media. 'You've figured out how to harness the sun's power for a better, more efficient, prosperous future for all of America – and in the process you're creating more jobs.' Only Solyndra hadn't figured it out. Or at least not the business side of it.

In 2011 Solyndra ran out of money, filed for bankruptcy and laid off around 1,100 of its employees. The $535 million government loan was never repaid and the American taxpayer was forced to swallow the loss. And so began years of investigations into the company and its relationship with the Obama administration, including one from the FBI for fraud.[31] The Washington air was thick with accusations from Republicans and conservative American media outlets of cronyism and corruption. The US Department of Energy's Office of Inspector General ultimately found in 2015 that Solyndra's executives had made misrepresentations to the government about its order book, though it also criticised federal officials for not being sufficiently rigorous in their analysis of the company.[32] Regardless of who was more to blame, Solyndra soon became a byword in the US for the folly of government involvement in the private sector. As for Solyndra's unused inventory of some 8 million unused glass tubes, around 1,000 were sold and became part of an outdoor art installation at the University of California Botanical Garden.[33] Given the millions of dollars of taxpayers' money spent on Solyndra, Republicans called it the most expensive artwork ever produced. But Solyndra's legacy went further. Its failure dealt a severe blow to the Obama administration's hopes of stimulating large-scale solar panel manufacturing on US soil. Yet on the other side of the world, it was a very different story.

Starting in the mid-2000s, Chinese local governments began pushing state subsidies into conventional silicon solar panel manufacturing in the form of discounted land, subsidised energy and cheap loans from state-owned banks with mandates to fund the industry's growth.[34] The results of this industrial strategy were formidable. At the turn of the millennium around 40 per cent of solar panels were manufactured in Japan, around 20 per cent in the US and around 10 per cent in Germany, which had built up a notable production cluster in the former East Germany. By 2016 the combined share of all three nations was less than 10 per cent. China had gone from zero to producing 70 per cent of the global total. By 2021 China's share had hit 85 per cent and accounted for a similar share of all the world's exports of solar panels.[35] One of the reasons Solyndra went bust was because the American firm simply couldn't compete on price with conventional Chinese silicon solar panel imports to the US. It was a similar story in Germany, whose manufacturers wilted in the fierce glare of Chinese competition. Even the imposition of European Union tariffs on panel imports between 2013 and 2018, justified by claims of unfair domestic subsidies from Beijing, and strong financial support for solar from the German government did little to arrest the decline of the German solar industry.

In January 2024 the price of Chinese solar panel exports had fallen to just $0.15 per watt of generating capacity, a 60 per cent decline on the price in 2017 and around half the equivalent prices of US- and European-manufactured solar panels and a third cheaper than Indian-made ones.[36] The Chinese solar export boom shows no sign of waning. Chinese exports of solar power rose almost sixfold between 2017 and 2024. They are going to markets all across the planet: to Brazil, Pakistan, Japan, Saudi Arabia, Thailand and countries in Africa.

The biggest customer, though, is Europe, which absorbed half of China's solar exports in 2023.[37] The only major market that did not import solar equipment directly from China in that year was the US, although the domestic American solar industry complained Chinese equipment was still coming into the country via Chinese factories in places like Malaysia, Cambodia and Vietnam, which imported Chinese panels and shipped them on with only minor modifications.[38]

Is it wise for Europe to be such a big customer of China for solar panels? Or is this the Russian natural gas story all over again? 'Once again, our European allies are selling their security for cheap energy,' argued an analyst at America's Center for Strategic and International Studies in 2024.[39] 'The US must not make the same mistake.' A similar challenge, or opportunity, depending on your point of view, is presented by wind power.

Blowing in the Wind

It's quite something to stand directly underneath a modern wind turbine and look up. I performed this neck-spraining exercise in 2022 at a wind farm in the English county of Lincolnshire, run by a Scottish renewables company, SSE, when I was interviewing the company's chief executive, Alistair Phillips-Davies, about the energy crisis. He was explaining to me how domestic wind power could replace the UK's 'volatile and expensive' imports of oil and gas, but I confess to having been somewhat distracted by the giant white blades spinning over my head.

Wind turbines are the largest pieces of rotating machinery made by man. Yet the truth is that those 90 m-diameter windmills in Lincolnshire, made by the Danish company Vestas, are small fry in the modern world of wind turbines. In 2023, the Chinese manufacturer Ming Yang unveiled plans for a new offshore wind turbine with a 310 m-diameter rotor to be built by 2025.[40] To get a sense of the scale of that, try imagining the Chrysler Building in New York spinning around and around on a central axis. This monster would be almost twice the size of the largest commercially deployed turbines elsewhere in the world, and generate twice the power.

China has invested almost as heavily in its domestic wind turbine-making capability as it has in solar energy. It doesn't today dominate global wind turbine manufacturing in the same way that it dominates global solar panel construction. Wind equipment manufacturing plants tend to be located relatively close to their end markets because of the cost and difficulty of transporting the gigantic blades and towers by sea and road. In December 2023 a video of a 65-m-long turbine blade being carried upright on the back of a lorry through the quaint streets of a town in the Scottish Borders en route to an onshore farm hit the headlines in Britain because it resembled something from a Hollywood movie about an alien invasion.[41]

Transport issues notwithstanding, there are signs of China pushing into global markets here too. Chinese wind turbine manufacturers exported around 4 gigawatts of wind turbine capacity in 2023, a 60 per cent rise on exports in 2022.[42] That year the EU bought around a third of Chinese wind power exports, and in 2022 China could produce wind turbines at roughly half the cost of Western firms. The share of total global orders of wind turbines was roughly equally divided between Western and Chinese wind turbine manufacturers in 2021. But in 2022 the share of Chinese manufacturers, led by Ming Yang, Envision and Goldwing, leapt to 66 per cent. The share of Western manufacturers, including the Spanish-German firm Siemens Gamesa, America's General Electric and Denmark's Vestas, in that year slipped to just 22 per cent.[43] Chinese firms seem to be more innovative too. In the four years to 2023, more than 400 new Chinese turbine models were released, compared to around thirty outside China.[44] All that Chinese wind dynamism has prompted a political reaction. In April 2024 the European commissioner Margrethe Vestager announced an investigation into Chinese state subsidies on wind industry components bound for Europe amid heightened expectations of tariffs to follow.[45] But is it really such a problem for the world to deploy cheap Chinese wind turbine imports and solar panels?

The world's governments agreed at the COP28 United Nations climate meeting in Dubai in December 2023 to triple global renewable power generation by 2030.[46] Let's examine what that means in numbers. At the end of 2023 all the countries of the world combined had around 1,500 gigawatts of solar generating capacity. By 2030 the International Energy Agency (IEA) projects that this capacity needs to quadruple to around 6,000 gigawatts for the planet to be on course for net zero emissions in 2050.[47] Meanwhile global electricity generating capacity from wind power in 2023 was around 1,000 gigawatts. To be on course for net zero, that needs almost to triple to 2,700 gigawatts by 2030.[48]

The world needs to massively increase solar and wind power generation capacity to be on track for net zero

Total installed global capacity, gigawatts

■ 2023   ▨ 2030 target to be on course for net zero in 2050

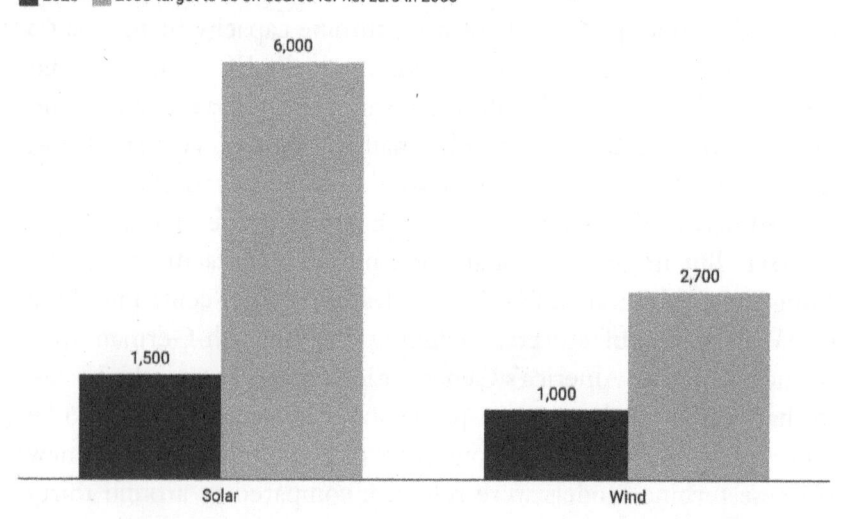

	Solar	Wind
2023	1,500	1,000
2030 target	6,000	2,700

Chart: Ben Chu • Source: IEA • Created with Datawrapper

Figure 7

Chinese manufacturing could enable Europe and much of the world to achieve that huge solar and wind rollout at a relatively modest cost. But as much as nations want to decarbonise for the lowest price possible, they also fear being reliant on China for the technology that would enable them to do so. The Danish prime minister, Mette Frederiksen, summed it up in September 2024: 'We were too dependent on Russian gas and oil and now we're repeating the same with China on many technologies, which is a big mistake.'[49] But the Western neuralgia about Chinese solar panels and wind turbines is mild next to its fears about Chinese electric cars.

Electric Nightmares

When our family's beloved twenty-year-old petrol-powered Volkswagen Golf finally gave up the ghost in 2022 we decided that the time had come to take the plunge and go electric. But our budget was limited. Scanning the used-car websites, we soon became aware that there were two EV models in our price range. One was a Nissan Leaf. The other was the MG ZS EV. We went for the MG and have been very happy with our choice. It's not as swanky or technologically advanced as a Tesla, but it was half the price and it is comfortable and reliable. MG (Morris Garages) is an old British marque from the 1920s. Along with the rest of the British motor manufacturing industry it sank into decline in the 1970s, following decades of mismanagement, and the brand was ultimately acquired and resurrected by the Shanghai Automobile Industry Corporation (SAIC) in 2007. So I drive a Chinese EV. Is it spying on me?

Gina Raimondo, Joe Biden's commerce secretary, argued it might be. 'A sophisticated EV . . . is filled with thousands of semiconductors and sensors,' she warned at an event hosted by a US thinktank in January 2024.[50] 'It collects a huge amount of information about the driver, the location of the vehicle, the surroundings of the vehicle. Do we want all that data going to Beijing?' She also raised the prospect of something even more worrying: 'Imagine if there were thousands or hundreds of thousands of Chinese connected vehicles on American roads that could be immediately and simultaneously disabled by somebody in Beijing.'[51] Given the frequency with which the connection of the car's entertainment system to my smartphone cuts out, such levels of reliable connectivity seem far-fetched. But Chinese EVs are, without doubt, at the heart of one of the most remarkable global industrial stories of the 2010s.

Motivated by a desire to put China at the forefront of an emerging technology, the Beijing government created powerful financial incentives to spur EV demand among Chinese households.[52] And, as with wind and solar, China subsidised domestic EV production heavily and its domestic companies have achieved formidable economies of scale in recent years.[53] All that has enabled China to roll EVs out domestically at an impressive rate. Around 38 per cent of all new car sales in China in 2023 were electric, well ahead of the proportions in the US (10 per cent) and the EU (22 per cent) in that year. Around half of all the 45 million electric cars on the world's roads in 2023 were made in China. It is the most mature EV market in the world, with ninety-four brands offering more than 300 models.[54]

Key to the success story has been Chinese investment in battery manufacturing, not just vehicle assembly. A significant share of the value in an EV derives from its battery. China accounted for 75 per cent of global battery production in 2022, with production led by a Fujian-based firm called Contemporary Amperex Technology Co. Limited, or CATL. And whereas Western car companies have been buying batteries made by others, some of their Chinese rivals, led by a firm called BYD (Build Your Dreams), are what they call 'vertically integrated', often manufacturing their own power sources. That's one of the factors that has enabled China's automotive firms to make EVs much more efficiently than Western car manufacturers and to sell them at far lower retail prices.

The average sticker price of a new Chinese EV in China in 2023 at $30,000 was less than half of its equivalent in the US and Europe.[55] Whereas European and US car makers, including the global leader, Tesla, have focused on high-end, more profitable EVs, Chinese firms have built for the mass market. One of BYD's models, the Seagull hatchback, sells in China for just $10,000. In most developed countries in 2023 the cheapest EV was more expensive than its petrol or diesel equivalents, usually around double the price (something I discovered when I was car shopping). In China the electric version was around 8 per cent cheaper. With such a price advantage, it's not surprising Chinese-made EVs are being imported in large numbers by countries such as Thailand and the Philippines. In 2023 China shipped 1.5 million EVs abroad, almost double the exports of Germany and around ten times the total of Japan and the US.

But the rich world has been erecting barriers to Chinese EVs. Raimondo made a security argument against them. Yet for others the real concern is jobs. Sherrod Brown, a Democratic senator for Ohio, made no bones about it in a letter to Joe Biden in April 2024. 'Chinese electric vehicles are an existential threat to the American auto industry,' he wrote. 'The US must ban Chinese electric vehicles now, and stop a flood of Chinese government-subsidised cars that threaten Ohio auto jobs, and our national and economic security.'[56] The following month Biden responded with 100 per cent tariffs on Chinese EV imports. That made little difference in itself. American imports of EVs from China were negligible in 2023, at around 12,000 vehicles only. But imports of Chinese EVs were much more substantial in Europe, at 500,000 vehicles, accounting for around a third of China's EV exports. Tariffs tend to beget further tariffs. So in July 2024 the European Union also announced tariffs on Chinese EV imports of between 17 per cent and 38 per cent on the grounds of unfair production subsidies.[57] Canada followed the US lead in August 2024 with a 100 per cent tariff on Chinese EVs.[58]

It was, though, Turkey that had moved first. In 2023 the government of Recep Tayyip Erdoğan imposed an additional 40 per cent customs duty on Chinese EVs and stringent new import regulations, including the requirement that any vendor had to have an extensive network of repair garages spread across Turkey. It was a move widely seen as part of an effort to protect its indigenous electric car brand Togg, a favoured Erdoğan project, from Chinese competition.[59] Brazil also imposed 10 per cent import tariffs on EV imports in January 2024, which are set to rise to 35 per cent by 2026. The government in Brasília said the goal was to rely less on imports and stimulate domestic production.[60]

The vision in Brazil, Turkey, America and parts of Europe is apparently one of greater national self-sufficiency in automotive manufacturing and other clean technologies. So will countries make their own EVs, their own solar panels, their own wind turbines? Would that mean true independence in the clean technologies of the twenty-first century? There's a problem with that logic, a critical one.

Critical Minerals

On 7 September 2010 a Chinese fishing trawler bumped into a Japanese coastguard vessel in the East China Sea. There were no injuries. Anywhere else and the collision would have been unremarkable. But it happened near the Senkaku chain of islands, known in China as the Diaoyus. Both countries claimed sovereignty over the uninhabited chain of barren rocks and the issue had been a growing source of tension between the East Asian neighbours. Nationalist indignation was unleashed in China after the boat's crew were taken into custody by the Japanese amid suggestions the collision had been deliberate. The flames of the row were fanned by Chinese state media, which reported that the crew had been forced by the Japanese to sleep sitting up and to drink dirty water and that the captain's grandmother had 'died from shock upon learning of the detention'.[61] Chinese demonstrators descended on the Japanese embassy in Beijing, burning Japanese flags. A Japanese school in the Chinese city of Tianjin was vandalised. Four Japanese businessmen were arrested for allegedly trespassing on a Chinese military facility.[62] But the most significant move was when the Beijing government acted to unofficially block exports of something called 'rare earth' elements to its East Asian neighbour.

Rare earths – elements with obscure names like cerium and samarium – aren't, in truth, that rare, but mining them involves the use of toxic materials which had made countries with strict environmental standards happy to see the business offshored. In 2011 China was almost the only country doing the dirty job of digging them up and processing them. In that year it was estimated to have a 98 per cent share of the rare earths market. If deliveries to Japan hadn't been restored after the row over the trawler crew calmed down, there were fears that the Japanese glass-making and automotive industries, which require these particular minerals, could have been hobbled.[63] Yet what really focused minds in the US was the fact that rare earths were also used in the manufacture of defence equipment, such as tanks' rangefinders, submarines' sonar systems and smart bombs' control vanes. And the US had relied on Japan for the supply of semi-processed rare earths, having watched its solitary rare earth mine, in Mountain Pass, California, close down back in 2002 after a toxic waste spill. If Japan were cut off from Chinese rare earths, then so, indirectly, would be the US. And this meant the US's military capability would be weakened, potentially disastrously.

The world was thereby introduced to 'critical minerals'. Minerals matter for the global economy just as much now as they did in 2011, indeed more so given the pressures of the energy transition. A typical EV currently requires six times the mineral inputs of an equivalent fossil fuel-powered vehicle in terms of weight, including rare earths, lithium, cobalt, graphite, copper, nickel, zinc and manganese. And an offshore wind farm requires thirteen times more mineral inputs than a gas-fired power plant, including copper, chromium and zinc. The wind turbine's large permanent magnets are built with rare earths, such as neodymium and dysprosium. Electrolysers to produce clean hydrogen – vital for certain heavy industrial sectors to decarbonise – will require lots of platinum. There will be huge demand for such minerals if we are to roll out clean energy technologies aggressively and hit net zero in 2050. The International Energy Agency estimates that between 2023 and 2050 global annual demand for copper for clean energy technologies could easily rise fivefold. For graphite and cobalt, it sees a potential sixfold increase. For nickel, it contemplates a tenfold increase. For manganese and lithium, it models the possibility of a seventeenfold increase.[64]

Demand for critical minerals is expected to shoot up due to the energy transition

Multiples of 2023 annual demand for clean energy technologies projected for 2050 in net zero emissions scenario

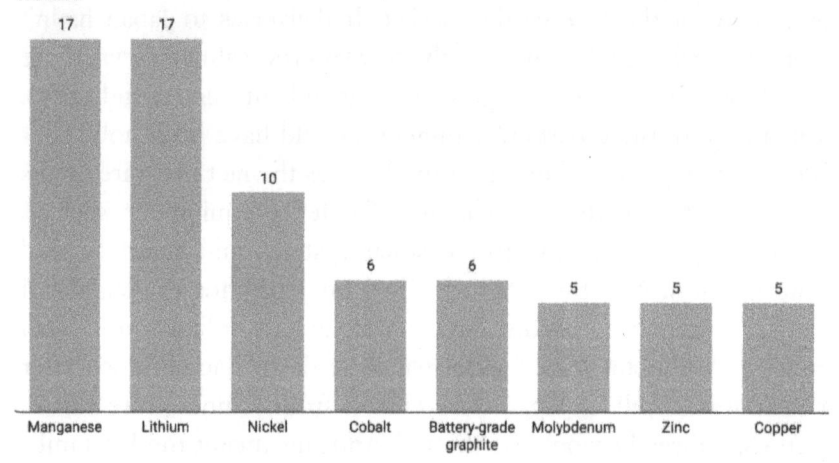

Manganese	Lithium	Nickel	Cobalt	Battery-grade graphite	Molybdenum	Zinc	Copper
17	17	10	6	6	5	5	5

Chart: Ben Chu · Source: IEA Critical Minerals Dataset · Created with Datawrapper

Figure 8

Such mineral demand projections are inherently uncertain because of the unpredictability and pace of technological change and the policies followed by governments, but the overwhelming likelihood is that there will be considerable growth in demand. All the minerals highlighted above are not especially rare in the Earth's crust, but as readily accessible resources they tend to be geographically concentrated, much more so than fossil fuels. China is by far the biggest national miner of graphite. The Democratic Republic of the Congo is the largest source of cobalt, accounting for around three-quarters of global supply. South Africa is similarly dominant in platinum mining. Indonesia and the Philippines are vast in global nickel production. Australia and Chile are the leading producers of lithium. Chile has also been called the Saudi Arabia of global copper production because it supplies around a third of the total.[65] It's only necessary to read this list and see where reserves of these critical minerals for the energy transition are located to realise that self-sufficiency for the vast majority of countries in the world in producing the key technologies of the twenty-first century within their territories is simply impossible.

That applies just as much to superpowers as smaller countries. 'Whether it's for the US or China, even though both are large countries, self-sufficiency is clearly just a fantasy,' says the materials researcher Seaver Wang.[66] Absent a thriving global trade in these minerals, these crucial technologies simply won't be produced on a sufficient scale for the world to decarbonise. So-called 'resource nationalism' in this context threatens to be dangerous. Some analysts are already warning that a scarcity of Chilean copper relative to demand could be a growing source of tension between states.[67] And this relates purely to the mining of these critical minerals. The refining of them – turning them into industrial inputs – is currently utterly dominated by China, which refines 40 to 80 per cent of all the critical minerals, including cobalt, graphite, lithium and copper, needed for the energy transition.

Even if these elements, minerals and ores were spread equally over all the countries of the world (which they are very much not), the centralisation of refining in China makes any trade restrictions and resource nationalism a major hazard for global industry and something potentially very damaging for the world's decarbonisation ambitions. In January 2020 Indonesia's president, Joko Widodo, banned exports of the unrefined nickel ore mined in the country in an effort to effectively force refining companies to establish processing plants inside Indonesia and to create local jobs and investment and capture more of the value of the supply chain. To some extent it has worked, with Chinese firms setting up local smelters. Yet the ban initially created a global nickel shortage. And if other countries follow the same strategy in the years ahead, using natural resources as a development lever, we could face crippling bottlenecks. The Democratic Republic of the Congo was exploring a similar ban on unrefined cobalt exports in response to the crash in global prices for the metal in early 2024.[68]

We had another sobering glimpse of how such critical mineral supply chains could be used not for economic but for geopolitical purposes in July 2023. In response to the previous year's bans by the US on the most cutting-edge microchips being sent from Taiwan to China, the Beijing government imposed new controls of its own on exports of two metals called germanium and gallium.[69] China produces 80 per cent of the world's gallium, a by-product of aluminium smelting, and 60 per cent of its germanium, a by-product of zinc production. Gallium is needed to make some special forms of semiconductors that can generate and detect light, facilitating high-speed communication. These semiconductors could be a central feature of future global markets, from self-driving cars and advanced medical sensors to 6G wireless and super-fast quantum computers. Germanium is used to manufacture the solar cells in satellites. They also both have uses in military applications such as missile systems and radar.

China didn't completely end exports of gallium and germanium. Beijing was requiring companies henceforth to apply for a licence in order to export the two metals and their related compounds, and to relay details of the prospective overseas buyers to the Chinese government. But the move was seen as a shot across the bows of the US and its allies, demonstrating what it could potentially do if antagonised. Two months later China pulled a similar move with new controls on exports of graphite, a mineral vital for battery manufacturing.[70] It was a worrying echo of what happened in 2011 when China held its rare earth exports hostages in its dispute with Japan.

How effective is such a weaponisation of supply chains? Some argue that export restrictions simply stimulate more supply from mines in other countries and ultimately prove self-defeating for the country that uses such tactics. They point to the fact that China's dominance over the rare earth supply chain declined considerably after 2011 and the row over the Chinese fishing boat. The shock stimulated mining for rare earths in the US and Australia, and by 2022 China's share of production had fallen from 98 per cent to an estimated 63 per cent.[71] The same could happen again with gallium and germanium production. China is currently the only producer, but historically they've been derived from minerals mined in Africa and Latin America and could be again. As for graphite, while China currently dominates its production, more could potentially come from Brazil, Turkey and Madagascar, which have mines and reserves.[72]

There is a case for a greater global geographical diversification in critical mineral mining and refining. An overreliance on any single country for a resource is potentially dangerous even without supplies being deliberately weaponised. Accidents or natural disasters could conceivably badly disrupt global industries when supply is so geographically concentrated. Technological innovation could help mitigate such risks. Demand for relatively scarce lithium resources could potentially be eliminated if, for instance, battery manufacturers shifted from lithium-ion to sodium-ion technologies. Sodium can be manufactured from seawater, which is obviously not in short supply. There is intense research taking place in this area.[73] Even if that doesn't pay off, a technological breakthrough in super-efficient solid-state batteries could radically reduce the demand for metals such as nickel and cobalt.

Yet while diversification is sensible, aiming at self-sufficiency is a different story. The idea of every country producing or even refining its own critical minerals is, as we've seen, a non-starter. And we also need to be realistic about the feasibility of rapid and extensive diversification. Bringing new mines and processing plants onstream will be costly and time-consuming. The International Energy Agency estimates that it takes an average of sixteen years to move a mine from discovery to production. 'Multidimensional challenges make the development of mines a generational endeavour, spanning decades and requiring hundreds of billions of dollars,' warns one group of analysts.[74] And the stark fact is that the world has neither money nor time to waste in the energy transition.

Too Much of a Good Thing?

When US treasury secretary Janet Yellen rose from an oddly oversized white armchair in a hotel in the southern Chinese megacity of Guangzhou in April 2024 to deliver a speech, she had one overriding message for her Chinese hosts: stop manufacturing more than your own economy can absorb. 'Overcapacity can lead to large volumes of exports at depressed prices,' she explained. 'This can undercut the business of American firms and workers, as well as of firms around the world, including in India and Mexico. And it can lead to overconcentration of supply chains, posing a risk to global economic resilience.'[75]

The big complaint in Western capitals is Chinese 'overcapacity', specifically in clean technology, and the consequent 'dumping' of equipment like solar panels, wind turbines, electric cars and batteries in overseas markets. Dumping means selling items at a price that is below the true cost of their production, undercutting the ability of Western countries to build up their own manufacturing base in these key technologies. It's an understandable fear when one looks at the bare numbers.

China manifestly has very high capacity in what Beijing has identified as the *xin san yang* or 'new three' technologies of the twenty-first century, namely solar, EVs and batteries. In 2023 China's manufacturing capacity for solar panels was three times the size of estimated global demand in that year, according to the Economist Intelligence Unit.[76] Similarly, China's battery manufacturing capacity alone in 2023 was roughly equal to global demand and was set to outstrip it several times over by 2025, according to the research group Bloomberg NEF.[77] Analysts at the US investment bank Goldman Sachs estimated that China's EV factories in 2024 were running at only 58 per cent capacity.[78]

But before we engage with the vexed question of 'overcapacity', it's important to pause to appreciate how much of a planetary benefit heavy Chinese investment in these clean technologies over the past fifteen years has been. First, in terms of the sheer reduction in global carbon dioxide emissions. China at the end of 2023 had domestically installed around 600 gigawatts of solar energy-generating capacity, more than the US and Europe put together.[79] New solar installations in China during 2023 alone were more than 200 gigawatts. To place that in context, it's more new solar than the rest of the world combined added in 2023.[80] Indeed, it's more than the US had installed in its entire history prior to that year.[81]

China has rolled out wind in prodigious quantities of turbines at home too. In 2023 it had 440 gigawatts of installed wind energy capacity nationwide, again roughly equal to the installed wind power capacity of the US and Europe combined.[82] As with solar, it added twice as much additional wind power capacity as the rest of the world combined in that year. If China had not installed renewables on this scale at home – and instead used coal, the most polluting of fossil fuels, for producing its domestic power – its national carbon emissions would have been roughly 25 per cent higher in that year than they actually were, according to the climate thinktank Carbon Brief. Similarly, if China hadn't put 22 million EVs on its roads by the end of 2023 and instead used petrol and diesel vehicles, its national transport emissions would also have been considerably greater. This matters deeply because the Chinese economy is the world's largest emitter of greenhouse gases, accounting for 30 per cent of the total in 2022. All told, in a counterfactual scenario in which China had not rolled out clean technologies so aggressively, global carbon emissions would have been perhaps 1.2 gigatonnes, or 3 per cent, greater.[83] The prospect of meeting the international goal of decarbonisation by 2050 would then be far more remote. Uncomfortable as it might be to accept for some in the West, China has led by example on renewables.

The second planetary benefit from China's huge clean energy investment push flows from the development of these technologies. Chinese solar panel manufacturers have relentlessly driven down their production costs as they've scaled up. The cost of an average commercial solar panel has fallen by an astonishing 90 per cent since 2010, making the cost of electricity from this form of renewable energy now lower than power derived from fossil fuels.[84] Similarly, between 2009 and 2019 the price of electricity from wind power fell

70 per cent. Battery prices are down even more, by 95 per cent.[85] And, as we've seen, China is now able to sell its cheapest EVs at lower prices than fossil-fuel cars.[86] These technologies are not just cheaper to produce, but vastly more advanced. The capacity factors of Chinese wind turbines and solar panels, the efficiency with which they convert sunlight and wind into electricity, have shot up. Chinese investment into research and development has raised the energy density of batteries, making the range of vehicles on a single charge substantially greater.

These collapses in clean technology costs and the great strides in their efficiency did not happen by accident. They were due to China's big state-sponsored push into these technologies. As its firms deployed more and more, they achieved economies of scale and moved up the technological learning curve, meaning they could manufacture superior products more efficiently. That led to falling prices, which stimulated new demand, in a virtuous circle. 'China's strategic support for its solar industry is the reason the solar industry is not a cottage industry anymore,' observes the solar analyst Jenny Chase. 'It's the entire reason why solar is now the largest source of new installed [electricity-generating] capacity every year.'[87]

It's time for a thought experiment. Imagine the projected costs (which would ultimately, of course, be borne by households) for the world of moving from fossil fuels to renewable energy if China had not invested so heavily in these areas since the turn of the millennium. The positive global spillover benefits of Chinese clean energy industrial strategy are hard to overstate, especially for developing countries, where the relative cost of clean energy and transport technologies is central to the question of the rate at which they will adopt them in preference to fossil fuels. Chinese investment in these technologies has the potential to be one of the greatest global public goods of this century.

Compare the record of China in rolling out renewables with that of Western countries. An offshore wind auction for UK government subsidy in 2023 failed to attract any bids from industry after ministers set the reserve price too low to make bidding profitable, despite loud warnings by the industry in advance that this would be the

ENERGY

case.[88] There were also disappointing results from similar auctions in France, Spain, Greece and Poland. A number of wind farm construction plans were cancelled in 2023 in the US and Europe due to rising costs and slow permitting times. The head of renewables for the Anglo-American energy giant BP described US offshore wind as 'fundamentally broken' on account of problems with permitting.[89] This was despite the financial incentives created by the US Inflation Reduction Act and the EU's REPowerEU Plan. There has been similar Western sluggishness on solar. To meet its accelerated 2030 goals for renewable energy generation, Germany needs to install around 20 gigawatts of extra solar power capacity a year. But in 2023, despite the recent shock of the Russian gas crisis, the country managed to install only an extra 14 gigawatts.[90] Europe as a whole added just 70 gigawatts of total new renewable power generating capacity in 2023 and the US 31 gigawatts. China, on the other hand, added 298.

China has been building out renewable electricity much more rapidly than Europe and America

Additional renewable power generating capacity added by year, GW

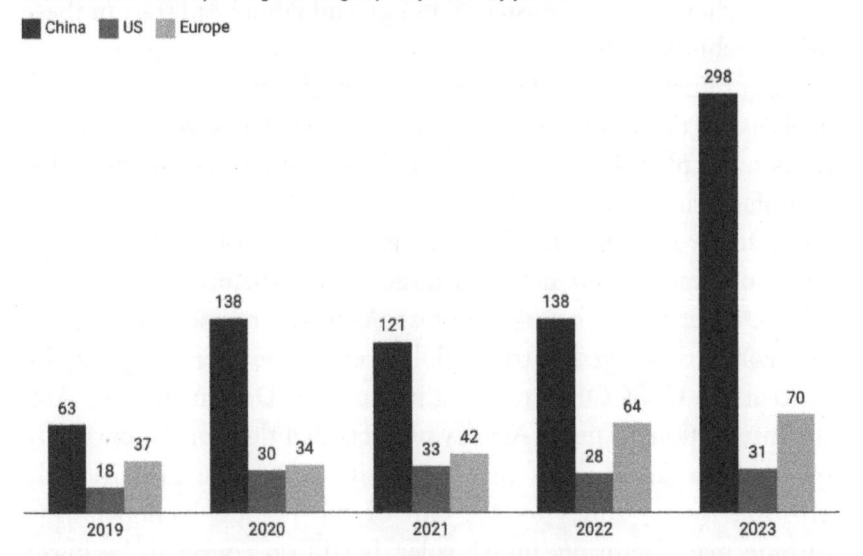

■ China ■ US ▨ Europe

Year	China	US	Europe
2019	63	18	37
2020	138	30	34
2021	121	33	42
2022	138	28	64
2023	298	31	70

Chart: Ben Chu · Source: International Renewable Energy Agency · Created with Datawrapper

Figure 9

When it comes to EVs, there has also been strategic drift from Western car manufacturers. While their Chinese counterparts have been intensely focused for more than a decade on making mass-market electric cars, Western car makers have often dragged their feet on the electric transition and, when they have finally moved, have concentrated on high-end vehicles with larger margins. According to a growing number of car experts, Chinese EVs are now simply superior in quality to Western-made ones.[91] Is it fear of powerful competition, rather than concerns about espionage or sabotage, that is the motivation for tariffs on Chinese EVs? 'If you can't beat them, ban them!' is the sceptical way the energy analyst Michael Liebreich sums up the Western policy.[92]

One country's industrial strategy is another's unfair trade practice. 'American workers and businesses can outcompete anyone – as long as they have fair competition,' proclaimed the White House in May 2024 as President Biden imposed fresh tariffs on Chinese EVs, solar cells and batteries. Yet Western nations now want to implement their own industrial policies to promote the domestic production of solar, wind, batteries and EVs. The simple fact is that China acted earlier with its industrial strategy and got a head start in these clean technology fields.

Let's return to those Chinese overcapacity figures. It's true that analysis by the International Energy Agency, based on announced investment plans by corporations and governments, suggests global manufacturing capacity in solar and battery production by 2030 is likely to be running ahead of where it needs to be for the world to be on track to hit net zero targets, overwhelmingly thanks to China.[93] But remember the context. As we've stressed, the world's governments pledged to triple global renewable energy capacity by 2030 at the UN COP28 meeting in Dubai in December 2023. And the International Energy Agency projects that the world is currently on track to fall short of that goal, with renewable capacity only growing by 2.7 times by the end of the decade.[94] Global wind turbine manufacturing, unlike solar, is still on course to be lower than required by 2030.[95] The Global Wind Energy Council has warned that a lack of turbine manufacturing capacity for onshore wind turbines in Europe and the US risks bottlenecks from 2026. Its forecast is for the international turbine fleet to be generating 2,000 gigawatts of power by 2030.[96] But that's only two-thirds of what's needed for us to be on track for net zero.

Most experts agree there are simply too many unprofitable Chinese EV manufacturers and that there will need to be a major industry consolidation at some stage. Yet the global rollout of EVs also needs to speed up. The Biden administration was aiming for half of new car sales to be electric by 2030. The UK and the EU want to end sales of new fossil-fuel-powered cars entirely by 2030 and 2035 respectively. Global demand in 2025 is projected by the IEA to be around 21 million vehicle sales. But to be on course for the IEA's 2050 net zero trajectory, global sales ought to be closer to 30 million, and the stock of EVs on the roads needs to rise by around 30 per cent every year thereafter.

In that context, a surplus supply of EVs from China is a preferable headache to the alternative of too few of them being made. Similarly, with wind and solar, in a world in which demand is below the required trajectory for decarbonisation by 2050, Chinese overcapacity in these clean technologies should arguably be seen as a blessing, not a curse. If demand rises, as we should hope it does to put us on track for net zero, we will need additional supply capacity – and China is there to help fill the gap.

The signs are, though, that measures in the West to keep out Chinese supply of clean technology are likely to intensify. If Western protectionism results in more global industrial capacity to produce clean technologies – and more productivity-enhancing innovation in these sectors – that might end up being beneficial. It's better to be overachieving in green technology production than underachieving. Yet the fragmentation of clean technology supply chains on national lines or into geopolitical blocs would come at a price. One study of the solar sector has estimated that if countries require their domestic manufacturers to supply a growing share of their domestic demand, solar panel prices by 2030 could plausibly be up to 25 per cent higher than if we saw a continuation of globalised production and supply.[97] That is a cost that Western households will have to absorb at a time when there are already signs of popular opposition to the costs imposed by the green transition.

We've already seen the negative impact of protectionism in the solar sector. Between 2013 and 2018, when the European Union imposed tariffs on Chinese solar panels, there was no resurgence in domestic manufacturing. Rather, the rate of new solar installations in Europe dropped dramatically. The installation rate only picked up when the tariffs lapsed. In 2018 the US, under Donald Trump, jacked up tariffs on Chinese solar panel imports. The result has been a lower rate of installation in the US than in Europe since then.

The idea that protection boosts domestic renewables production in developing countries is also doubtful. The Modi government in India imposed a 40 per cent tariff on Chinese solar panel imports in 2022 on the justification that this would stimulate domestic manufacturing.[98] But in 2023 the Indian rate of new installations fell almost 30 per cent to 9 gigawatts, down from 13 gigawatts in 2022, as the cost of imports jumped and domestic production failed to fill the gap.[99] The danger is that more protectionism will inflict further delays on clean energy rollouts, and not just in India but around the world.

Some Western politicians seem to grasp this danger. Mairead McGuinness, the European commissioner for financial stability, pointed out to the European Parliament in February 2024 that because Europe relies 'to a very important degree' on imported solar panels, any measure to restrict imports 'needs to be weighed against the objectives we have set ourselves when it comes to the energy transition'. But the danger is that such voices of caution get drowned out in the rush for jobs and a dubious sense of energy security and national self-sufficiency.

What about those concerns about national security when it comes to digitally 'connected' Chinese EVs' cameras and data-collection capabilities? This frankly seems overblown and based on a hypothetical scenario rather than on actual evidence of harm or likely risk. If China is looking to utilise its technology exports for mass espionage, it has a more promising candidate in the form of the hundreds of millions of China-assembled smartphone handsets in the West. As for the fears of smart Chinese EVs on Western roads being switched off remotely from Beijing in a devastating automotive cyberattack, that seems at odds with the reality that China hopes to make money in these markets. Such an act of sabotage – or even the emergence of the possibility of it – would permanently destroy Western sales at a stroke. But if national security is a genuine concern over imported connected Chinese EVs there are a number of potential safeguards, such as mandating restrictions on the data they could send out of the country, requiring it to be stored locally or monitoring the sourcing of the semiconductor chips that they use.

Human rights are another justification for trade restrictions when it comes to Chinese-made solar panels. It's estimated that between one-third and one-half of the world's polysilicon, the base material needed for solar panels, is produced in the Xinjiang region of China, where there is credible evidence of the use of forced labour from the Muslim Uyghur people there. It was through the Uyghur Forced Labor Prevention Act that the US limited direct solar imports from China in 2021. This undoubtedly represents an ethical dilemma. But the Uyghur human rights question does have to be weighed against the human costs of slowing the fight against global warming.

There's another important piece of context. In 2023 the value of China's exports of electronic items such as laptops and smartphones, often assembled for Western firms, dwarfed that of its combined sales of EVs, solar panels, batteries and wind turbines.[100] But there have never been any complaints about Chinese overcapacity in those devices. The difference is that most of the profit from the sale of electronics assembled in China flows to Western firms, whereas China captures most of the value added when it comes to manufacturing clean technologies. In the end it's difficult to resist the conclusion that the Western antipathy to Chinese clean technology exports owes more to concerns about competition and jobs than to ethics.

Build Back Closer

On 8 July 1986 a white car rolled off the production line of a new factory in the north-east of England. Its registration plate read 'JOB 1'. This Bluebird 2.0 GTX was the first completed car from the Sunderland plant of the Japanese car manufacturer Nissan. This was a moment the UK's then prime minister, Margaret Thatcher, had spent almost a decade trying to make happen. She had lobbied the Japanese firm assiduously, encouraging it to invest in Britain, writing letters and visiting Tokyo to court politicians. She had even carved out a secret financial deal with the company to get the investment over the line.[101] Amid a general panic over the rising automotive might of Japan and the implications for Western car makers, Thatcher had taken the view that it was better to invite them in than to keep them out. It was a decision that sparked the resurrection of car manufacturing on UK soil. Other Japanese automotive giants including Toyota and Honda also invested in new manufacturing plants in the UK in the following years. That Nissan Sunderland factory is today the UK's largest car plant, employing 6,000 people. It produced the Leaf, which was one of Britain's bestselling electric cars in 2023.[102] America, in the end, did something similar in the 1980s, despite the complaints of US car makers. Honda, Nissan and Toyota also built factories in America to serve the US market, creating tens of thousands of jobs in the process.[103]

What this suggests is that there is an alternative to protectionism in the era of EVs. Instead of discriminating against Chinese-made electric cars, Western governments could encourage Chinese companies to build the vehicles in factories locally to keep the supply chains shorter and jobs closer to home. This approach would be a way to stimulate local manufacturing and address concerns about national security. It would be easier to monitor the technology going into Chinese EVs if they were being assembled in Western countries. For many automotive industry analysts, further integration makes far more sense than attempts at separation. And some European governments are taking the Thatcherite view that it would be better to encourage overseas car manufacturers to set up plants locally than to try to keep out their products. 'France welcomes all industrial projects. BYD and the Chinese auto industry are very welcome in France,' declared the French finance minister Bruno Le Maire in May 2024 when Xi Jinping made a state visit to the country. There have already been investments by Chinese EV and battery firms in Hungary, Germany, Slovakia and Spain.[104] Brazil and Turkey also seem content for Chinese firms to evade their new tariffs by offshoring EV production to their territories.[105]

Perhaps it seems naïve to suggest this approach for the US given the political climate between China and Washington. But it's notable that at least one US car maker – Ford – was looking into the possibility of a joint venture with the Chinese battery maker CATL on US soil in 2023.[106] China's BYD in early 2024 was reported to be exploring the possibility of opening a factory in Mexico to sell into the US and so avoid the Biden-imposed tariffs.[107] Donald Trump's re-election has likely destroyed that idea, after the Republican candidate explicitly pledged to prevent it happening in October 2024 by imposing unlimited tariffs on Chinese-made auto imports from Mexico. 'I'll put 200 or 500 [per cent tariffs], I don't care. I'll put a number where they can't sell one car,' Trump told Fox News.[108] Yet even Trump suggested at a rally in Dayton, Ohio in March 2024 that he might be amenable to Chinese car makers manufacturing *directly* on US soil. 'If they want to build a plant in Michigan, in Ohio, in South Carolina, they can, using American workers,' he riffed, seemingly off the cuff. 'They can't send Chinese workers.'[109] Whether this amounts to a firm policy position from the newly elected president or not is, at the time of writing, as clear as the muddy Ohio river.

One justification used in the West for a trade war, rather than cooperation, over EVs is that China itself has discriminated against Western car manufacturers for years. It is true that domestic subsidies available to Chinese brands were not made available to their US and European counterparts that were seeking to sell into the

Chinese market. It is accurate to argue that China has been more protectionist than the West when it comes to its domestic automotive industry. Yet it is also worth bearing in mind that a large proportion of Chinese EV exports in 2023 were Chinese-built Teslas, emerging from Elon Musk's Shanghai factory.[110] The cars were assembled in China but the brand was American. So is a Tesla that's imported from Shanghai and driven, for example, in London or Berlin a Chinese EV or an American EV? Would an electric Volvo, a Swedish marque bought by a Chinese company, manufactured in South Carolina be a Swedish, American or Chinese EV? When supply chains are globalised the concept of the 'nationality' of a manufactured product is rarely as clear cut as the economic nationalist discourse implies. And the dependence goes both ways. The US in 2023 was a major importer of lithium-ion batteries from China, accounting for a fifth of all China's exports of this product.[111] Most went into EVs assembled in America. The battery accounts for between a quarter and a third of the price of a typical EV.[112] So were these US EVs or Chinese EVs?

A similar offshoring approach, perhaps in the form of joint ventures, could be beneficial in relation to wind power. Building out regional manufacturing hubs for Chinese-designed turbines in Latin America, Europe and Asia would ensure more secure access to needed components and assuage fears of excessive reliance on a single country. Rather than obsessing about creating local employment directly in wind turbine or solar panel manufacturing, the West could focus on creating new 'green' jobs in installing Chinese-made solar panels and integrating them into smart local energy systems. A company called Solarwatt, based in the former East Germany, once the centre of German solar, announced in 2024 that it would cease making panels. However, its management said it would focus instead on creating systems that connect the power generated by solar panels to wall boxes that can charge cars and heat pumps to warm homes and would move as many existing workers as possible into these divisions.[113] This is the kind of green jobs transition that could be at the heart of Western governments' industrial strategies.

The energy crisis of 2022 sparked a global rush for national energy self-sufficiency. It was a vision that seemed to dovetail with the need to decarbonise the global economy by the middle of the century: the perfect union of industrial protectionism and protecting the planet. The danger, though, is that the opposite outcome is more likely. Exile economics risks slowing – perhaps even derailing – the global energy transition and the adoption of clean technology, while doing very little for energy security.

We've seen the case against exile economics when it comes to food, and now we've seen its pitfalls in relation to clean energy. But should we be thinking differently when it comes to the very highest form of technology on the planet? How should we consider national resilience when it comes to the microelectronic brains of almost all modern technology: silicon chips?

5
Silicon

Imagine a laundromat – but for dogs. You enter a small hut with your mucky hound, insert your money into a machine, and you are granted access to a bathing tub and time-limited hot water, shampoo and a drier. A family-run company from rural Illinois, CCSI International, manufactures such customisable 'dog-wash systems' and sends them to parks, beaches and pet stores all around the US. But in 2021 CCSI's boss was told that the usual silicon chips suddenly weren't available for its electronic circuit boards - they couldn't be sourced for love nor money.[1]

Dog-wash systems were one of the more unlikely victims of 'chipageddon' – a global shortage of silicon chips.[2] The most high-profile casualty was the car industry. In 2021 dozens of plants across the world had to be idled – essentially powered down and the workers sent home – because of the shortage of these micro-electronic components. The average modern car contains between 300 and 1,000 chips, for everything from adaptive braking to climate control.[3] It's estimated that global car makers missed out on around 8 million vehicle sales and $200 billion of potential revenue that year because of the chip shortage.[4]

The consumer electronics sector also suffered conspicuously. Americans who needed a new broadband router were being forced to wait more than a year.[5] The Korean electronics giant Samsung warned it would have to delay the launch of its next Galaxy smartphone.[6] Meagre stocks of Microsoft's new Xbox Series X game console ran out so quickly in the UK that some opportunistic gamers were putting them up for resale on Ebay for ten times the retail price.[7] The Wall Street bank Goldman Sachs counted 169 different sectors of business in total that were likely adversely engulfed in chipageddon.[8] Chip production came into balance with demand again in the following year, but the shortage provided an unpleasant revelation.

As the dog-washing booth underlined, chips are everywhere these days. As well as being embedded in modern cars, planes, computers, smartphones, televisions and video-game consoles, they're now standard in medical devices and wifi-connected smart appliances, from doorbells to microwaves and fridges. The digital revolution has created a global chip industry that made $500 billion of sales in 2023, a figure that's projected to rise to $1 trillion by the end of the decade, powered by the rise of cloud computing data centres, 5G telecommunications, the 'internet of things' and the rise of artificial intelligence (AI) applications.[9] But even these figures don't really do justice to the economic importance of the chip sector, without which relatively little in our $100 trillion modern global economy could continue to function effectively for very long.

The great chip dearth was a financial headache for everyone. But for one group of people – the US military – it was something more. It was a strategic wake-up call.

The Dragon's Jaw

The challenge from the US military to Texas Instruments (TI), a US semiconductor firm, during the Vietnam War was simple: create a new aircraft-delivered bomb capable of destroying a strategic bridge in North Vietnamese territory known as the Dragon's Jaw which 638 conventional American bombs had somehow missed. TI's Paveway, a laser-guided bomb using a primitive microchip to direct its flight path, managed the task. The bridge was finally destroyed by twenty-six Paveways on 13 May 1972.[10] From the moment the Dragon's Jaw was broken everyone in the US military grasped the importance of silicon chips and the strategic importance of being at the cutting edge of microelectronics.[11]

Chips are used in all modern weapons systems. They are still the backbone of the guidance system for missiles. A portable shoulder-mounted Javelin missile system, of the sort supplied by the US to the Ukrainian military (and known by the local defenders as 'St Javelin' for its protective qualities) contains around 200 chips.[12] Chips also allow military radar and communications systems to function. They will be the brains of potential AI military applications and autonomous armed drones, which are seen as the next major military strategic battleground. 'If a potential adversary bests the United States in semiconductors over the long term or suddenly cuts off US access to cutting-edge chips entirely, it could gain the upper hand in every domain of warfare,' warned a 2021 report by a bipartisan National Security Commission established by Congress, whose commissioners included the former CEO of Google and the boss of Amazon's cloud computing arm.[13]

The fast-growing digital connectivity of infrastructure, from ports and water sanitation plants to power stations and hospitals, makes the secure supply of chips to run these civilian utilities a national security consideration. What the events of 2021 brought home to America's military was the possibility that their supply of these vital components was potentially insecure. And when they examined the supply chain in more detail, the more insecure it seemed.

The most advanced chips needed for those weapons systems are almost exclusively manufactured on the island of Taiwan, only 130 km from the coast of China and also claimed by China as its own territory since 1949. A Chinese invasion of Taiwan, the US military realised, would effectively cut off America from a technology it needed to defend itself. And so was born the Creating Helpful Incentives to Produce Semiconductors ('Chips') Act, a $53 billion US government grant and tax-break programme passed by Congress in August 2022 with the intention of incentivising companies to reshore advanced semiconductor manufacturing to the continental United States.[14]

Many lauded it as a homecoming. The transistor had been invented in America in the 1950s by scientists working at Bell Labs, the innovation arm of the US telephone monopoly AT&T, which had strong government ties. And the nascent integrated circuit industry, which turned these transistors into microchips, was nurtured by large, lucrative orders from the US military, including the contract for the Paveway laser-guided bomb, and from NASA. In 1965 three-quarters of all integrated circuits produced were being purchased by the US military. 'The Pentagon had created Silicon Valley,' in the words of the author of *Chip Wars*, Chris Miller.[15] One might argue this was just the kind of 'military-civil fusion' that alarms US Defense Department hawks today when it comes to China.

Most of the software-based design work for chips still takes place in America, and the lion's share of the profits of the semiconductor industry are still captured by US companies such as Intel, Broadcom, TI, Qualcomm, AMD and Nvidia. The US stock market-listed (though UK-based) firm ARM provides the chip design software that underpins most of the world's smartphone processors. But in order to cut costs and boost profits the actual manufacturing of the chips for US and some European firms was outsourced to Asia, primarily Taiwan. In 1990 the US directly manufactured around four in ten of the world's computer chips. But by 2019 its share had fallen to just one in ten.[16]

The CHIPS Act's goal was to ensure that at least a fifth of advanced logic chips – the sort with high-technology military and AI applications – will be produced in the US by 2030. 'Instead of relying on chips made overseas that could be delayed because of a pandemic or some global disruption, now they're going to be able to have those chips available on the spot,' proclaimed President Joe Biden. 'It's a game changer.'[17]

This was not the limit of Washington's efforts to secure itself. Up to the early 2010s the US had taken the view that it didn't need to be too concerned about absolute technological progress in China as long as America maintained a lead over its rival. But the mood in Washington fundamentally shifted over the following decade. By 2021 the view had taken hold across the political spectrum that a lead wasn't enough – China's level of capability had to be degraded. And this applied in spades to semiconductors with potential military uses. 'Given the foundational nature of certain technologies, such as advanced logic and memory chips, we must maintain as large of a lead as possible,' said Biden's national security advisor Jake Sullivan in September 2022.[18]

The objective of the Biden administration, picking up where the Trump administration left off, was to prevent these chips going to China to be deployed for use in Beijing's missile and military AI programmes. The fact that these advanced chips are based on designs and technology mostly owned by US corporations enabled the US Commerce Department in October 2022 to impose a de facto ban on these components being exported from Taiwan to China.[19] The control ratchet was tightened up another notch exactly a year later.[20] But if the goal was to stop Beijing getting access to cutting-edge chips, Washington realised it had to go further still and open up new points of pressure in its 'chip choke' on Beijing.

Nanotechnology

The majority of advanced logic chips are manufactured by a Taiwanese company called the Taiwan Semiconductor Manufacturing Company (TSMC). And to make its chips TSMC uses machines from the Dutch company Advanced Semiconductor Materials Lithography (ASML), an offshoot of the lightbulb manufacturer Philips. ASML machines project transistor patterns at tiny scales onto silicon wafers using extreme ultraviolet light. Photolithography is the full term: printing with light. To give a sense of the scale, the most advanced chips have transistors, the basic building block of the chip, etched onto them which have shapes that are less than 10 nanometres long. A nanometre is one billionth of a metre. The diameter of a typical human hair is around 90,000 nanometres. The width of a human red blood cell is 7,000 nanometres. Modern transistors are smaller than viruses. These machines which can operate at that nanoscopic, almost atomic, level are so sophisticated and complex that ASML has no competitors.

No other company on the planet has the expertise to replicate what it does. The Biden administration realised there was no point simply preventing TSMC selling to China if it didn't also stop ASML selling its chip-making machines to China and potentially enabling Beijing to build its own advanced chip factories. So Washington leaned on the Dutch government, leveraging its geopolitical influence as the de facto guarantor of European defence via NATO. The Dutch government and ASML – after some resistance – complied in June 2023 and restricted exports to China.[21] Japan, whose own firms also supply crucial equipment needed for manufacturing semiconductors, also fell into line with US policy and imposed its own new export restrictions in 2023.[22]

But the indications are that the ratchet has many turns to come. In April 2023 the US national security advisor Jake Sullivan announced that his country's policy would not be indiscriminate in its restrictions on trade with China, but that it would have a 'small yard, high fence' policy.[23] In other words, the restrictions would be very tight (high fence) but they would only apply to a relatively small number of critical products (small yard). In reality the 'yard' has been getting steadily larger. In 2024 the US started to apply pressure on the German firms Trumpf and Zeiss – which make the sophisticated lasers and almost impossibly smooth mirrors used in ASML's lithography machines – not to trade with China directly as well.[24] It was also trying to persuade ASML not to allow its staff to maintain the older lithography machines that it had already sold to Chinese chipmakers, despite the fact that this ongoing service is as important as the delivery of the physical machines.[25] In addition, Washington was applying pressure on Germany to prevent its firms exporting key chemicals required for chipmaking to China.[26] There have been reports too of attempts to prevail on South Korea to reconsider its commercial relations with the US rival.[27] If a technological embargo is the objective, the long and complex nature of the advanced semiconductor supply chain – and the fact that so much knowledge about how to make things work is in people's heads due to their practical experience – would seem to lead to an ever-widening sphere of prohibitions.

Another inevitable consequence of the Washington chip choke is countervailing action. We think of China as a giant exporter of electronics, which it is. Yet it mainly assembles products with chips inside them, rather than manufacturing the key components on its own territory. Indeed, China has long spent more on importing chips than it does on crude oil, its next biggest commodity import.[28] It's estimated that China's own domestic chip-manufacturing industry supplied just 6 per cent of its total domestic needs in 2020.[29] The shock of the US advanced chip export ban in 2022 prompted China to accelerate its own efforts to become self-sufficient in chip production. China manufactures a lot of products containing chips, but at the moment it has no substantive capacity to manufacture the most sophisticated logic chips, those packed with billions of transistors with features below 10 nanometres in size, each of which takes several months of work in the chip factory to produce.[30] And it has a share of just 3 per cent of global production capacity of the trailing-edge products, those with features between 10 and 22 nanometres long.

Does the difference between 2 nanometres and 10 nanometres really make that much difference? Aren't these literally nanoscopic differences? To illustrate, take the logic chips at the 7 nanometre 'node', which first emerged in 2018, and compare them with the 5 nanometre chips which first came out in 2020. The 5 nanometre chips have roughly twice as many transistors and thus twice the computing power.[31] In the industry, the gap between nanometres is regarded as being as wide as the Pacific Ocean when it comes to computing power and efficiency.

If the goal is building data centres, 5G smartphones or developing AI and machine learning, the brutal fact is that only the absolute bleeding-edge chips will do the job well. And it's important to bear in mind that it's the relentless miniaturisation of the transistors on chips – and the resulting explosion of processing power for ever-lower costs – that propelled us, in the space of just fifty years, from computers that filled rooms, to PCs, to the internet, to smartphones. A smartphone today contains millions of times more processing power than the mainframe computers used by NASA to send the first humans to the Moon in 1969, and as much memory storage as entire data-centre servers as recently as 2005.

When it comes to today's geopolitical chip wars, there is a danger of fixating on the Washington–Beijing dynamic. Despite being a US ally, the new superpower struggle over this technology has also sparked defensive action from Europe, which is just as dependent on chip imports as China. Like China, it also currently has no capacity to produce cutting-edge chips and has only around 12 per cent in the trailing-edge category. In February 2022 the EU unveiled a €43 billion European Chips Act, which aims to more than double its share of global chip production to 20 per cent by 2030. The logic of self-sufficiency and national security would seem on the face of it to justify a dash for advanced-chip-manufacturing capacity in both Europe and China.

And why not elsewhere too? The Indian government in 2021 pledged $30 billion in state support to create a domestic chip industry and boost its semiconductor 'self-sufficiency'.[32] In 2023 the South Korean government brought forward its own 'K-Chips Act', full of the promise of tax credits and state assistance in kind for domestic chipmakers, including its national champion, Samsung. The head of a special panel on chips for the ruling party in Seoul prophesied that 'the winner of the global chip battle will control the economic security order, while the loser will end up becoming a technological colony'.[33] Many other countries, including the UK, are feeling the pressure to come up with their own semiconductor strategies. Yet there's a problem with assuming that siting a chip fabrication plant in a particular territory confers security.

Golf Balls on the Moon

When you explore the microchip supply chain you find more and more firms – and more and more geographical diversity. An ASML machine has 100,000 parts which the company sources from 5,000 direct suppliers spread across Europe, the US and Asia. It has no realistic alternative supplier for many of its key inputs, whether vacuum systems from the UK or ultraviolet light source components from America. This includes the ultra-high specification mirrors and lasers from Trumpf and Zeiss as well as special chemicals called 'photoresists' from Japan which undergo a chemical reaction upon exposure to light. Zeiss's equipment is so precise it boasts that, scaled up, it could direct a laser to hit a golf ball as far away as the Moon.[34] Its mirrors are so smooth that, if they were expanded to the size of a country, the highest bump on their surface would be less than half a millimetre high.[35] The firm acknowledges it has no competitors when it comes to supplying ASML.[36]

Similarly, just four Japanese companies together have a near-monopoly on the photoresists required for the most advanced chipmaking.[37] And then there is a single separate Japanese company, Tokyo Electron, which has a 100 per cent monopoly on the production of the equipment that enables the ASML machines to interact with those chemicals.[38] This is by no means the full extent of the complexity. There are dozens of other processes in advanced-chip manufacturing with names such as 'etching', 'doping' and 'deposition', all with very limited numbers of firms capable of providing the necessary equipment, and spread all across the globe.[39] It's vital to understand that the key to the most advanced chipmaking does not lie solely in the machines themselves, but in the ability to operate them and efficiently integrate them with other vital processes – an ability only Taiwan's TSMC and South Korea's Samsung currently possess. And then there is the scientific expertise required to invent the ever more advanced lithography techniques demanded by the industry. The Interuniversity Microelectronics Centre (IMEC), a research institute in Leuven, Belgium, is regarded as almost indispensable in this regard.

But we're getting ahead of ourselves. First we need to look at the issue of where the raw materials used to make these chips are actually located. The silicon from which chips are made is not rare. It's the second most abundant element in the Earth's crust after oxygen; you find it as silicon dioxide in rock called quartz, but you might know it better as sand.[40] It's mined at scale in more than sixty countries, and could be sourced from most others.[41] But there's a lot more to the chipmaking story than such digging up sand.

Spruced Up

Spruce Pine is a small town high up in the Appalachian mountain range as it passes through the state of North Carolina. It's relatively poor but there are great natural riches on its doorstep – natural riches on which the entire $500 billion per year silicon chip industry rests. Up a narrow mountain road from the town, a notoriously secretive mine run by a Belgian company called Sibelco quarries white quartz rock. The quartz from Spruce Pine is the purest silicon dioxide ever found on Earth. It's pretty much only quartz from this quarry that is currently good enough to be used in the manufacturing process for the silicon wafers that are used to make all the world's semiconductor chips.

Spruce Pine quartz is fashioned into an industrial crucible in which a highly refined form of silicon called 'polysilicon' is melted down and turned into a long ingot from which the silicon wafers are cut, ready to be turned into microchips. If the crucible has even the tiniest impurity in it, that wrecks the quality of the wafers and they can't be used. Spruce Pine quartz is 99.99999999999 per cent pure (thirteen nines), meaning there is just one impurity for every 10 trillion parts that are pristine.[42] Spruce Pine and the estimated 180,000 to 200,000 tonnes of quartz it produces per year is more or less the only show in town for semiconductor crucible-making.[43] That makes it, in financial terms, a licence to print money, akin to a gold mine. Unsurprisingly, geologists have been tasked with searching the Earth for other sources of equally high-grade quartz. But, so far, none of any comparable size has entered the supply chain.[44] Spruce Pine has a de facto monopoly.

'Here's something scary,' an industry veteran told the journalist Ed Conway in an interview for his book *Material World*. 'If you flew over the two mines in Spruce Pine with a crop duster loaded with a very particular white powder you could end the world's production of semiconductors within six months.'[45] Mercifully, he didn't specify what the powder would be.

A secretive Appalachian mine is by no means the only potentially weak link in the chip supply chain. Virtually all of the metallurgical-grade polysilicon used to make semiconductors is produced in China.[46] The melting of the processed silicon (using those Spruce Pine quartz crucibles) often takes place in Japan, where companies specialise in producing ingots and turning them into wafers.[47] The final production process, carried out in Taiwan and South Korea, also requires purified neon gas, a byproduct of steel production. Ukraine was a major supplier of neon to the chip industry until the Russian invasion in 2022. Now most of it comes from China. 'A prolonged ban of neon exports from China would shut down a significant portion of semiconductor production after inventories are exhausted,' warns the boss of one industrial gas supplier.[48] Chip production also requires tungsten, again sourced primarily from China.

One assessment defined a potential chip chokepoint as occurring where 65 per cent or more of a particular item is concentrated in a single country or region. It identified at least fifty in the global semiconductor supply chain.[49] 'There's always something you need to import and ship from another place, country or even continent,' says one Taiwanese chip industry supplier.[50] This is potentially dangerous for every nation involved, but it also creates a form of technological balance of terror. As far as China and the US are concerned, damage to the semiconductor factories of Taiwan would be disastrous for both their electronics industries and wider economies. And when it comes to raw materials for chipmaking, China could cut off the flow of polysilicon, neon or tungsten and the US could in turn put an embargo on the export of Spruce Pine quartz. In the medium term, they might well be able to adjust and find alternative raw material sources. But in the short term, the two countries have their hands around the other's neck and the ability to squeeze.

The New Oil

In recent years the phrase 'chips are the new oil' has become popular.[51] 'Where the oil reserves are located has defined geopolitics for the last five decades. Where the chip factories are for the next five decades is more important,' the chief executive of Intel, Pat Gelsinger, claimed in October 2022.[52] And some analysts have suggested that countries that produce advanced chips like Taiwan and South Korea are 'the new OPEC', referring to the oil-producing cartel.[53] The logic of this kind of rhetoric leads to the reshoring effort. If a country wants to control its destiny it has to control its chips. But the oil analogy is fundamentally misleading. While oil pumped out of the ground in one part of the world is broadly the same as oil pumped in another, advanced chips are products that cannot be used interchangeably.

Indeed, they are the most complex products ever created by human hand and brain, involving scarcely comprehensible levels of intricacy, whose design is pushing the limits of our knowledge of the physical world. Their production, as we have explored, is a form of nanotechnology. They are the product of hundreds of raw materials and complex fabricated inputs from dozens of countries, involving the expert scientific knowledge and deep practical know-how of people from all around the world. The software design skills are every bit as important as the physical manufacturing process.

They are truly global products; indeed, the most global products in human history, when you take into account the full supply chain. A chip can cross international borders more than seventy times before completion. They are estimated to be the world's fourth most globally traded product – after crude oil, refined oil and cars – with trade flows adding up to $1.7 trillion in 2019.[54] Chips are the epitome of twenty-first-century economic and technological global interdependence. That's why the disruption of the 2021 chip shortage cut right across the global economy, contributing to the post-pandemic inflationary surge which generated popular discontent in so many countries.

The sophistication and cost of the production processes involved in making chips (and indeed to produce the raw material inputs) constitute nigh-on insurmountable barriers to most new firms and countries breaking in to the business. Indeed, it's de facto monopolies all the way down, from TMSC, which manufactures almost all the most advanced chips, to the Dutch firm ASML, which makes the lithography machines, to the German firm Zeiss, which supplies the lithography mirrors, to Sibelco in Spruce Pines, which mines the ultra-pure quartz, to the Japanese firms that manufacture the photoresist chemicals. And so on.

Can national industrial policy really reconfigure such a complex and inherently global system? The Biden administration claimed in 2024 that it was making good progress towards its 2030 goal of having a fifth of advanced chips manufactured on US territory. Drawing on American state subsidies, Taiwan's TSMC has announced a $65 billion cutting-edge chip-manufacturing complex in Phoenix, Arizona.[55] The giant Korean chipmaker Samsung is building a new facility in Texas.[56] There have been a host of other announcements of new electronics and computing plant investments, from Ohio to Idaho.[57] The CHIPS Act has certainly helped to get America building, with US total manufacturing construction investment doubling in the two years after its enactment in August 2022.[58]

But everything we've discussed in these pages shows why the idea that the entire supply chain of semiconductor production can be totally nationalised by any single country is regarded by industry experts as hopelessly unrealistic. And the costs of even attempting to achieve this are likely to be extortionate. To supply all of America's semiconductor needs domestically would require an additional upfront investment of $350–420 billion, according to estimates from Boston Consulting Group and the US's Semiconductor Industry Association. For Europe to do the same for its own domestic demand would require an additional upfront investment of $240–330 billion. Globally, a move to semiconductor self-sufficiency for the major regions would add up to $1 trillion in additional upfront investment.[59] And this is assuming, implausibly, that all the required raw materials in each region could, in fact, be sourced locally.

Further, this doesn't actually capture the overall cost of such an effort to achieve self-sufficiency. The speed of change at the advanced end of the chip production industry – and consequent need for additional investment – will make your head spin. A facility to fabricate the most advanced logic chips costs around $20 billion to build, almost twice as much as a new US aircraft carrier and three times as much as a new nuclear power station. But at the current rate of technological advance, it will only be cutting-edge for a couple of years. It's estimated that around half of the industry's annual revenues from chip sales have to be reinvested in research and development and put into new capital expenditure on plants simply for firms to remain at the technological frontier. In other words, reshoring will require not only a huge one-off investment, but continuous investment too, year after year.

Morris Chang, the father of the Taiwanese chip industry and the founder of TSMC, delivered a blunt reality check in 2022 when he predicted that efforts to increase onshore manufacturing of semiconductors by the US and others would prove 'a wasteful and expensive exercise in futility'. He believes America will manage to make more chips on its territory but 'all of that will be [at a] very ... high unit cost. It will be noncompetitive in the world markets.'[60]

For semiconductor regional self-sufficiency, it's estimated that the US would have additional annual ongoing costs of $5–15 billion, Europe of $25–60 billion and the world of $45–125 billion. This would push up the cost of semiconductor production by between one-third and two-thirds, which would inevitably feed into price rises for consumer products, from smartphones to cars. It's an open question whether populations would be willing to accept all those additional costs in exchange for the feeling of security that might arise from moving production from Asia to the US and Europe. And this is before factoring in the loss of dynamism an attempted major contraction of global supply chains would be likely to impose on productivity growth in this most historically innovative of sectors. Imagine forcing Usain Bolt to run in flip-flops.

Christmas Cancelled

The structural architecture of the Newport semiconductor wafer factory in South Wales pokes out cheerily from its body. Bright blue support struts and a large, snaking yellow pipe are visible from the main road. The building was designed in the early 1980s by the architect Richard Rogers to be 'inside out', like his perhaps best-known work the Pompidou Centre in Paris. But when I visited the plant, which mainly makes power regulating chips for automotive firms and wind turbine manufacturers, in May 2023, a miasma of fear and anger was hanging over the plant. The UK government had recently ordered its Dutch owners, Nexperia, to put it up for sale because it, in turn, had a Chinese owner with links to the Beijing government.

The logic of the London authorities was that, like their US allies, they did not want the factory and its semiconductor technology to fall into Beijing's hands. The factory is part of a cluster of expertise in Wales, linked to the local university, in a field called 'compound semiconductors', which has many potential applications in self-driving cars, advanced medical sensors and quantum computers. I was sent by the BBC to report on the crisis and the 600 local Welsh jobs the government's divestment order had put at risk. Tony Hill, an equipment engineering manager, told me that the workers were dismayed by the decision because the firm's current owners had, unlike the previous regime, invested in the plant. 'It's a little bit like being given a Christmas present and suddenly it's been taken away again and nobody really knows whether we're going to be getting it back again.' The struggle over Newport highlights a dilemma, particularly for smaller countries like the UK, when it comes to semiconductors.

The UK state can't compete with multibillion-dollar American, EU or Chinese semiconductor state subsidies. The British government's National Semiconductor Strategy, published in 2023, pledged around £1 billion ($1.3 billion) of public money over a decade – a sum dwarfed by the commitments of Brussels, Washington and

Beijing.⁶¹ If the UK wants to grow its own chip industry, it needs foreign investment. So the government was faced with a difficult choice: forgo badly needed foreign investment at the potential cost of jobs or risk compromising national security? The Newport plant was eventually sold to an American firm in early 2024 and the jobs saved.⁶² But the day I visited Newport it felt like there had to be a better way than security-driven semiconductor nationalism.

But is there, and what would it look like? It's worth recognising that there are legitimate concerns about the fragility of the system we have. The multiple de facto commercial and geographical monopolies and potential single points of failure in the global semiconductor supply chain are understandably and appropriately a cause of concern among policymakers. An earthquake in Taiwan, a fire in the Netherlands, floods in Germany, a tsunami in Japan, a landslide in the Appalachians: any single one of these natural shocks could be catastrophic for the semiconductor supply chain and that's without even going into the risk posed by military conflict or a terror attack. Geopolitical risks to supply chains – particularly a Chinese invasion of Taiwan – obviously need to be taken seriously. Even supply chains between allies cannot be taken for granted. In 2019 a diplomatic row between Japan and South Korea over Second World War compensation led Tokyo to temporarily impose export controls on South Korea on chemicals critical to its semiconductor production.

The public might not like the costs of reshored supply chains, but they will not like the costs of fragile ones either. The 2021 chip shortage offered a taste of what could be to come. When you consider that the boss of ASML, the supplier of the indispensable machines needed to make advanced chips, was told by some of his suppliers in 2021 that they were having trouble delivering key components because they couldn't get hold of the chips they needed in order to be able to manufacture, it becomes clear how precarious the system is.⁶³

Yet reshoring chip production is a potentially dangerous quest for politicians to embark upon without clearly defining what they are trying to achieve in terms of national security. In fairness, at times US and European leaders appear to recognise this reality.

And so far, the impact of programmes such as the US and EU chips legislation has been broadly positive in increasing geographical diversification in global chip production and cross-border investment.[64] But at other times the rhetoric – and sometimes the policies themselves, such as the widening US yard – veer towards crude deglobalisation and protectionism. Whether the Biden CHIPS Act will survive a second Trump presidency is, at the time of writing, entirely unclear to everyone. On the 2024 campaign trail Donald Trump described the Act's subsidies as a 'bad deal' for America and suggested that his cure-all of a new tariff wall would compel foreign firms like TSMC and Samsung to make the same semiconductor factory investments at zero cost to the US taxpayer.[65] However, some analysts think the legislation will ultimately survive because it fits with Trump's onshoring drive and was passed with the support of many Republicans lawmakers.[66]

Whatever happens to the CHIPS Act, many analysts think US and European leaders should target a deeper partnership with geopolitical allies in Asia on chip production rather than trying to go it alone. To deal with the very specific Taiwan concentration problem, it might make more sense for the US to encourage the building-up of advanced chip production in allied countries such as South Korea and Japan, which already have considerable semiconductor manufacturing infrastructure, rather than focusing on constructing new factories in America itself. In other words, this strategy would entail more globalisation of supply chains, not less. It would involve more cross-border corporate investment, not less.

A key question concerns the kind of policy interventions that would deliver the greatest bang for each invested buck in terms of building supply chain resilience. In terms of state spending, it would likely be more efficient to use it to develop alternative global sources of the ultra-pure quartz that is needed for the production of chips. Research into lowering the cost of synthetic varieties would also reduce the risk of chokepoints. More state funding for domestic semiconductor basic scientific research in universities and for enhancing the skills base of workers might also deliver better results than tax breaks for construction projects. One thing guaranteed to be wasteful is lack of coordination between allied countries in terms of common objectives and the policies pursued to get there. Some estimates put the total cumulative state financial support for the chips industry from America, China, the EU – and also Taiwan, Japan, South Korea and India – in recent years at around $700 billion. Given the market power of the biggest commercial players, the risk of a subsidy race is uncomfortably high.[67] And in a highly cyclical industry like chips, where booms and busts are common, there is a danger that the economics of many of the dozens of new chip factories being planned will simply not work. The other risk is that governments feel compelled to force the economics to work by imposing requirements on domestic firms to buy locally, no matter the price.

When it comes to building up a domestic industry through sheer financial and political force, the meagre results of China's chip self-sufficiency drive – which has been in operation since 2014, when Beijing launched the China Integrated Circuit Industry Investment Fund, known as the 'Big Fund' – serve as a lesson. Despite an estimated $140 billion in expenditure from the centre, the main result has been mass bankruptcies and abandoned projects.[68] The original target was to raise Chinese self-sufficiency in chips from 16 per cent in 2015 to 70 per cent by 2025.[69] The outcome will likely be closer to 20 per cent.[70] Despite excited headlines about a 7 nanometre Chinese-built chip being deployed in a Huawei smartphone in 2023, all the evidence points to China remaining firmly stuck in producing second-tier chips for the foreseeable future.[71] There are ways for countries to enhance chip supply security other than onshoring.

Just in Time to Just in Case

On 11 March 2011 at 2.46 pm Japan Standard Time, two tectonic plates briefly broke free from each other's immense friction some 115 km off the Oshika Peninsula, releasing centuries of pent-up energy in seconds. The power of the Tohoku earthquake was ten times greater than that of the largest nuclear bomb ever tested.[72]

Hundreds of billions of tonnes of water were displaced, sending waves up to 40 m in height rushing towards the coast of north-eastern Japan. The tsunami, which hit land around fifteen minutes after the 9.1 magnitude earthquake, devastated the Japanese coastline, levelling 120,000 buildings and killing some 18,000 people. The waters flooded the Fukushima nuclear power plant and its cores melted down, resulting in Japan's worst ever nuclear accident.

Among the biggest industrial casualties from the fallout from the Tohoku quake was the Japanese automotive giant Toyota. For two weeks Toyota was forced to halt production at its Japanese plants entirely, and it was a further three months before its production levels fully recovered. Yet it wasn't Toyota's manufacturing plants that were taken offline by the Tohoku quake. Toyota's plants were in the south of Japan, some distance from the region engulfed by the tsunami and shaken by the earthquake. The firms directly affected were Toyota's supplier companies, including the chipmaker Ranesas Electronics.[73] This chastening supply chain rupture, which effectively cost Toyota a quarter of its annual production, prompted the firm to build a database of all its suppliers and their suppliers. It ultimately went ten firms deep and covered around 400,000 separate components.[74] The exercise prompted Toyota to implement a major overhaul of its historic industrial practices.

A Toyota executive, Taiichi Ohno, had visited a US supermarket in 1950 and been impressed.[75] The story runs that the sight of workers restocking the shelves with new deliveries as they arrived at the store, rather than from stock held on site, made Ohno realise the possibilities of applying this model to Toyota's factories, resulting in large savings on its warehousing bills and thus boosting its profits. Whether the supermarket visit really provided the inspiration, the 'just-in-time' (JIT) manufacturing model that Ohno pioneered in Japan, where components would be delivered to Toyota's plants only hours before they were deployed on the assembly line, was an industrial phenomenon and was at the heart of the famous Toyota Production System (TPS).[76] The system played a considerable role in helping Toyota to become the largest global automotive manufacturer over the subsequent decades. Other global car makers eventually adopted the JIT practice too.

Yet the 2011 Tohoku disaster prompted the JIT pioneer to shift away from it. In the years that followed, Toyota began to ask its suppliers to stockpile the most critical components, partially rebuilding the inventory system that JIT had largely abolished half a century earlier. Just-in-time morphed into just-in-case. Toyota also started to source its components from multiple suppliers rather than relying on a single one, as well as developing a closer and more collaborative relationship with more of its suppliers on the basis that this would help it to pivot more easily in the face of shocks. So when chipageddon struck in 2021 Toyota found itself well served by its new methods. It was considerably less affected by the chip shortages than the other large auto makers.[77] While Volkswagen and Renault saw their sales contract by 5.5 per cent and 1.3 per cent respectively over 2021, Toyota's sales grew by 12 per cent.[78] Toyota's latest industrial revolution shows how silicon supply chain resilience can be enhanced without adopting the exile economic policies of contraction and withdrawal.

Governments worried about semiconductor supplies could work with firms to map supply chains and stockpile. Investment could be targeted in building inventories of raw materials including gases and chemicals. And stockpiled semiconductors will not always be the most advanced ones. Here it's worth returning to that 2021 chip shortage and examining what happened in greater detail. Despite the scramble by governments in recent years to onshore the production of advanced chips, the semiconductors that were often most lacking in 2021 were not leading-edge specialist logic chips with high-tech military or AI applications but rather trailing-edge 'legacy' chips – often interchangeable commodity products – which do rather more mundane jobs such as operating car windscreen wipers and the driers in dog laundromats.[79] Around two-thirds of all the chips being produced in 2019 were at nodes above 28 nanometres.[80] The odd thing about chipageddon was that, despite the headlines, the actual shipments of integrated circuits in 2021 amounted to a record 394 billion units, a 24 per cent increase on the previous year.[81]

Despite chipageddon, 2021 saw a new record number of integrated circuits shipped globally

Volume of integrated circuit shipments, billion

[Bar chart showing volume of integrated circuit shipments from 2012 to 2024, with 2021 highlighted at 394.2 billion]

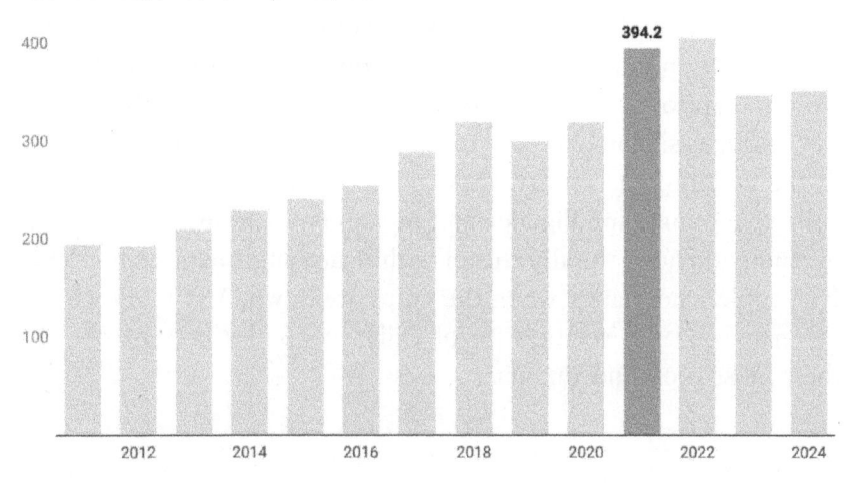

Chart: Ben Chu • Source: Tech Insights • Created with Datawrapper

Figure 10

The shortage had been real – but it had been primarily created by a spike in demand rather than a contraction of supply. The demand for personal computers and other devices had shot up in the pandemic lockdowns as people were forced to work from home. Many big car makers had cancelled their orders in anticipation of reduced sales due to those lockdowns. As lockdowns eased and people started buying vehicles again, these big customers suddenly ramped up orders, contributing to a major imbalance between available supply and demand.

There was, it is true, some bad luck that crimped chip supply in 2021. A fire at a semiconductor plant in Japan came at precisely the wrong time.[82] A severe drought in Taiwan curtailed factory production (chip plants use a lot of water).[83] An extreme winter storm in Texas, the centre of US chip manufacturing, had a similar effect on production there, as power had to be diverted from chip factories to freezing households.[84] Yet the remarkable thing was how little impact these events had on aggregate production. Chip factories had stretched to meet the greater demand, using more of their capacity than ever. The globalised production system for microchips arguably stood up pretty well to the massive test in the shape of the whiplash demand patterns of the pandemic. The irony is that many politicians drew a misleading exile economics lesson from the episode – that they couldn't rely on those supply chains.

Central as silicon chips are to the economy and national security in the twenty-first century, these components are the fruit of our collective human intelligence and ingenuity – and intelligence and ingenuity do not naturally cluster within any single nation's borders. It's people who matter when the chips are down. And that's where the nativism and isolationism of exile economics present one of their most profound threats.

6

People

On 8 December 2020 a ninety-year-old woman wearing a grey cardigan and a disposable face mask sat in a large blue armchair in a hospital in the British city of Coventry, looking a little nervous. A nurse approached and administered a small injection into the patient's upper left shoulder. Photographers' flashes went off and a cheer went up. With that Margaret Keenan became the first person in the world to receive an approved Covid-19 vaccine.[1] What was thought to be impossible had been achieved. Within a year of the virus first being identified scientists had developed a vaccine – something never done so quickly before. Normally the process takes years. Four had elapsed in the making of a mumps vaccine in the 1960s.

But Margaret Keenan's jab was more than a spectacular triumph for medical science. The administration of that first dose in Coventry's University Hospital was a signal that the national lockdowns, which had confined billions of people around the world to their homes, could come to an end. Once a sufficiently large population had been vaccinated they could safely mingle again – in offices, in restaurants, in theatres, in sports stadiums, on public transport – without the risk of a lethal surge in infections. The door to that global liberation had been opened, in no small part, by an immigrant.

Uğur Şahin was born in Iskenderun, a Turkish city on the eastern Mediterranean coast, in 1965. He migrated to Cologne in Germany as a four-year-old, coming over with his mother. He studied medicine at the local university and received his doctorate in immunotherapy in 1992. Şahin trained as a doctor and worked at

Cologne's main hospital in the oncology department. In the early 2000s he started exploring whether a novel biotechnology known as 'messenger RNA' – which uses specially designed molecules to essentially teach a patient's body to produce the proteins needed to fight a disease – could be used as a cancer vaccine. In the city of Mainz, where Johannes Gutenberg built the first printing press, Şahin founded a firm called BioNTech with his wife, also the daughter of Turkish immigrants, with this cancer-battling goal in mind.

But when the Covid pandemic was declared in March 2020 Şahin pivoted and put all his energy into creating a vaccine for the new coronavirus. 'It felt not like an opportunity, but a duty to do it, because I realised we could be among the first coming up with a vaccine,' he recalled.[2] Within days BioNTech struck a development deal with the US pharmaceutical giant Pfizer, who would mass-produce the drug and do the expensive and important job of testing it in trials all around the world. Results from those trials unveiled on 3 November 2020 showed that BioNTech's vaccine worked, protecting those that received the jab with an impressive 90 per cent efficiency. It was the BioNTech/Pfizer vaccine that was injected into Margaret Keenan's arm that day in Coventry. More than 4.6 billion doses have been delivered to 181 countries since then.[3] The drug that Uğur Şahin conceived and developed had played a central role in bringing the pandemic to an end.

Şahin baulks at the idea of being held up as an immigrant role model. 'I think we need a global vision that gives everyone an equal chance,' he has said.

> Intelligence is equally distributed across all ethnicities, that's what all the studies show. As a society we have to ask ourselves how we can give everyone a chance to contribute to society. I am an accidental example of someone with a migration background. I could have equally been German or Spanish.[4]

But the fact is that he was someone born in Turkey who was working in Germany and doing work of great importance to humanity. To many in that country – and also around the world – his life story served as a powerful lesson in the benefits of migration. 'Here's to the immigrant heroes behind the BioNTech vaccine,' wrote one columnist, referring to Şahin and his wife.[5] Another spoke of their 'immigrant ingenuity'.[6] Yet some insist on presenting immigrants not as a cure, but a poison.

Poisoning the Blood

Donald Trump glided down the mirror-clad escalators into the atrium of Trump Tower in New York City on 16 June 2015 to announce he was running to be US president. The real estate tycoon and TV personality had been speaking for less than three minutes when he accused Mexico of sending 'rapists' to the US.[7] He followed that up six months later with a promise to enact what he called a 'complete shutdown' on Muslims entering the US.[8] At a rally in New Hampshire in December 2023 Trump's rhetoric took on a still-darker tone. Illegal immigrants, he claimed, are 'poisoning the blood of our country'.[9] The presidential candidate repeated the line on his social media platform and once again in another rally in Iowa.[10] Trump campaigned in the 2024 presidential election on a promise to deport all undocumented migrants from America, estimated to be around 11 million people (though other credible studies put it at double that).[11] At the time of writing it's unclear whether his second presidential administration will be able to make good on that, given it would constitute an unprecedented operation in US history, requiring enormous financial and logistical resources.

Trump's anti-immigrant and nativist sentiments resonate among Europe's populist right. Germany's Alternative for Germany advocates 'net zero migration'. In France Marine Le Pen's National Rally has proposed the abolition of France's *droit de sol*, which allows individuals born in France to immigrant parents to acquire French nationality. 'For us migration is not a solution but a problem, not medicine but a poison. We don't need it and won't swallow it,' thundered the Hungarian prime minister, Viktor Orbán, in 2016.[12] Austria's Freedom Party, which came first in the country's elections in September 2024, has suggested that the EU should appoint a 'remigration commissioner'.[13] 'We have to think about our own people first now. Borders closed. Zero asylum-seekers,' says Geert Wilders, whose Party of Freedom won the largest share of the vote in the 2023 national elections in the Netherlands.[14]

The Covid pandemic led to a plunge in global mobility as cross-border travel was severely restricted to prevent the spread of the virus. New Zealand and Australia more or less entirely closed their borders to foreign citizens and non-residents. But since then global mobility has come surging back, and with it long-term migration. In 2023 the number of permanent immigrants moving to the countries of the OECD – comprising the majority of the world's wealthiest nations – reached a record high of 6.5 million. This was up 10 per cent from the 6 million in 2022, which itself had been a record.[15] And these figures do not include some 5 million refugees created by the Russian invasion of Ukraine, the largest displacement of people in Europe since the Second World War.

Amid this surge of people moving across national borders, sentiment on immigration across the world has grown more hostile. A giant poll by Ipsos of 48,000 people in countries all around the planet in the autumn of 2022 found that 64 per cent agreed that there were too many immigrants in their country.[16] That was up from 55 per cent who answered that way in 2016.[17]

In many countries there is manifestly a rising restrictionist mood when it comes to migration. In the summer of 2024 around 17 per cent of people polled by Ipsos across twenty-nine countries cited 'immigration control' as one of their top three worries.[18] That summer a different poll found the proportion of Americans who said immigration rates should be decreased hit 55 per cent, the highest level since 2001. Reducing immigration in 2024 was also, according to polling, the top public priority in Germany, with sharp rises in support of that policy also recorded in the Netherlands, France, Norway and the UK.[19] There is a growing view in some countries not only that immigration levels are too high, but that immigration is damaging in itself. In the summer of 2024 the proportion of Americans who said immigration was a 'bad thing' for their country rose to 32 per cent, up from 19 per cent in 2020.[20] In the UK the share of the public seeing immigration as 'mostly bad' for their country was 40 per cent in September 2024, up from 30 per cent four years earlier.[21] The history of the Second World War, though, tells a different story.

Mussolini's Gift

In the late summer of 1938 a thirty-seven-year-old man and his family were driving in the Italian Alps. At each town they passed through the man would jump out and find a post box and deposit a letter to an address in America. The letters were essentially the same. They were asking for a job.[22] One survives. It reads:

> I must confess that I expect rather difficult times in the years to come. In my personal case, my wife being of Jewish origin might lead to a disagreeable situation for the children. I am writing to you this, mainly in order to inform you that in case there should be in America a convenient position for me, I would gladly accept it.[23]

The man was Enrico Fermi. He was one of the world's most respected and pioneering nuclear physicists and he was trying to leave Italy because the Fascist regime of Benito Mussolini had started to target Italian Jews with discriminatory laws, following the lead of Nazi Germany. Fermi was writing to American universities to ask for an academic position so he and his family could get out of Italy for good. And he was sending letters from four different towns to reduce the risk of the plan being detected by the Rome authorities, who might confiscate the family's passports. Multiple job offers soon arrived. And four years later, in a squash court under a disused football stadium on the South Side of Chicago, Fermi and his colleagues created the first self-sustaining nuclear chain reaction in a large-scale physics experiment, giving the US military a crucial technological breakthrough in the race against the Nazis to create an atomic bomb. 'More than any other man of his time, Enrico Fermi could properly be named "the father of the atomic bomb",' concluded his obituary in the *New York Times* in 1954.[24] The physicist Isidor Rabi called him Mussolini's greatest gift to America.

The reality was that Fermi was just one particle in the brain drain from Europe. Other luminaries who fled European Fascism and antisemitism included Leo Szilard, Emilio Segre, Edward Teller and Niels Bohr. All contributed their brain power to the Manhattan Project to construct the atom bomb. Most had doubts about the morality of using their skills and genius to create such a potentially apocalyptic weapon. But they accepted that a worse fate would befall the world if the Nazi regime developed the technology first. Sir Ian Jacob, who had been Winston Churchill's military secretary, is reported to have quipped that the Allies won the war 'because our German scientists were better than their German scientists'.[25] It does seem fair to say that if the racist authoritarians of Europe had not driven out many of their best minds world history might conceivably have been very different.

This pattern of immigrant contribution to science has continued in the decades since. One of Uğur Şahin's BioNTech collaborators on the mRNA Covid vaccine was the Hungarian-born biochemist Katalin Karikó. She moved to the US in 1985 and was awarded the Nobel Prize in Physiology or Medicine in 2023. Between 2000 and 2023, forty-five of the 112 Nobel Prizes won by Americans in chemistry, medicine and physics were won by immigrants to the country.[26] A similarly outsized proportion of the researchers in Britain, Germany and France who have been awarded Nobel Prizes were also immigrants. The contribution of migrants extends well beyond pure scientific research. As we saw with semiconductors, the role of technology in shaping our world is difficult to overstate. Technology is created by people, and those people are very often migrants.

Morris and Jensen

Morris Chang was born in 1931 in China, the son of a middle-ranking Shanghai banker, but he was on the move from almost the day he was born. By the time he was eighteen Chang had lived through the Sino-Japanese War, the Second World War and the Chinese Civil War – upheavals and violence that had pushed his family all around China, from Ningbo to Guangzhou, then on to Hong Kong and Chongqing and back to Shanghai. Finally, when Mao's Communist regime took power in 1949, Chang crossed the Pacific Ocean and landed in America, where, after a year studying Shakespeare at Harvard, he switched to mechanical engineering at the Massachusetts Institute of Technology. After graduating he joined the semiconductor firm Texas Instruments (TI), based in Dallas. Over the next twenty-five years Chang greatly improved the efficiency of TI's chip-manufacturing operations, which directly expanded its market share and profitability, and he rose up the company ranks. He expected to be made chief executive but was passed over for the top job and handed in his resignation in 1984. 'I left because I felt that essentially I had been put out in the pasture,' he recalled.[27]

So the fifty-four-year-old was interested when the Taiwanese government came calling a couple of years later and asked the industry veteran to set up a semiconductor manufacturing plant on the island controlled by the successors of the Chinese Nationalist forces defeated by Mao's Communists back in 1949. Chang took up the offer, emigrated to Taiwan and created the Taiwan Semiconductor Manufacturing Company (TSMC) in 1986, with the radical idea that it would only make chips for other semiconductor firms, wherever in the world they were, rather than designing or selling them for itself. It was an idea he'd proposed to his bosses at TI in the 1970s but they'd not taken it up. The Chang 'pure-play foundry' model of chip manufacturing turned into one of the most significant developments in twentieth-century industrial globalisation.

On the back of TSMC's extraordinary technological ability to squeeze ever more transistors onto pieces of silicon and, just as important, to deliver a high and reliable yield of chips from each wafer, it became the go-to chip-manufacturing company for the world's biggest electronics firms. And as we explored in the last chapter, TSMC is now the largest advanced chipmaker in the world, the firm at the very technological forefront with few, if any, potential rivals. Without the pipe-smoking Morris Chang, it would never have happened and Taiwan would not today have its 'silicon shield', with both Washington and Beijing – two superpowers – being economically reliant on the island's chip-manufacturing prowess. If the board of TI hadn't passed over Chang to be CEO in 1984 the US government might not today be paying TSMC to build chip foundries in Arizona via the CHIPS Act.

If what happened with Morris Chang might be considered a form of brain drain out of the US in the age of globalisation, Jensen Huang was the opposite: a 'brain gain'. Huang was born into a relatively poor Taiwanese family in 1963 and sent to America in 1972, along with his brother, to live with an uncle in Washington state. But the nine-year-old Huang had not been in Washington long before he was dispatched by his uncle to a boarding school called the Oneida Baptist Institute in rural Kentucky, which had been set up in 1899 to try to heal the murderous feuds raging between Appalachian clans by providing a strict religious education for their children. Huang's uncle apparently believed Oneida was a prestigious boarding school. In reality it was more like a reform school, where students were required to work, including cleaning communal bathrooms, as well as to study. 'The kids were really tough,' Huang has recalled. 'They all had pocket knives and when they get in fights, it's not pretty. Kids get hurt.'[28] It must have been bewildering for a nine-year-old Taiwanese migrant with broken English to be dropped into such an environment, and contemporaries recall that the bullying of Huang was relentless. Yet Huang says that the experience toughened him and that he ultimately thrived at Oneida, saying he 'loved the time' he was there.[29]

After school, Huang went to study electrical engineering at Oregon State University and, from there, moved to Silicon Valley to design chips. A fan of early video games, he founded Nvidia in 1990 to make Graphic Processing Units (GPUs), before pivoting to design advanced chips with AI applications. Nvidia is one of the so-called 'fabless' chip designers that the pure-play foundry model of TSMC enabled to exist. On the back of the burst of investor enthusiasm for AI in 2023 the stock price of the Nasdaq-listed firm shot up. In November 2024 it hit $148, giving the company a paper worth of $3.6 trillion. Nvidia was, at that point, the most valuable publicly listed company in the world. And it has a symbiotic relationship with TSMC, sometimes described as the most important company in the world.[30] Two companies at the heart of the twenty-first-century economy: both founded by immigrants.

Chang and Huang are spectacular outliers by their nature. But can we read across from these two examples to the impact of immigrants more generally? The evidence suggests this is possible. Several studies suggest immigrants are more likely to start a business than the native-born.[31] This means they create more jobs than would exist otherwise. 'Immigrants contribute disproportionately to employment creation' is the view of the OECD.[32] That might be because, having travelled from their homeland, migrants tend to have a greater entrepreneurial drive than the average native. The case shouldn't be overstated. Relatively high rates of self-employment among immigrants might not be because they are inherently more entrepreneurial but because they have fewer options in the regular employment market due to language and cultural factors or discrimination. And some research suggests the businesses migrants found might not employ that many people relative to others and might be less likely to survive.[33] Part of the story might be that immigrants are more likely to be of working age, so you would expect them to be more likely to start a business. But the job-creation impact of immigration is generally seen by economists as positive. Evidence from the US also suggests that the presence of a larger number of migrants with science, technology, engineering and maths (STEM) degrees in an area is associated with an increase in native wages; though a larger share of the benefits go to more educated native-born workers.[34] And outliers matter. Brilliant individual immigrants to the US – such as Alexander Graham Bell (Scotland), the pharmaceutical magnate Charles Pfizer (Germany), Andy Grove of Intel (Hungary) and Google founder Sergey Brin (Russia) – have made an extraordinary impact on the world of business and the global economy.

Oxygen in the Relationship

I met Eugene in Glasgow in 2022. The postgraduate student at Glasgow University from western China was gregarious, fluent and thoughtful. 'I have different personas when I'm speaking Chinese and English,' he told me, as we chatted in one of the city's high-ceilinged tenement apartments. 'I don't know why but you tend to talk about something you're not willing to talk about in your mother tongue.' It's estimated that around 1 million Chinese people like Eugene are currently studying outside China. They thus represent a considerable proportion of the estimated 6 million students studying abroad globally, with 4 million in OECD countries.[35] And many of these Chinese students end up in the UK, learning at British universities. There were around 150,000 in Britain in 2022, up 50 per cent on five years earlier. That's been a great financial benefit to UK universities.

But it's also generated concerns. Some MPs in the Conservative Party have argued that the increasing financial reliance of British universities on the tuition fees of Chinese students, some of whom have hardline nationalist views, risks compromising the academic freedom of these institutions.[36] Michelle Shipworth, an academic at University College London, reported in 2024 that one of her teaching modules, which contained a slide asking 'Why does China have so many slaves?', was removed by her employer after complaints from some Chinese students. 'Some of my colleagues are hyper anxious about losing income from overseas students to a point where they will be prepared to do almost anything to keep our students happy,' she has said.[37] There are suggestions that these students themselves are manipulated by Beijing. A parliamentary committee with responsibility for oversight of the UK intelligence community was told that Chinese-embassy-funded Chinese Students and Scholars Associations (CSSAs) attempt to 'monitor and control' overseas Chinese students' behaviour.[38]

The sense that Chinese students pose a national security threat has been fuelled by the intelligence services. The head of MI5, Ken McCallum, has called British universities 'magnetic targets for espionage and manipulation' and reported that fifty Chinese students linked to the People's Liberation Army had been removed from the UK.[39] The UK government also operates an Academic Technology Approval Scheme (ATAS), which vets overseas students applying to study in areas of research with potential 'military technology' applications, including physics, maths, engineering and AI. Chinese students have increasingly fallen foul of this system in recent years. A freedom of information request from the Bloomberg news organisation showed that the rejection rate hit 5 per cent of applications in 2023, a tenfold increase on 2019.[40]

It's a transatlantic phenomenon. America is an even more popular destination for Chinese students, with 290,000 studying in the US in 2023.[41] The concerns there are even louder. In 2022 the then Republican senator for Florida Marco Rubio called for links between Chinese and US educational institutions to be 'discouraged'.[42] Christopher Wray, the former head of the FBI, warned in 2022 of some Chinese graduate students in the US, with clandestine links to the Beijing regime, of 'stealing innovation'.[43] The first Trump administration launched a 'China Initiative' in 2018 to root out supposed Chinese spies in US academia. It resulted in no espionage convictions, but plenty of wrongful arrests.[44] The scheme was ultimately wound up in 2022 but the crackdown has continued in other ways. Bloomberg has found evidence of at least twenty Chinese science students with valid visas being denied entry to the US between November 2023 and May 2024. The first Trump administration's 2020 rule still stands. This says that any Chinese graduate students who studied at any university in China with a connection to the country's military, whether or not any negative information exists about the individual, can be denied a visa.[45]

Glasgow is one of the most popular destinations for Chinese overseas students in the UK, with more than 6,000 studying on its campus. I spent time with some of them, listening to their perspectives and stories, for a 2022 BBC radio documentary.[46] What I found belied many of the stereotypes of students being intolerant Communist Party mouthpieces who impose their views on others. I discovered, more often, a reticence when it came to getting involved in political discussions at all. 'Even if we have more access to different opinions about democracy and other political topics we don't talk about it that much because we will get in trouble,' Eugene told me. 'We can have some opinions in our own hearts, in our own minds, but we don't talk about this.' The strongest message from our research was that Chinese students in the UK should not – despite the political and media narrative around them – be considered a homogeneous bloc.

It would be misguided to dismiss national security concerns, or to downplay the risk of intimidation by some Chinese students and attempts by the Chinese government to influence free speech on Western campuses.[47] The proposals from Human Rights Watch to impose various safeguards on Western university campuses – such as monitoring Chinese government-linked organisations and explicitly committing to academic freedoms – seem well judged and proportionate.[48]

Yet it would also be misguided not to balance those concerns against the benefits of openness, not only in terms of academic exchange but cultural and political understanding. 'People-to-people exchange is like oxygen in the relationship,' Amy Gadsden of the University of Pennsylvania and a former special advisor for China at the US State Department has observed.

> When you have it you don't even notice it's there. When you don't have it you can't breathe. What we're seeing is, as we lose the people-to-people part of our relationship between the United States and China, it will become harder and harder to breathe, the relationship will have a harder time breathing.[49]

One of the most striking points from my conversation with Eugene was when he said one of the attractions of a UK university, at least for him, was that it allowed more individuality and self-expression than higher education in China. 'You don't have to be a product on an assembly line,' as he put it.

Eugene returned home in 2022, not long after our meeting, but told me that he had greatly enjoyed his experience in Scotland and would like to return one day to work. That goodwill is an asset to Britain. But such assets can also be undermined. The Nobel Prize-winning American scientist Steven Chu, whose parents migrated to the US from China, has warned of the hostility of political discourse in America towards Chinese students. 'For many decades we were viewed by the rest of the world as a welcoming country, a country of immigrants,' he said in 2022. 'This is at risk now because there are mixed messages now being sent.'[50]

The vice-chancellor of Cambridge University in the UK, Deborah Prentice, has a similar warning about the British state's increasing restrictions and rising immigration fees on foreign students which, she argues, 'send a not-so-subtle message that foreigners are not welcome here'.[51] Adam Posen of the Peterson Institute in Washington argues the West should have an open-door policy to regime critics of the Chinese government, similar to the welcome extended to dissidents of the Fascist regimes in the 1930s like Enrico Fermi:

> Let us welcome every bloody scientist, every entrepreneur, every investor, every business who wants to partially or wholly exit China. Let them come to the US, let them come to the UK, let them come to Singapore and Australia and suck out some of their talent and let it come here.[52]

There is also a straightforward economic consideration in the US, especially since it wants to reshore semiconductor manufacturing. Around 40 per cent of the high-skilled semiconductor workers in the US were born abroad. And international students comprise around two-thirds of graduate students in electrical engineering and computer science, of whom a large majority currently stay in the country after completing their degrees.[53] A 2023 study by the Semiconductor Industry Association found that even if the CHIPS Act succeeded in reshoring a considerable chunk of advanced chip-manufacturing capacity, the country would face a shortage of 67,000 technicians, computer scientists and engineers to work in those factories by 2030, equivalent to around 60 per cent of the new jobs projected to be created.[54]

As well as investment in training more domestic workers, the association's strong policy recommendation to deal with this ominous skilled labour shortage was an immigration policy that enabled more skilled workers to come to – and remain – in the US. 'America's efforts to onshore critical supply chains will not succeed unless it also onshores the talent necessary to compete,' as a 2022 letter from a host of senior former national security officials to US Congressional leaders put it.[55] In other words, either the US can reshore semiconductor manufacturing or it can close itself off to immigration – but it can't do both. The same applies to European states with technological ambitions of their own in the coming years.

China is often looked on with envy in the West for its high numbers of science graduates: the country is projected to produce 70,000 scholars with STEM PhDs in 2024 compared to around 40,000 in the US.[56] Yet, according to one of its government-linked thinktanks, China itself still has 200,000 fewer software engineers and chip designers than it needs to deliver on its ambitions to substantially boost the country's semiconductor self-sufficiency. Nor is a brainpower shortage a new problem for China. Since 2008 Beijing has had a plethora of incentive schemes to encourage Chinese-born scientists who have studied and worked abroad to return. The latest iteration offers returnees signing bonuses of 3 to 5 million yuan – $420,000 to $700,000 – according to research by the Reuters news agency.[57]

China is producing more science doctorates than the US

Science, technology, engineering, and mathematics PhDs awarded per year, thousands

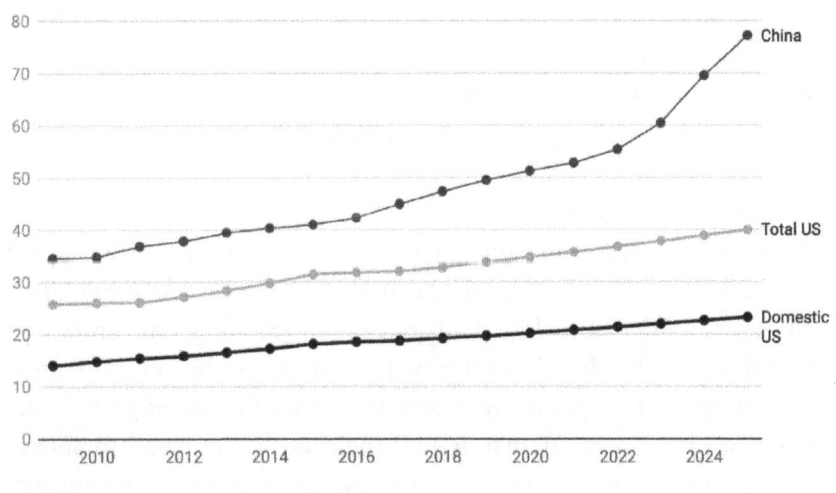

2020-2025 = forecasts
Chart: Ben Chu • Source: CSET • Created with Datawrapper

Figure 11

These efforts seem to have had some success, though the effect of China's sharply authoritarian turn under Xi Jinping has worked in the opposite direction.[58] What some are calling a new Cold War between the US and China is also a tussle over 'human capital'. It's not just in the field of semiconductors that America is reliant on immigrant science students. More than two-thirds of full-time US graduate students in AI-related disciplines, widely seen as the most important new frontier in technological progress, are international.[59] But what about immigrants who aren't science students, or people with technological expertise and advanced degrees, or successful entrepreneurs? What about the less skilled?

Marielonomics

The distance between the island of Cuba and Key West in Florida, the southernmost point of the continental USA, is 144 km. In 1980 for many Cubans that was the distance between repression and liberty, between poverty and prosperity. But there was no way across for them, except by taking desperate measures. On 1 April 1980 an unemployed Cuban bus driver called Hector Sanyustiz and four others drove a bus through a fence at the Peruvian embassy in Havana in an effort to escape the forces of his own country and seek asylum in Peru. The Cuban police guarding the embassy opened fire on the bus, injuring two of the would-be refugees and also killing one of their own due to a ricocheted bullet.[60] The authorities in Havana demanded all the men be returned to stand trial over the police officer's death. The Peruvians refused, prompting the Cuban dictator Fidel Castro to withdraw protection from the embassy. The effect was not what Castro had anticipated. After the withdrawal of the police some 10,000 Cubans, desperate to leave the impoverished island, rushed into the embassy's gardens, also pleading for asylum.

On 20 April, Castro, humiliated by the chaotic scenes, announced that anyone insufficiently loyal to the Cuban nation that they wanted to leave could do so via the port of Mariel, provided they could get someone from the US to pick them up by boat. The émigré Cuban community in America – many of whom had managed to flee in the previous years – scrambled to take advantage of the opportunity to get their relations and friends to freedom, renting fishing boats in places like Key West. Over the next few months, some 125,000 Cubans crowded into 1,700 boats at Mariel, which then motored them across the straits to Florida, overwhelming the US coastguard in the process. It became known as the Mariel boatlift.

Physicists like the great Enrico Fermi can study subatomic particles by deliberately manipulating them with laboratory equipment. But economists, who study people's interactions in a complex society, can't manipulate them in a comparable way to see the reactions. So they are always on the lookout for so-called 'natural experiments' – sudden changes in normal economic conditions in a specific place or time period which can be statistically analysed to draw out some wider lessons about economic forces. One Canadian-American economist, David Card, realised that the Mariel boatlift represented a golden opportunity to study the impact of migration on local employment and wages. More than half of the new Cuban arrivals, for the most part less-skilled workers, went to live in the city of Miami, increasing its labour force by 7 per cent almost overnight. So, Card asked, what happened to the wages and employment levels of existing workers in the city as a result of this extremely large and sudden influx?

In 1990, a decade after the arrivals, Card looked at local jobs market data for the period between 1979 and 1985.[61] The standard economic assumption before then was that supply and demand applied just as much to labour markets as to any other market. So a large influx of less-skilled migrants into a local jobs market like Miami was expected to push down average wages for existing workers without college qualifications and also to increase unemployment in this group. But to Card's surprise he found that there was no such effect. The 'Marielitos' were successfully integrated into the workforce, taking jobs on construction sites, in warehouses and restaurants – and existing lower-skilled workers were left no worse-off. The results were a major challenge to prevailing assumptions about the impact of migration. Card's findings were challenged by another economist, George Borjas, in 2015, with Borjas suggesting there was indeed a negative impact on the wages of the lower-skilled in Miami. The academic debate entered the political spotlight when the first Trump administration cited Borjas's work to justify its immigration curbs. But the Borjas challenge itself has been undermined by detailed statistical analysis.[62]

Whether the Mariel findings apply universally to all labour markets or not – whether such an influx would always have such benign results – is still open to debate. As Card has accepted, it's possible that there were specific circumstances in Miami, such as the previous waves of Cuban migrants, that made it easier for the Marielitos to integrate economically. Yet the Mariel study has thrown doubt on the idea that the arrival of relatively large numbers of less-skilled immigrants is inevitably economically negative for existing workers in the same category. A landmark report by the US National Academies of Sciences, Engineering, and Medicine in 2016 concluded that the impact of immigration on the wages of US-born workers overall is 'very small'.[63] The UK experienced large flows of lower-skilled migration after around 1 million Eastern Europeans arrived in the years after the expansion of the EU in 2004. Studies of that episode likewise suggest that the impact on wages of UK-born people in lower-skilled occupations was extremely small, albeit negative.[64] The UK government's Migration Advisory Committee concluded in 2018 that migrants have had 'no or little impact' on the overall employment and unemployment outcomes of the British-born workforce.[65] This is because lower-skilled migrants can fill specific gaps in the labour market or be complementary to higher-skilled natives. For instance, one study in Italy found that migrant workers who entered sectors such as childcare and cleaning enabled women who would otherwise have had to stay at home to go to work and earn.[66]

Donald Trump, back in that June 2015 speech given in the lobby of Trump Tower, accused Mexican immigrants of 'bringing drugs' and 'bringing crime' to the US. And the claimed link between immigrants and criminality is a frequent trope among populists. But there is little evidence to support it in developed countries. Studies from Britain, America and Italy have identified no connection between higher immigration rates and an increase in crime.[67] Indeed, the increase in immigration to many OECD countries has coincided with a decline in both violent crime and overall crime, which peaked in the most developed of those states in the middle of the 1990s and has been coming down steadily since for reasons that remain something of a mystery.[68] Some researchers did find that immigrant groups in Britain who face poor labour market opportunities, like asylum seekers, are more likely to commit property crime, though this is also true of disadvantaged native groups. Moreover, the size of the effect was not particularly large.[69] So what is the problem with migration if it's not an economic or a criminal one?

Numbers

It's worth going back to the overall numbers. The United Nations estimates around 280 million people were living in countries where they were not born in 2020, up from 113 million in 1985. As a share of the world's population that's an increase from 2.3 per cent to 3.6 per cent, with a clear step-up coming after 1990 and the fall of the Soviet Union.[70] The proportion of foreign-born people in developed countries is higher and has been rising more rapidly. In OECD countries the total share of people born abroad was 14.7 per cent in 2023, up from 11.7 per cent in 2013.[71] But people's perceptions of demographic change are outstripping reality. Surveys have found that the public's average guesses of the share of first-generation migrants in the populations of countries like the US, the UK, Italy, Germany and France are often considerably higher than what the data shows. The immigrant population share in all of these states is between 10 and 20 per cent but people tended to estimate it at between 25 and 35 per cent.[72]

How many people would move to live and work in different countries if they could? An international Gallup survey in 2021 suggested around 900 million adults, or 16 per cent of the global total, wanted to do so, up from 12 per cent a decade earlier.[73] We shouldn't take this number at face value, however. People might say they would emigrate if they had the chance but, as the Nobel Prize-winning economists Abhijit Banerjee and Esther Duflo have noted, there are formidable psychological barriers to them actually doing so, even if it were possible.[74]

But imagine some 900 million adults did move countries to work, what would the impact be? The economist Lant Pritchett estimates that when someone with a low level of schooling in a poorer country moves to a richer country, with higher levels of productivity, their

Migration has pushed up the foreign-born population in most developed countries since 2013

Foreign-born share of total population %

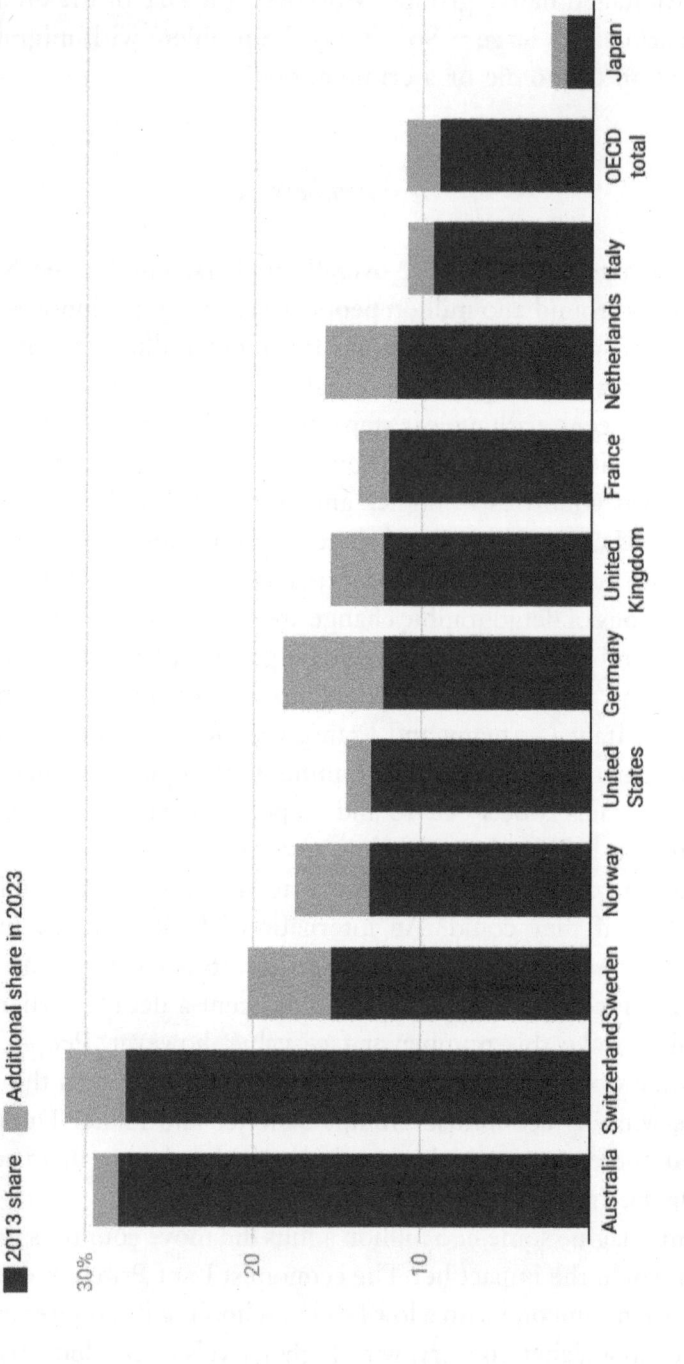

■ 2013 share   ■ Additional share in 2023

Australia, Switzerland, Sweden, Norway, United States, Germany, United Kingdom, France, Netherlands, Italy, OECD total, Japan

Chart: Ben Chu • Source: OECD • Created with Datawrapper

Figure 12

wages increase by around $15,000 per year on average.[75] That implies an increase in global incomes of around $13.5 trillion per year if every adult in the developing world (with the desire to) was able to move to the richer world, equivalent to around 7 per cent of global economic output. Such a huge increase in income – and tax revenues – would enable richer countries to cover their current foreign aid budgets, which amounted to $220 billion in 2023, dozens of times.[76] Some economists' estimates of the gain from eliminating restrictions on free movement are even larger, implying a potential doubling of global income.[77]

Wouldn't the countries from which the migrants left be harmed by the emigration, especially if skilled workers like doctors, nurses and scientists left these nations? To some extent perhaps, but they would also benefit from these migrants sending back money to their families. Such migrant cash 'remittances' in developing countries are already, at $650 billion in 2022, considerably larger than Western government aid flows and would also likely increase substantially if millions more were able to emigrate.[78] One piece of analysis in 2023 suggests that the benefits for countries in Africa from a 10 per cent increase in skilled outward migration would be many multiples of the costs.[79]

But open borders, whatever the hypothetical economic benefits, are plainly politically untenable for richer countries. Studies suggest the million Eastern European migrant arrivals in the UK after 2004 – however benign their labour market impact – contributed to the rise in support for the UK Independence Party (one of the predecessors of Reform UK, which called in the 2024 general election for a 'freeze' on all non-essential immigration) and, ultimately, to the 2016 referendum result, which led to Britain leaving the EU and its regime of freedom of movement for workers across the bloc.[80] Of the people who voted for Donald Trump in the 2024 US presidential election, exit polls suggest 90 per cent saw immigration as the most important issue in determining how they cast their ballot, beating even the economy (80 per cent).[81] In Canada, the share of the population who agreed with the statement 'Overall, there is too much immigration to Canada' jumped from 27 per cent in September 2022 to 58 per cent in September 2024.[82] In the

June 2024 European Parliament elections, in which far-right parties made gains, 'migration and asylum' was cited as a motivating issue by 28 per cent of the electorate.[83] The post-pandemic pick-up in migration to the rich world, both legal and irregular, has pushed the issue of migration up the political agenda in multiple countries and helped fuel the rise of the populist right globally. The pace of migration clearly matters to host communities.

Part of this negative reception might be due to the failure of governments to plan and provide the housing and other infrastructure needed to accommodate incomers in certain areas. But anxiety about immigration is also inextricably linked to fears about cultural and ethnic change and debates about assimilation. For high-income countries, international migration was a bigger contributor to population growth between 2000 and 2020 than population growth resulting from the balance of native births over deaths – and it is projected by the United Nations to be the sole driver of population growth over the coming decades due to low fertility rates in these nations.[84] When it comes to asylum and refugees, who often have no option but to enter richer countries irregularly, migration engenders profound fears around border control and national security, whether at the US–Mexico boundary, in the Channel or in the Mediterranean, separating Europe and Africa. There were over 2.7 million new asylum applications made in OECD countries in 2023, the highest level on record and more than double the claims in 2019. This has been ascribed to a combination of worsening conflicts, growing state failures, intensifying repression, heightened climate-related stresses and the opportunities resulting from the easing of pandemic travel restrictions.[85] This atmosphere of threat has prompted growing calls from many on the populist right for migration flows to be entirely severed.

Yet the economic consequences of a major drop in migration rates, let alone 'net zero' migration in rich countries, would likely prove politically untenable too. Developed nations with rapidly ageing populations and fertility rates below population replacement levels are likely to continue to need at least some lower-skilled migration to work in sectors such as health and social care in the coming decades, sectors that are already suffering from considerable numbers of unfilled vacancies. It's sometimes suggested governments should welcome skilled immigrants – graduates, STEM students and relatively wealthy entrepreneurs – but largely exclude the rest, including most lower-skilled economic migrants and asylum seekers. Countries such as Sweden and Finland have shifted policy in this direction since the pandemic.[86]

This kind of discrimination based on skill level appears to be a plank of exile economics. It's something that even Donald Trump, despite his anti-immigrant posture, toyed with in 2024 when he suggested, to the apparent surprise of his team, that every foreign college graduate in the US should be given a Green Card, allowing them to immigrate permanently.[87] Whether this will actually happen or not is, as with so much in the second Trump term, utterly opaque at the time of writing. Regardless, the problem is that, as the last century's history attests – from the Jews of the 1930s to the Mariel boatlift – the distinctions between economic migrants, asylum seekers and scholars are not always clear cut. Moreover, it's not just immigrants themselves who can make a positive economic contribution, but their children too. The father of Uğur Şahin of BioNTech was a so-called 'guest worker', part of a wave of mostly lower-skilled workers from Turkey who were allowed to come to West Germany in the 1960s to help fill gaps in the labour market, generally working in factories. Şahin senior came to work in the Cologne Ford car plant. The guest workers, as their name implies, were only initially expected to stay for two years. But around half stayed for their whole lives, including the Şahin family.[88] And that's why Uğur, fifty-five years later, was in a position to help unlock the pandemic in December 2020 from his laboratory in Mainz. An embrace of exile economics would make such multigeneration immigrant success stories rarer.

In exile economics lower-skilled migration is the great fear. But it's one of the ironies – or perhaps consistencies, depending on your point of view – that when it comes to the movement's industrial priorities, it is sectors that tend to rely most heavily on lower-skilled workers, especially steel production, that are front and centre.

7

Steel

Andrew Carnegie was the Elon Musk of his day, at least in terms of his personal wealth. When the Scottish-born American business tycoon sold his industrial interests in 1901 to the Wall Street banking titan J.P. Morgan, the transaction made him the richest man in the world. Carnegie's peak personal fortune, as a result of that deal, has been estimated in today's money at around $310 billion.[1] That's close to Elon Musk's $335 billion peak net worth in late 2024 as a result of the post-US election jump in the market value of his Tesla stock.[2] Carnegie gave away most of his fortune in one of the biggest philanthropic bequests in history, funding public libraries, concert halls, educational institutions and research programmes. 'The man who dies thus rich dies disgraced' was Carnegie's philosophy.[3] Musk used a considerable chunk of his riches to buy the social networking platform Twitter and unblock white supremacists (and often amplify their voices) in the name of free speech.[4] Musk's wealth flows from electric cars. But Carnegie's came from steel.

The tie-up of J.P Morgan's existing steel interests with those of the Carnegie Steel company produced an industrial leviathan: the United States Steel Corporation. At its creation, the volcanic foundries of U.S. Steel were churning out around 9 million tonnes of steel a year, more than half of all the steel consumed in the US, which was at that time the planet's fastest-growing economy. The Pittsburgh, Pennsylvania-headquartered company duly became the world's first corporation with a market valuation of more than $1 billion. It was arguably the jewel in the crown of America's Gilded Age.

But U.S. Steel's influence was more than simply financial. The company's workforce in 1901, at 168,000 strong, accounted for

0.6 per cent of the country's total employment.[5] By comparison, the American-based workforce of the world's most valuable company in late 2024, the advanced-chip designer Nvidia, is 13,000, or just 0.007 per cent of total national employment, making U.S. Steel at its birth almost 100 times more significant in terms of the American jobs market.[6]

And this was only the beginning for U.S. Steel. Its workforce peaked in the Second World War at 340,000, when the company estimates it manufactured a third of the steel equipment used by the American armed forces. By the end of the conflict, America was producing over 60 per cent of the entire planet's steel, some 66 million tonnes.[7] And most of that was from U.S. Steel. Yet that was as good as it got for the leviathan. The story of the following decades was one of decline as its complacent managers failed to respond to growing domestic and international competition, running the company for short-term cash rather than innovating with new, more efficient, production techniques.[8] Its market share declined in tandem with its profits, and in August 2023, with other corporate predators circling, U.S. Steel decided to put itself up for sale through auction.[9]

Four months later Japan's Nippon Steel, a far more efficient and profitable rival, came out on top in that competition, with a bid for the ailing company of $15 billion.[10] That offer was actually a sizable premium on U.S. Steel's stock market valuation of $9 billion, which, as commentators noted, was less than that of the restaurant chain Texas Roadhouse. How the mighty are fallen. And that might have been that for one of the most storied names in American industrial history. But members of the US Congress had other ideas. To some of them the idea of the icon of American industry being swallowed up was simply unconscionable. 'It's absolutely outrageous that U.S. Steel has agreed to sell themselves to a foreign company,' declared John Fetterman, the Democratic senator for Pennsylvania. 'I am committed to doing anything I can do, using my platform and my position, to block this foreign sale.'[11] A trio of Republican senators – J.D. Vance, Josh Hawley and Marco Rubio – agreed. They complained in a letter to the US treasury secretary Janet Yellen that the Japanese company 'does not share U.S. Steel's storied connection to the United States' and pressured her to use the federal government's powers to intervene.[12] Soon after, Donald Trump pledged he would block the deal if he became president again.[13] That prompted Joe Biden to publicly oppose the takeover from the formidable bully pulpit of the American presidency. 'U.S. Steel has been an iconic American steel company for more than a century, and it is vital for it to remain an American steel company that is domestically owned and operated,' Biden asserted in March 2024.[14] And in January 2025, as one of his final acts as outgoing president, Biden finally drove a stake through the heart of the deal, by formally blocking it. 'This acquisition would place one of America's largest steel producers under foreign control and create risk for our national security and our critical supply chains,' he declared. The episode emphasises that steel, in the eyes of politicians, is special.

Special Metal

And steel really is special. When the English inventor Henry Bessemer developed a reliable method for the mass-production of this amazingly tough alloy of iron and carbon in 1856 it's no exaggeration to say this son of a fugitive from the French Revolution unlocked the modern world, at least in its physical manifestations.[15]

Today steel, which is a thousand times stronger than the iron our ancestors used, is a fundamental component of our buildings, our factories, our pipelines, our pylons, our bridges, our rail tracks, our vehicles, our monuments and our domestic appliances. It's in medical equipment, cutlery, barrels, ships, jets, submarines, weapons and nuclear missiles. And it makes the tools that make just about everything else. Of all the metals we mine on the planet each year, more than 90 per cent by weight is iron ore for steel.[16] Steel is so ubiquitous, so fundamental, that it can be a struggle to fully appreciate its role in our lives. Steel is everywhere, though the biggest consumer by far is the construction industry, followed by vehicle and mechanical equipment manufacturers.

U.S. Steel might have dwindled as a force, but the steel industry globally has never been larger, employing 6 million people and bringing in $2.5 trillion in revenues a year.[17] In 2023 the planet's steel mills produced around 1.9 billion tonnes of metal, equivalent to around 200 kg for every man, woman and child on Earth.[18] Such volumes of production – which usually involves melting down a mixture of iron ore and the dirtiest of fossil fuels, coal – explains why the steel industry is estimated to be responsible for around a quarter of all industrial carbon emissions and around 7 per cent of our total greenhouse gas emissions.[19]

National Strength

Donald Trump's verbal intervention over the future of U.S. Steel was perhaps the least surprising development of his campaign for a second presidency. One of his most resonant economic policies in his first term as president was the announcement in March 2018 of new 25 per cent tariffs on steel imports into America. These applied not only to steel imports from Trump's bête noire of China but, initially at least, also to allies such as Canada, the EU and South Korea. The justification was that these metal imports constituted a threat to American 'national security', though beyond vague references to defence and critical infrastructure the precise nature of this threat was never spelled out by the US Commerce Department.[20] For Trump, steel production is more than just a metal, it's a gauge of national power. As he summed it up on social media in March 2018: 'If you don't have steel, you don't have a country.'[21] It's a perspective that Park Chung Hee, South Korea's military dictator in the 1960s, nicknamed 'the rat' by opponents, shared.

The Pohang Iron and Steel Company (POSCO) integrated steel mill next to the South Korean city of Gwangyang is a monument to the conviction of Park that 'iron and steel is national strength'. With its five giant blast furnaces, the POSCO Gwangyang site covers almost 5 million sq m and has a 14,000-strong workforce.

It can produce 23 million tonnes of steel annually.[22] For a long time it was the largest steel-producing site in the world.[23] Yet if the technocrats of the World Bank, the multilateral lender whose remit is to assist poor countries to industrialise, had had their way in the 1960s, it would never have existed. In 1960 South Korea had a national income per head roughly equal to that of Kenya.[24] Its economy was heavily reliant on fishing and its rudimentary manufacturing sector produced items like wigs made from human hair and textiles.[25]

When Park asked the World Bank to lend him funds to create a giant new steel mill in the country as part of an ambitious industrialisation drive, it said no. The technocrats, not unreasonably, cited recent failures to develop similar integrated mills by other developing countries including Brazil, Mexico and Turkey, and also the fact that natural-resource-rich South Korea would have to import iron ore and coal across vast distances from the likes of Australia, Canada and the US.[26] The Korean economist Ha-Joon Chang labels Park's steel dream 'one of the worst business proposals in history'. But Park was undeterred by the World Bank's decision and persisted, persuading Japan to channel its Second World War reparations payments to financing his plan.

He then launched one of the most successful industrial policies in history. He supported POSCO through the carrot of state subsidies: cheap energy, cheap credit, copious transport infrastructure and tax breaks. On top of this he guaranteed POSCO a domestic market by imposing a 25 per cent tariff on imported steel. At the same time there was a stick approach in the form of relentless political pressure on the company to increase production, increase efficiency and, above all, export. By the 1980s POSCO was world-leading in efficiency, exporting 30 to 40 per cent of its production. Today the subsidies have gone, the company has been privatised, POSCO is the seventh-biggest steelmaking company in the world and South Korea is the sixth-largest national producer of the metal.

Moreover, Park presciently saw the development of steel production as the foundation stone of a wider South Korean industrialisation strategy. The steel exports brought in foreign currency that could be invested in other manufacturing industries such as shipbuilding and, eventually, car making and consumer electronics. Developing a domestic steel industry, initially with expert foreign assistance, enabled South Koreans to 'learn by doing' and, over time, successfully transfer the industrial and managerial skills they had acquired from steel manufacture to other sectors. Today South Korea's GDP per head is roughly twenty times higher than Kenya's and it is firmly established among the developed nations of the world.[27] And it's in no small part due to steel.

So are the lessons of this a Trumpian one that rich nations should protect and build up their steel plants? Do, as Park insisted, iron and steel represent national strength? If that's true, the outlook looks bleak for the nation where the Industrial Revolution began.

Port Talbot

The Port Talbot steelworks are not on the scale of South Korea's Gwangyang. They boast only two blast furnaces rather than five, and 4,000 workers rather than 14,000. But it's nevertheless an impressive site. Its ziggurats of blackened piping loom over the South Wales town, visible from the back gardens of many of its pebble-dashed houses. And that's precisely how most of the locals want it to stay. In September 2023 the mill's owner, Tata Steel, dropped a bombshell on the town, announcing that it was closing down Port Talbot's two blast furnaces. The Indian company was going to build an electric arc furnace on the site instead – a less polluting and more efficient form of steel production using recycled steel – but this would still result in almost 3,000 job losses, three-quarters of the workforce.

I was sent to interview some of the steelworkers for the BBC. Their dismay was palpable. 'I've been here just over forty-one years, started on the blast furnaces as a sixteen-year old,' Mark Davies, a solidly built union official, told me in the shadow of the site by a busy road. 'I wouldn't like to lose my job but it's the youngsters [that most concern me]. My son works here, he's twenty-six, I'd like him to have at least the opportunities I had.'[28] This was a common story. Steelmaking in this part of South Wales is a multi-generational profession and the fear was that the redundancies would mean not just the loss of jobs, but the destruction of a community and the end of a whole way of life.

In truth this move by Tata did not come as a great surprise. UK steel production has been in long-term decline. Production in 2023 at 5.6 million tonnes was the lowest since the Great Depression of the 1930s.[29] The number of British steelworking jobs was more than 300,000 in the 1970s. Today's workforce, including Mark Davies and his son, is just a tenth of that.

The talk today is of an existential threat to British steel industry after another company British Steel, owned by China's Jingye Steel, announced a few months after the Tata decision that it too was planning to decommission its blast furnaces in the Lincolnshire town of Scunthorpe – threatening to leave Britain, as some pointed out, as the only major economy without the ability to make so-called primary steel from iron ore and coal.[30] This has set off alarm bells not only about job losses but, as in the US, about national security too. 'We are on the brink of losing our full ability to make our own steel, vital to our defence industry – not least in building warships. It's utter folly,' warned an official of the GMB Union, which represents steelworkers, in a letter to the UK's defence minister, calling for government intervention to keep the blast furnaces open.[31]

It's an argument that apparently has some traction in London, just as in Washington. In 2021 the Conservative government pushed through the nationalisation of the financially ailing steel firm Sheffield Forgemasters, which, though small and niche, produces some critical components for the Royal Navy's nuclear submarine fleet.[32] Even a Conservative government, opposed on principle to state ownership since the 1970s, struggled to hold the line when the defence of the realm was felt to be at stake.

It's not just Britain that has been watching its steel industry decline. The EU has lost nearly a quarter of its steel workforce – some 86,000 workers – since the global financial crisis in 2008, when the continent experienced a sudden 20 per cent fall in steel demand which has never come back. Between 2007 and 2019 the number of steel industry jobs in Spain fell by 10,000, in Italy by 8,500, in France by 8,300 and in Germany by 6,300.[33] All across Europe – whether in South Wales, France's Moselle, Germany's Ruhr or Spain's Basque Country – one hears the same anxieties about working-class communities being hollowed out by deindustrialisation and an undermining of national strength and security due to the long and melancholy retreat of steelmaking.[34]

Steel City

Over the past forty years, multiple administrations in Washington have implemented protections for the steel industry. Trump was the first to use Section 232 of the 1962 Trade Expansion Act explicitly for steel tariffs but he joined a long line of presidents – including Jimmy Carter, Ronald Reagan and George W. Bush – who acted in response to heavy lobbying from the sector and fears of the impact of foreign competition. Even before Trump's 25 per cent tariffs in 2018, steel benefited from much higher levels of protection from international competition than other sectors of US manufacturing.[35] But you would not know it from looking at the production or employment data, for there has been a similar seemingly inexorable downward trend in steel production in the United States as there has been in Britain and Europe. American steel production by weight has halved since the 1970s.[36] And employment in steel mills has also more than halved since the mid-1980s, falling to just 83,000 workers in 2022.

Why does it matter? The impact of the loss of US manufacturing jobs, including in steel, was for much of this period, despite the protections offered, seen by many in Washington as part of the inevitable churn of free markets. Those steelworkers, it was assumed, would be re-employed in other jobs, and other sectors of the economy would expand. Politicians in Washington looked at the statistics showing that unemployment remained low and that GDP continued to grow as a vindication.

But a 2016 study by the economists David Autor, David Dorn and Gordon Hanson shattered those assumptions. It suggested that the impact of the loss of manufacturing jobs from the 2000s onwards had created persistent harms to specific areas in the US 'rust belt', the historic industrial American heartlands. They called it the 'China shock' because it coincided with China's rapid integration into the global trading system and the areas most severely impacted were subject to the greatest competition from Chinese industry.[37]

The town of Weirton in West Virginia is a good example. A steel mill was established there in 1909 and it became the state's largest employer. In 2003, after years of financial decline, it entered bankruptcy and closed down most of its operations; the workforce slumped from 15,000 to just 800.[38] My former colleague on the *Independent* newspaper Andrew Buncombe reported from Weirton during the 2016 US presidential election between Donald Trump and Hillary Clinton.[39] Ed Sutton, a city government worker, was quoted as saying he would be voting for Trump because 'nothing had replaced the steel jobs' that had disappeared. 'They talk about creating all these jobs. But they're just retail jobs that pay minimum wage, or just above.' Locals blamed the 1994 North American Free Trade Agreement (NAFTA), which had eliminated tariffs on Mexican and Canadian steel imports and which had been signed by Bill Clinton as president. 'Her [Hillary Clinton's] husband introduced NAFTA,' a former steel worker told Buncombe. 'If anyone in this state votes for her, they're crazy.'

But it's a city some 56 km east of Weirton, in neighbouring Pennsylvania, that is often seen as the archetypal American rust belt tragedy. Pittsburgh, the 'Steel City', the adopted home of Andrew Carnegie and U.S. Steel, boomed between 1870 and 1950, with its population shooting up from 80,000 to 676,000 on the back of the success of US steelmaking. Yet from the 1970s, as national steel production waned and scores of local mills closed down, the city's population fell off a cliff. By the late 1980s 150,000 Pittsburgh steel mill workers had been laid off and many more had moved out. By 2020 the city's population was down to just 300,000, less than half its peak in the middle of the twentieth century. In

2021 Pittsburgh had the highest natural population loss, meaning more deaths than births, of any American metropolitan area.[40] The city is now estimated as hosting one of the most concentrated populations of elderly adults in the entire US.[41]

So does this vindicate Donald Trump's economic approach to steel? Is international trade the enemy? Is the right way to help American workers, like those in Weirton or Pittsburgh, to impose enormous and permanent tariffs on foreign steel and, in the words of Trump's former chief strategist Steve Bannon, to attempt to 'jack up' domestic steel mills once again?[42] We've already seen how South Korea catapulted itself into the rank of rich nations in just forty years through its promotion of domestic steel. Indeed, economic historians argue that tariff protection was important in the development of the American iron and steel industry in the late nineteenth century, when Andrew Carnegie was importing Henry Bessemer's technology to the United States.[43] Given that scholars have found a statistical link between support for Trump in the 2016 presidential election and the areas subject to the China shock perhaps this is a protectionist project that even liberals ought to be backing?[44]

And does the same pro-production prescription apply in the UK and the EU? Should European governments be trying to reverse the post-2008 decline in steel manufacturing as part of a continent-wide industrial, social and security policy? Given that steel jobs across the developed world, despite the fact they have been declining in number, tend to pay considerably more than the national average, is supporting domestic steel the right way to support working-class livelihoods?

How Much Is Enough?

To grapple adequately with these complex questions, it is important to start with a more basic one: how much steel do we need as a planet? The International Energy Agency (IEA), a multilateral organisation based in Paris and formed to help countries respond to the global oil price shocks of the 1970s, provides us with one way of answering it.

Add together all the steel in all those structures and appliances across every country on the globe and divide the sum by a global population of around 8 billion. The IEA calculates that the global stock of iron and steel in use in the world currently equates to around 4.2 tonnes for every person on the planet. So how much more do we need? The IEA thinks that by 2050 we will require around 6.5 tonnes per person.[45] By 2050 the global population is projected to be around 9.7 billion. Put all those figures together and the estimated global stock of steel will need to rise from around 32 billion tonnes today to 63 billion tonnes in 2050. So, on that basis, we will require much more steel in the decades ahead.

But some countries, of course, have much bigger stocks of steel than others. Think of the steel buildings, cars, weapons and personal appliances of a high-income country like Germany relative to the amount of infrastructure and material wealth in a country like Mali, many of whose roads are still made of packed earth.[46] In Germany there is around 12 tonnes of steel per person. In Mali it's less than 0.1 tonnes. Analysts estimate that developed countries have around 10 to 15 tonnes per person.[47] And they estimate that 13 tonnes is, roughly, steel saturation point for a country. This doesn't mean that people in rich countries won't want new appliances, cars or rebuilt homes but rather that they won't need more steel to supply these wants because the steel they require can be sourced by recycling the metal they already have. And if the whole planet were to have the 13 tonnes per person seen in rich countries today, by the time the global population peaks in 2080 at around 10.4 billion people the stock of steel would need to be 135 billion tonnes, or roughly four times the quantity around today.[48] So, on this basis too, the world certainly needs more steel. But which countries should manufacture it?

As the British journalist and physical materials specialist Ed Conway points out, the stock of steel per person is a rather useful measure of human development in a country, correlating well with measures such as life expectancy, average income and health.

Analysts could do a lot worse when seeking to get a quick sense of the average standard of living in different countries than to look at estimates of steel per head.[49]

Yet national steel *production* is not always a useful proxy in this respect. Rich states with copious amounts of steel per head – plenty of infrastructure and home appliances – such as Singapore, Israel, Ireland, Denmark and Norway don't manufacture much steel; none in some cases. And despite what Donald Trump might say, they are still very much countries – homes to millions of people with some of the highest living standards on the planet. Indeed, only around seventy-one of the world's 193 nations recognised by the United Nations manufacture steel in any significant quantity.[50]

So how do states that manufacture little or no steel get their supply? They import it, of course. Between a fifth and a third of the steel produced globally is exported across borders: some 435 million tonnes in 2023. Because it travels so well – not perishing, not difficult to transport – steel is one of the most highly internationally traded of manufactured commodities.

Too Much Steel

At this point we have to grapple with the question of overcapacity. Global steel production in 2023 was 1.9 billion tonnes. But the world's foundries and furnaces and mills had capacity to produce 2.4 billion tonnes that year, giving an excess capacity of around 550 million tonnes or 25 per cent.[51] Overcapacity has been higher in the past. It was more than 800 million tonnes in 2009. Yet the essential point is that, at a global level, the world has the capacity to produce considerably more steel than it currently needs every year.

Some overcapacity is inevitable and, indeed, desirable. If potential supply exactly matched consumption, there would be no flexibility to meet unexpected spikes in demand. Yet when potential supply is 25 per cent higher than demand we have a problem. This is in part because of the particular nature of steel production. Giant blast furnaces, which turn iron ore into pig iron, the first

Global crude steelmaking capacity exceeds production

Million tonnes

····· Capacity — Production

2,432

1,888

Excess capacity

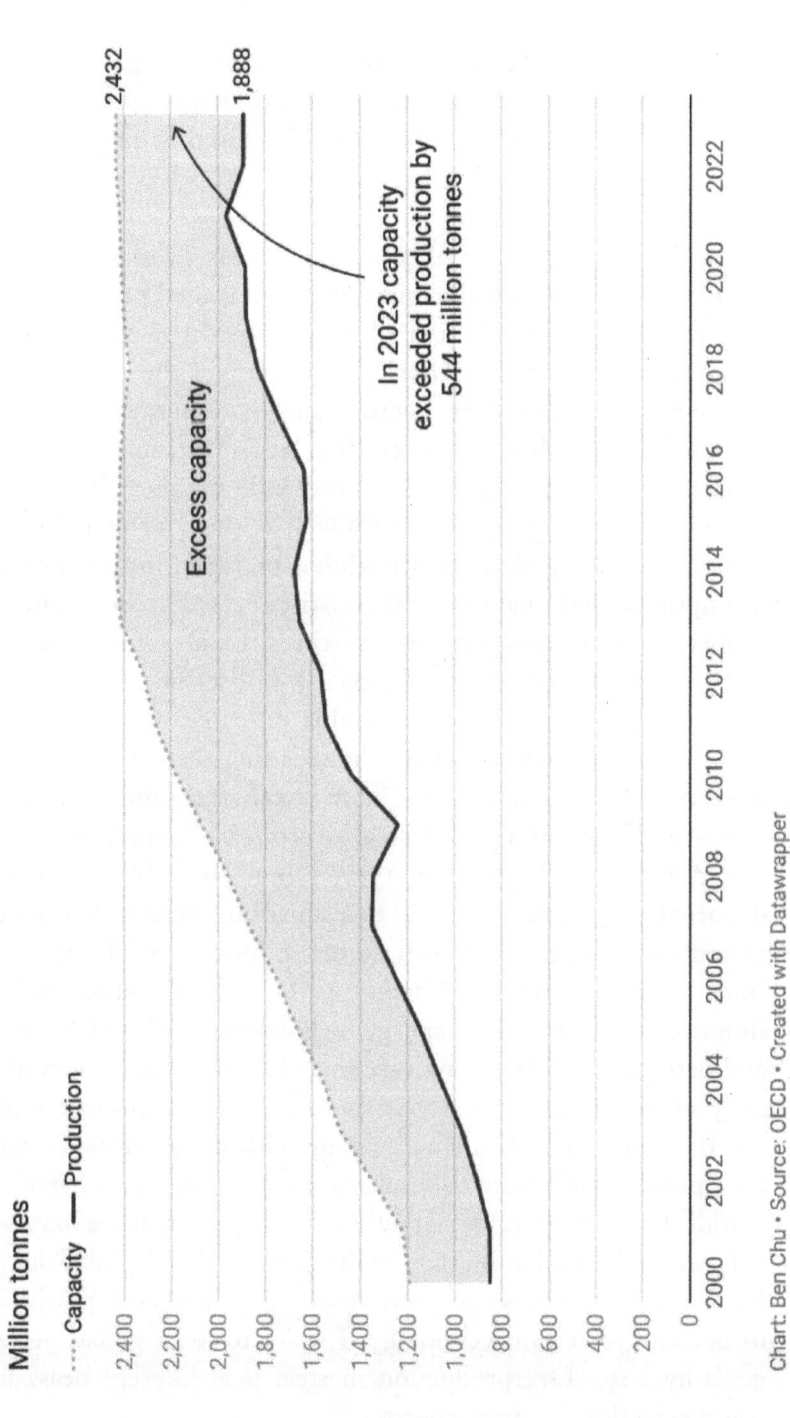

In 2023 capacity exceeded production by 544 million tonnes

Chart: Ben Chu • Source: OECD • Created with Datawrapper

Figure 13

stage in primary steel production, cannot be switched on and off like a computer, but must be run continuously, day and night, meaning that even if they are not being used to produce metal, excess capacity is a tremendous ongoing cost, which depresses the profitability of operations.

Excess capacity inevitably means excess production, which lowers prices domestically and the global traded price. This also crushes the profit margins of producers in every producing country and especially unfairly disadvantages the most efficient producers. Compared to sectors such as energy, mining and chemicals, steel has delivered the worst financial returns to shareholders since the turn of the millennium.[52] This excess capacity leads to geopolitical trade frictions and complaints of cheap steel being dumped on global markets, threatening jobs in important national political constituencies like Port Talbot or Pennsylvania or Gwangyang. As the OECD summarised in a 2023 report: 'Such levels of capacity utilisation are not in line with a healthy and financially viable industry.'[53]

So the central problem with the idea that the US or any developed country should 'jack up' its national steel production is that this would make the global steel overcapacity problem worse. It would make steel production even less profitable, even more distorted and, unless we moved to a situation where each producing country only supplied its own domestic market, would ratchet up trade tensions further. In Chapter 4 we explored Chinese production overcapacity in clean energy technologies such as solar panels and batteries and the strong case that this abundance could ultimately be beneficial for a planet that needs to decarbonise rapidly. On the face of it there is an analogy with the situation in global steel production. Doesn't abundance in cheap steel also benefit the world? The difference is that although the planet, as we have seen, will definitely need more steel in the decades ahead, global demand for the metal is not set to grow at anything like the explosive rate of demand for clean technology if we're to meet global net zero goals by 2050. Overproduction in steel is a different beast from overproduction in green energy.

So who is overproducing steel? It's hard to overstate how dominant China is when it comes to global steel production. Of the 1.9 billion tonnes of crude steel manufactured in 2023, more than half, 1 billion tonnes, was manufactured in China. The next-largest national producer was India, with 140 million tonnes, then Japan, with 87 million tonnes, followed by the US, with 81 million, and then Russia, with 76 million. All the other steel-producing countries in the world produced 486 million tonnes between them, less than half of China's production in that year.[54]

But that does not mean that half of the steel being used for construction in the average country is Chinese. Most construction steel is consumed in the country where it is manufactured. The vast quantities of Chinese production are mostly used in its own infrastructure development – new highways, new high-speed train lines and, above all else, property construction.

For the past decade China has been engaged in the biggest building project the planet has ever seen, with real estate and infrastructure development, directly and indirectly, estimated to be accounting for more than a quarter of its economic activity. And that building project has required steel in historically unprecedented quantities.[55] By the same token, some economists argue that the principal reason domestic steel production has contracted in countries such as the US and the UK and also in parts of Europe in the past fifty years is not foreign competition but rather because these countries are simply building less than they did, and even failing to maintain their existing stock of infrastructure and buildings adequately.

A regular report by the American Society of Civil Engineers on the state of US infrastructure has persistently given D grades, meaning 'poor or at risk', to the country's bridges, airports, dams and power lines ever since it began in 1998.[56] For years the International Monetary Fund has urged developed countries in Europe – including the UK, Germany, France and Italy – to step up investment in public infrastructure, on everything from roads to broadband provision and renewable energy.[57] More public and private infrastructure investment would increase the national demand for steel, primarily from domestic sources.

Yet even if producing countries are mainly consuming their own steel, the presence of even a negligible volume of imports can have a profound effect on prices and profitability given the interconnectedness of global markets. As you would expect given the sheer size of its steel sector, the largest volume of excess steel producing capacity is in China. According to OECD estimates, China had more excess capacity – at 132 million tonnes in 2022 – than the entire combined steel *output* of the US, the UK, France, Canada, the Netherlands and Austria in that year.[58] As a proportion of potential Chinese output, 132 million tonnes is around 12 per cent; indeed, some estimates put China's excess capacity as high as 20 per cent. Yet though it manufactures far less steel, estimated spare steelmaking capacity in the EU in 2022 was actually greater, at 36 per cent. In the US it was around 33 per cent and in Japan 22 per cent. The lowest excess capacity of the major steel-producing nations was in India, at 9 per cent.[59] All steel-producing nations are producing too much of it. And projections imply excess capacity is already set to grow, with more than 300 additional steel plants, equating to another 156 million tonnes of production capacity, planned around the world by 2026.

Self-Sufficient Steel

Let's return to the question of who should manufacture the steel the world needs. Should each nation seek to become self-sufficient in steel production, or is relying on imports a reasonable – perhaps even a sensible – choice?

First, it's important to recognise that self-sufficiency is something of a mirage when it comes to steel. On paper, countries such as China, South Korea and India are self-sufficient, producing more steel than they consume and being significant exporters. But even these surplus and exporting countries also *import* steel. Despite its gigantic domestic production, China in 2023 imported 10 million tonnes of steel. India imported 8 million tonnes and South Korea 16 million tonnes.[60]

Steel exporters are also often steel importers

2023, million tonnes

■ Steel exports ■ Steel imports

Country	Steel exports	Steel imports
Mexico	3	15
United Kingdom	3	5
Canada	7	7
Malaysia	7	7
Indonesia	8	13
United States	9	28
Taiwan	9	7
Turkey	11	18
India	11	8
European Union	24	34
South Korea	26	16
Japan	32	5
China	80	10

Despite being nominally self-sufficient in steel and exporting 11 million tonnes in 2023, India also imported 8 million tonnes

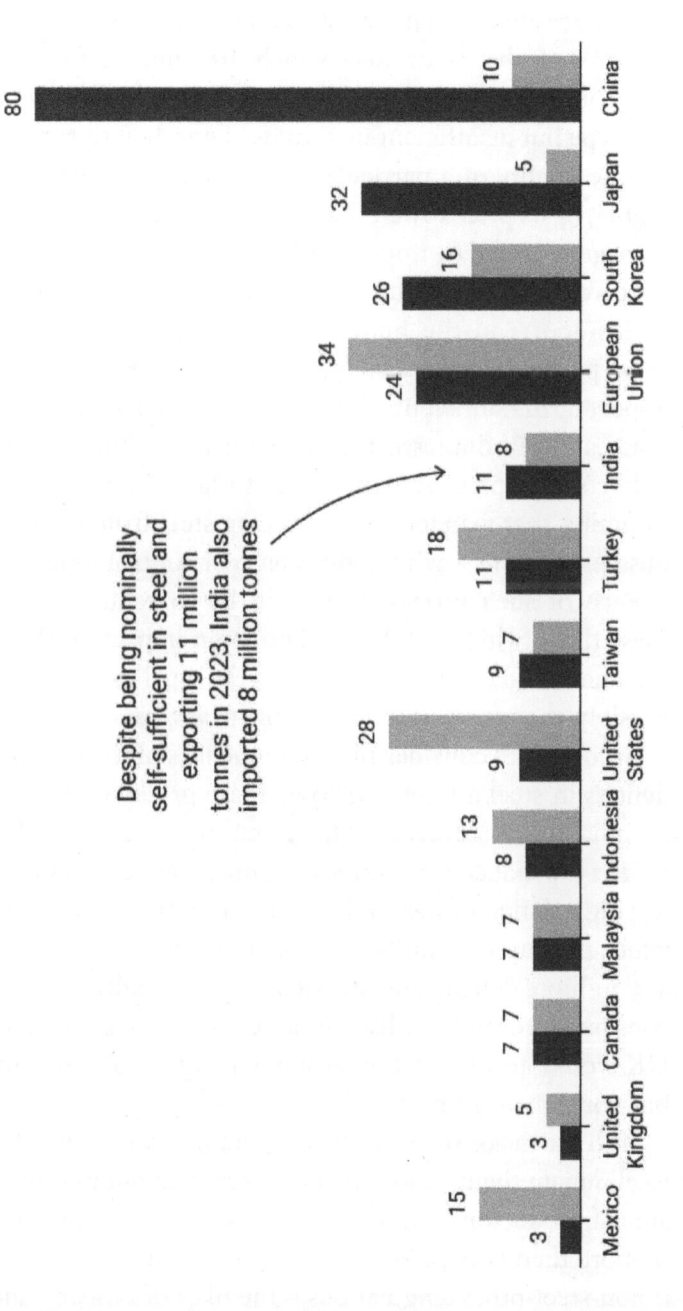

Chart: Ben Chu • Source: OECD • Created with Datawrapper

Figure 14

The reason is that not all steel is created equal. There are different grades and shapes of steel which are suitable for different tasks, and countries may be able to produce more than enough steel of one type but insufficient quantities of another, so requiring imports. Or the quality of a particular type of steel from overseas might be higher, or its price lower, than the domestic version and so company managers prefer to import rather than source domestically.

It would in theory be possible for government officials to block such imports in the hope of stimulating domestic production of those particular grades or types of steel, or for politicians to impose import tariffs sufficiently large enough to make such imports uneconomical for its domestic firms. Another possible avenue is to change public sector procurement policy to favour national suppliers. But assuming that managers are sourcing steel from overseas for sound business reasons – with a focus on cost control – the natural consequence of such interventions will be to reduce the efficiency of these firms, which will have a knock-on impact on their profits and the shareholders in the business, the quality of its products and possibly the wages and welfare of its workers.

Second, let's consider the consequences of nations that have trade deficits in steel attempting to increase production so as to become nominally self-sufficient. This group would include the US, which in 2023 produced 81 million tonnes but consumed 91 million, leaving a deficit of just under 10 million. It would also include Italy, which produced 21 million tonnes but consumed 24 million, leaving a 3 million deficit, and Mexico, which produced 16 million and consumed 29 million, leaving a deficit of roughly 12 million. The UK would also be in this group, having produced 6 million tones but consumed 9 million.

If all the major steel-producing countries with trade deficits sought to eliminate them, it would add roughly 40 million tonnes to global annual production.[61] In the context of a global annual spare capacity of more than 600 million tonnes, this might not seem dramatic. But if non-steel-producing nations – the likes of Norway and Singapore – sought to follow and become self-sufficient, the impact would be far greater.

Indeed, assume that all 435 million tonnes of annual steel imports fell away in a world of self-sufficient steel-producing and consuming nations, those production surpluses would have to be consumed at home, which would lead to an almighty crash in domestic steel prices for surplus nations such as China, Japan and South Korea, though also Brazil, India, Germany and Turkey. In reality, trade in steel would be unlikely to cease, but a drive to greater production would simply lead to greater overcapacity and more distortions, which would negatively affect every producing nation.

Research by the OECD already points to a kind of steel overcapacity doom loop. Its researchers have found evidence that when countries run large and persistent steel import deficits, often because of chronic overcapacity in some other countries, there's historically been a politically led drive in those deficit countries to step up domestic production, which in turn has led to still-greater overall overcapacity in the medium term.[62]

But is there an environmental trump card? One of the arguments in favour of greater national self-sufficiency in steel production is the need to decarbonise steel production, by swapping coal-fired blast furnaces for renewable-energy-powered electric arc furnaces, whose feedstock is not iron ore and coking coal but scrap steel from buildings and products that have come to the end of their natural lives.

At this stage it's worth exploring how fundamental recycling already is to the steel industry. This is far from intuitive given how long-lasting we tend to think of steel being. And steel is indeed exceptionally durable. In buildings it can last 100 years or more. But on average steel goods still only last for forty years before they need to be replaced.[63] It's estimated that most steel already gets recycled, with recycling rates from vehicles and industrial equipment well above 90 per cent.[64] And manufacturing throws off a lot of scrap: vehicle makers, for instance, only use around half of the steel they actually purchase.[65] Indeed, the World Steel Association estimates that since 1900 the global steel industry has recycled over 25 billion tonnes of steel.[66]

Steel recycling, it's suggested, represents a potential saving grace for the steel industry in a country like the UK. Britain's historical head start in industrialisation (it was of course where Bessemer's converter was born) means the UK is now generating 10 million tonnes a year of usable scrap steel. That's more than the country consumed in 2022. So could Britain not service all its domestic steel consumption needs by building new electric arc furnaces and recycling, rather than by importing? This seems an economically coherent vision of self-sufficiency. Indeed, it's one that the UK government is betting on, with its decision to publicly subsidise the construction of new electric arc furnaces in places like Scunthorpe and Port Talbot to replace the blast furnaces.

It's not just Britain. Analysts at Material Economics estimate that by 2050 the amount of available scrap steel arising in the EU will cover 80 per cent of its steel requirements.[67] So self-sufficiency in steel production from scrap also seems plausible on paper for the EU. The argument could also be made for the United States.

A fifth of steel production in the UK is already from the processing of recycled steel, although that's actually rather low by international standards. The proportion is 44 per cent in the EU. In the US, where electric arc furnaces are called 'mini mills', it's two-thirds. Globally around 29 per cent of steel production is from recycled steel in electric arc furnaces.[68] This share is projected to rise to around 50–60 per cent by 2050.[69]

Yet the steel recycling economy is only a coherent vision of self-sufficiency up to a point. Because unless developed countries successfully choke off all steel imports, the global overcapacity problem will not disappear and will likely intensify if other countries also seek to use the energy transition as an opportunity to bolster domestic steel production volumes.

While Britain, America and Europe might have a sufficient pipeline of scrap steel to envision a circular national steel production and consumption economy, the same is not true for developing nations. It's estimated that even in a radically more circular steel economy around 1 billion tonnes of new primary steel production (using iron ore as a feedstock as opposed to scrap metal) would be needed globally every year by 2050, between a third and a half of the supply.

Less-developed nations would also need iron ore to create this primary steel. Iron ore is not a scarce deposit. It's the second most common metallic ore, constituting around 6 per cent of the Earth's crust, behind only bauxite, from which aluminium is derived, at 8 per cent.[70] But as we saw with South Korea, iron ore is not found, or easily mined, in every nation. So it's worth asking what security benefit self-sufficiency in steel production would bring to a nation if it still had to import iron ore. In 2022 Australia mined 34 per cent of the planet's iron ore, Brazil 16 per cent, China 15 per cent and India 11 per cent. The top ten producing countries – also including Russia, South Africa, Ukraine, Iran, Canada and Kazakhstan – accounted for 92.4 per cent of the total, leaving all the other 183 countries supplying just 7.6 per cent.[71] The result is that iron ore is the world's most traded mineral by value.

If global trade in these metal-bearing rocks were to dry up, it's possible many countries could start mining locally and, over time, increase their own domestic production. But none could do so as cost-effectively as the current natural resource giants in this area and trying to achieve self-sufficiency would be prohibitively expensive.

Heavy Metal

Examine a chart of US steelworker employment over the past few decades and it's impossible to discern the impact of Donald Trump's 2018 steel tariffs. The line continued to go down after the tariffs were imposed, just as it was descending before, despite all the protection offered by previous presidents for steel. Notwithstanding the China shock of the 2000s, the largest destroyer of steelworking jobs in America since the 1960s has not been foreign competition but impressive productivity increases, thanks specifically to the proliferation of the efficient electric arc furnaces of U.S. Steel's American competitor Nucor.[72] There are some secular forces that policy struggles to counteract. It's theoretically possible that US steel-sector employment might have fallen further without the tariffs. But a detailed 2024 study of the impact of Trump's protectionism on individual sectors found no evidence that it increased employment in US steel manufacturing, even though this was its explicit justification.[73]

Trump's first term steel tariffs did not increase the number of domestic steel making jobs

US iron and steel manufacturing employment, thousands

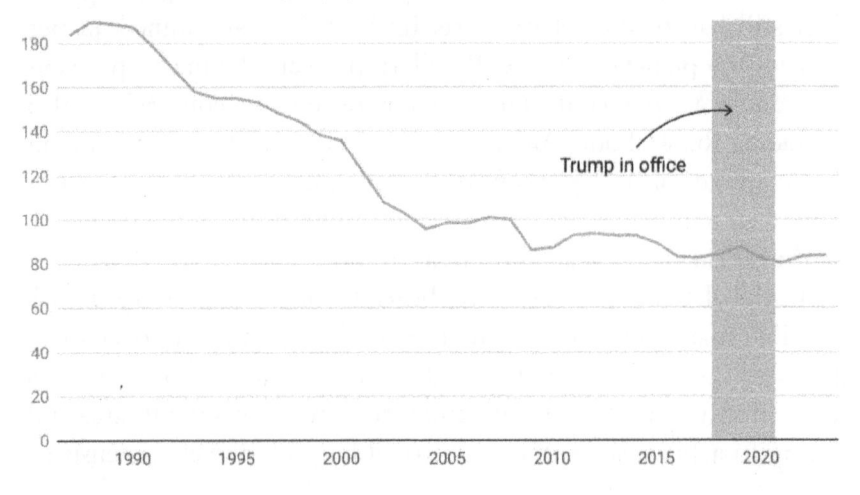

[Chart showing US iron and steel manufacturing employment from 1990 to 2020s, declining from about 180 thousand in 1990 to around 85 thousand, with "Trump in office" period highlighted]

Chart: Ben Chu • Source: FRED • Created with Datawrapper

Figure 15

For economic nationalists, of course, this only provides evidence that the tariffs were too low, or not comprehensive enough, or inappropriately watered down to exclude allies in Europe or Canada. Another, bigger push is required to bolster US national steel production. But what would the cost be of such a protectionist push? A separate analysis of the 2018 Trump tariffs – many of which were kept in place by the Biden administration – by the nonpartisan Tax Foundation thinktank estimates that they have reduced long-term US GDP, wages and employment by the equivalent of 166,000 full-time jobs by imposing higher input costs on other US manufacturers beyond steel. The impact of the retaliatory tariffs on US exports by China and others compounded the economic damage.[74]

To understand what full-on protectionism for the US steel industry would mean, it might be best to look to China itself. The Communist regime in Beijing has jacked up national steel production in recent decades far beyond anything that South Korea's General Park attempted. If steel production is a gauge of economic dynamism, then China is easily winning the global race. Yet that is not how it looks from Beijing. China now suffers, as we have seen, from chronic steel oversupply, all the more so as its domestic real-estate sector's demand for the metal has now slumped. As Adam Posen, the director of the Peterson Institute for International Economics in Washington, has put it: 'Subsidising steel until it reached vast overcapacity has been a sinkhole rather than a success for China, contributing to environmental degradation and helping to ensure an uncompetitive workforce.'[75]

Of the world's 1,023 operating coal-fired blast furnaces, around two-thirds are in China. And of the fifty or so currently under construction globally, thirty-seven are in China.[76] As clean steel production ramps up as part of the energy transition, Beijing is set to be landed with tens of billions of dollars' worth of 'stranded assets' – assets that won't generate a return because of the net zero transition – in the form of carbon-intensive blast furnaces that it won't be able to use.[77]

But can't China at least partially push this problem onto other countries by offloading its excess steel production capacity overseas? If ever that was a solution, its days now appear numbered. Between 2022 and 2024 countries such as Mexico, Brazil, Chile, Thailand, Vietnam and India imposed new tariffs on Chinese steel imports, or launched investigations into dumping.[78] Unless China reduces its steel production capacity it will likely face a new wave of protective tariffs from richer countries too.

The EU has already imposed tariffs on around twenty grades of Chinese steel, and an EU-wide tax on the embedded carbon emissions in imports, which will affect Chinese steel, is already set to be introduced in 2026.[79] Before the 2024 US election Brussels and Washington were exploring a coordinated transatlantic agreement to keep Chinese steel out of their economies. One of the few things about which we can be entirely confident in regard to Trump's second term is that he will not roll out the welcome mat for Chinese steel. All this means that excess iron and steel production might very soon start to feel like national weakness, not strength, for Beijing.

So what does the future of steelmaking look like? For poor countries, boosting domestic steel production just might still be a lever for broader development and 'learning by doing', as it was for South Korea, although sadly extreme global overcapacity today makes a similar steel export drive a much more doubtful prospect. For richer countries, there are likely to be opportunities in new clean steel production technology – in additional efficient electric steel recycling and also in rolling out currently experimental but promising plants using hydrogen gas (instead of coal) to convert iron ore into iron. Sweden is setting the pace when it comes to pioneering hydrogen steelmaking.[80]

A higher rate of public investment in developed countries in such clean steel production is not only vital for decarbonisation, but would also likely have the benefit of stimulating demand for local steel producers. And there might be scope for a country like Britain, which currently exports a lot of lower-value steel products and imports higher-value ones, to move up the steel production value chain. That could be beneficial for the incomes of domestic steelworkers.

Yet a developed world industrial policy built around jacking up primary steel production, especially from coal-fired blast furnaces, for the sake of job creation and a quest for national self-sufficiency is perilous. The frustration over Chinese steel dumping is legitimate. But to respond to Chinese overproduction with an increased glut in Europe and the US would make the international market oversupply problem still worse and not ultimately help those local communities around the world that are at risk from blast furnace closures.

But what of those national security concerns? Should a country be relaxed about its weapons or its critical infrastructure being made with imported steel, possibly from unfriendly states? Even if that is a legitimate source of anxiety, the more rational policy would arguably be to seek a *diversity* of overseas steel suppliers, including as many allied nations as possible, rather than striving for self-sufficiency. For the United States, suppliers would surely include Europe, Mexico, Japan and South Korea (and vice versa). It's hard to avoid the conclusion that that would entail politicians in Washington welcoming, not rejecting, Japanese corporate investment and expertise in a backward-looking relic like U.S. Steel.

The economic logic is unfashionable but simple: the global economy's demand for additional steel over the coming decades ought to be satisfied by those companies that are most efficient at producing the metal, and with the lowest greenhouse gas emissions. And those are likely to be in the states where there is the cheapest wind and solar energy. The question of which nation the world produces its steel in is not of zero importance, but it's hard to maintain that it should be a central economic or political consideration. And an underlying truth is long overdue for recognition: that the primary danger at the moment is not too little steel, but rather too much of it.

Beyond Steel

But where does that leave steelworkers in developed countries? Are they and their families and communities simply condemned to a future of unemployment and inactivity? What is there to offer the American rust belt or the deindustrialising regions of Europe if steel is in an inexorable state of decline as an employer in these places due mainly to greater production efficiency and technological advances? Bear in mind that even if the developed world's blast furnaces are ultimately replaced with electric arc furnaces, these new plants will typically require only a third as many workers.

Let's return to Pittsburgh, the city whose population collapsed along with its steel industry. Because despite the blows of heavy industrial retreat, the Steel City has, in fact, successfully pivoted in the direction of new industries such as technology, finance and healthcare.[81] Its unemployment rate in early 2024 was just 3.5 per cent, lower than the national average.[82] The city's Carnegie Mellon

University – named after its Gilded Age steel magnate benefactor – has world-class computer science and robotics programmes.[83] It regularly features in lists of the more livable and pleasant cities in America.[84]

This is not the typical rust belt story and achieving such phoenix-like resurrections will be anything but simple. To sketch out an industrial policy with a chance of achieving that holy grail for Western countries would require a whole different book. But Pittsburgh shows what can be achieved with strong civic and political leadership and a commitment to face forwards, not to try and turn back the economic clock. We will always need steel, but the political fetishisation of this iconic product and driver of industrialisation has turned into what can feel like an economic millstone. As the Steel City itself shows, there can be life – and prosperity – beyond steel.

And so, in our tour of exile economics, we discover complexity, nuance and even paradox. Too much steel production is a problem for the world, but too much solar power manufacturing capacity is not. National food insecurity is a consequence not of too many imports, but of too few. Greater national self-sufficiency in new technologies is impossible without greater openness to skilled migrants. But what are the lessons of trade and globalisation when it comes to one of our greatest modern sources of anxiety: medicine?

8

Medicine

Like many nurses around the world in April 2020, Teresa Jay Dranger was grappling with a shortage of medical face masks at work. In search of solutions, the forty-three-year-old from the small town of Collins in New York state had come across online videos of how to create a homemade mask out of an old bra. She uploaded the results of her own efforts to social media. The enormous makeshift mask covered not just her mouth and nose, but her entire face. 'I don't think I could catch the Covid through it – nothing's getting through that thing. That's what happens when you're blessed – you get smothered,' she laughed.[1] Such light-hearted online content – along with pictures of people in China making masks out of grapefruit peel and even large cabbage leaves – helped keep many of us sane in the pandemic.[2] But really the global shortage of personal protective equipment (PPE) – items like masks, gowns and gloves – was no joke.

For frontline healthcare workers treating people with Covid these masks – particularly high filtration N95 respirator masks – were seen as vital to protect them from contracting the disease themselves and potentially spreading it to non-infected patients.[3] What we learned in those days was that around half of the global supply of masks – 10 million a day – were being produced in China.[4] We also learned that, when demand spiked, as it did in January 2020 as the virus spread in the southern city of Wuhan, China would more than absorb its own capacious national supply of masks.

Yet demand for masks was spiking in other countries too in the following months as the virus crossed national borders. The

OECD estimates that global mask demand by the spring of 2020 had jumped to 28 million per day for careworkers alone and to around 240 million per day when manufacturing and transport workers were included. Rather than a formal prohibition on mask exports, China imposed a kind of compulsory state purchase which amounted to the same thing. And dozens of other states – starting with Taiwan, but then extending from Albania to Uzbekistan – did ban exports in those months and requisitioned supplies to prevent overseas orders being delivered.[5] One French supplier failed to fulfil an order to the UK's health service as a result.[6] A Swedish healthcare company was unable to send masks to Italy from its Lyon depot.[7] The response in many states was an emergency push to increase mask production at home. The British fashion house Burberry announced it would be retooling its trench coat factory in Castleford, Yorkshire, to make masks for patients as well as non-surgical gowns.[8] Louis Vuitton likewise said it would convert five of its French workshops to produce masks rather than luxury handbags.[9]

On 31 March 2021 the French president, Emmanuel Macron, visited the factory of Kolmi-Hopen near Angers in the west of France, one of the few large European face mask production facilities. 'The world has changed over the past few weeks,' he announced.

> The past choices were built on a certainty that we could import these masks very easily, that they were produced in very large quantities at the other end of the world, often in China, sometimes elsewhere. Our priority today is to produce more in France and to produce more in Europe.

Macron said that, by the end of the year, he wanted France to be 'fully and completely independent' in face mask production.[10]

The US government had a similar goal. The first Trump administration is estimated to have distributed around $1.2 billion in subsidies to US companies to build plants to make masks and other protective medical gear in the following months.[11] It invoked the Defense Production Act to stop US companies from exporting the equipment overseas, including to its allies in Canada and Mexico.[12] In February 2021 Joe Biden argued the lesson was simple: 'We shouldn't have to rely on a foreign country – especially one that doesn't share our interests or our values – in order to protect and provide [for] our people during a national emergency.'[13] If the early 2020 mask shortage made politicians question the wisdom of relying on global supply chains, that was only compounded by the international row over vaccines a year later.

Vaccine Nationalism

It was not the easiest day at the office for Pascal Soriot. The French-born chief executive of AstraZeneca was being called to testify before a virtual hearing at the European Parliament. The parliamentarians were not happy with the performance of the multinational pharmaceutical company when it came to fulfilling its orders for its Covid vaccines and this was their first chance to hold its boss to account in public. A few weeks earlier the news had emerged that AstraZeneca would be able to provide the EU with only 31 million doses in the first quarter of 2021, well below its initial commitment of 80 million doses, due to production problems at its Belgian production site.[14] The news had provoked fury in European capitals.

Making matters even worse from their perspective was the revelation that AstraZeneca, a Swedish-British company whose headquarters are in the UK, would still be supplying some 2 million doses every week from its European production plants to the government of the UK, which was now outside the EU because of Brexit. The German MEP Peter Liese warned:

> If there is anyone thinking that European citizens would accept that we give this high-quality vaccine to the UK and accept to be treated as second-class by a UK-based company, I think the only consequence can be immediately to stop the export of the biotech. Then we are in the middle of a trade war. So the

company and the UK better think twice. We need to tell other companies in the world, if we treat the Europeans as second class, you will suffer for this.

Such was the tension the EU Commission even threatened at one stage to use Article 16 of the Northern Ireland Protocol to prevent EU exports of the vaccine to that part of the UK, which was supposed to have a friction-free post-Brexit trade border with the EU. In the event the Commission backed down in a matter of hours.[15]

The EU Parliament hearing on 25 February 2021 might have been virtual because of the risk of infection, but it was no less brutal for Soriot. One Finnish MEP described him as 'a piece of soap', apparently on account of his slippery and conflicting statements, and demanded: 'How is it possible you had no clue of your production capacity?'[16] The unedifying row lasted for months, with a great deal of back and forth on the precise terms of the different contracts signed between AstraZeneca and the EU and separately with the UK. A court case brought by the EU Commission against AstraZeneca was inconclusive, with both sides claiming vindication.[17] The whole episode was, many observed, an ugly example of vaccine nationalism: countries jostling for position to increase their own access to vaccines at the expense of others.

Something similar was going on, although rather more under the radar, in the United States. The subsidy contracts created under the first Trump administration's vaccine development programme – part of its 'Operation Warp Speed' to develop vaccines – obliged manufacturers to fill massive US government orders first. This constituted a de facto ban on vaccine exports. When the Biden administration took office in January 2021, just as the vaccines became available, the White House did nothing to change those contracts.[18] It didn't begin delivering doses to other countries until the summer of 2021, despite the fact there was spare capacity and it meant some stockpiled vaccines went out of date.[19] The White House said it was prudent to hold on to these in case of another surge in cases.[20] But when it came to the vaccine, it was a clear case of 'Americans first'. The overarching lesson that many drew from this pattern of behaviour in the pandemic was that you can't trust other nations when it comes to vital medicines and equipment. And the answer? Produce as much as possible – whether vaccines, essential medicines, masks or surgical gowns – at home.

Since the pandemic, multiple countries, including the US, have announced plans to scale up their domestic vaccine production capabilities. 'The United States has relied too heavily on foreign materials and bioproduction,' said a White House statement in September 2022 at the launch of a new National Biotechnology and Biomanufacturing Initiative.[21] The US pharmaceuticals giant Pfizer has increased its production facilities in Kalamazoo, Michigan.[22] Its smaller counterpart Moderna has doubled its production capability in Norwood, Massachusetts.[23] In the EU, BioNTech's new Marburg facility in Germany will be able to supply 1 billion doses of its mRNA vaccine per year.[24] The UK's AstraZeneca announced a new vaccine manufacturing plant in Speke, Liverpool.[25] There are similar expansions, assisted by state subsidies, in Canada, Switzerland, Belgium, France and Japan. But the idea that shifting the final production of vaccines to a country's own territory confers absolute security has something fishy about it.

Shark Liver Oil

One of the stranger ingredients of some coronavirus vaccines is an adjuvant called squalene. An adjuvant is a substance that is added to make the other ingredients more effective. They boost the body's immune response to a vaccine's active ingredient. The most concentrated natural source of high-purity squalene is the livers of sharks, particularly those fish that live in deep water such as the Pacific near Japan or in the Atlantic. It's estimated that it takes around 3,000 sharks' livers to produce just under 1 tonne of squalene.

The Covid pandemic and the consequent surge in the demand for vaccines raised concerns among some environmentalists of an impending slaughter of 500,000 sharks, possibly including endangered species, to satisfy the demand for squalene.[26] Those predictions turned out to be overblown. Squalene can also be sourced from plants, albeit at a higher cost, and there are synthetic alternatives. In any case, far more squalene is used in cosmetics than vaccines. Yet the episode of the shark liver oil did underline something important about the length and complexity of vaccine supply chains.

As well as squalene, some vaccines contain items such as aluminium salts, another common adjuvant, mined in China, Australia and India. Some contain thiomersal, a mercury-based preservative, which is added to prevent the growth of bacteria and fungi when the vaccine is opened. This is mined in countries such as Spain, Italy and Kyrgyzstan. Then there are stabilisers such as gelatin, sourced from pigs and cows, often from herds in the US, Brazil and China. Another stabiliser is sucrose, a type of sugar, mostly from Brazil, India and Thailand. And this is all, of course, in addition to the crucial antigens in the vaccine made from cell cultures or fermentation processes in bioreactor facilities in the US, Germany, Belgium, India and China.

Messenger RNA (mRNA) vaccines require something extra: nanoparticles called lipids, which function as their delivery system for the mRNA into the immune system. A single batch of lipid nanoparticles might require ionisable lipids from America, polyethylene glycol lipids from China and cholesterol from Europe.[27] Making a batch of ionisable lipids requires ten different precise manufacturing steps and takes months.[28] 'We're talking about biology manufacturing here,' as Pascal Soriot put it. 'It's not like doing an orange juice.'[29]

What contains all these vaccine ingredients is just as important: the vials. Their production requires specialised production facilities in their own right, involving precise moulding and quality control. The raw materials are also highly specialised. Borosilicate glass and medical-grade plastics have to be sourced from specific suppliers.[30] From antigen production and bulk manufacturing to the fill-and-finish process, cold chain logistics and final distribution, a typical vaccine could easily pass through around six different countries. The Pfizer/BioNTech Covid vaccines, according to the International Federation of Pharmaceutical Manufacturers and Associations, utilised an estimated 280 ingredients sourced from nineteen different countries.[31] Other estimates are even larger. The Coalition for Epidemic Preparedness Innovations (CEPI) states that a typical vaccine manufacturing plant will use in total 9,000 different materials, sourced from 300 suppliers, spread across thirty countries.[32]

Final vaccine production is concentrated in around thirteen countries, including America, China, India, Japan, Switzerland, the UK and France.[33] But these complex international supply chains – with a long list of intermediate inputs – means that, for the vast majority of countries, total vaccine self-sufficiency is no more realistic than achieving self-sufficiency in the production of semiconductors, as we saw in Chapter 5. Any interruption along the way can upset production, which is one of the reasons AstraZeneca's Belgian plant ran into difficulties in early 2021. A surer way to greater security would be for countries and regions to collaborate and form their own vaccine purchasing and producing blocs, which would give them greater bargaining power in relation to pharmaceutical firms. But some insist there is no alternative to trying to go it alone when it comes to vital medical products.

China Crisis

Among China's top state-linked economists Li Daokui was perceived as one of the more West-friendly. So it came as something of a shock to hear reports of the man who did his PhD at Harvard and who was an assistant professor at the University of Michigan for seven years suggesting that China could impose a kind of medicine choke on the West in March 2019. 'We are at the mercy of others when it comes to computer chips, but we are the world's largest exporter of raw materials for vitamins and antibiotics,' Li was reported to have told the National People's Congress in Beijing.

'Should we reduce the exports, the medical systems of some western countries will not run well.'[34]

The remarks understandably generated alarm in Washington, especially as they reinforced some of the potential threats that politicians had been hearing about. A report by the bipartisan U.S.-China Economic and Security Review Commission in 2019 stated that the US was heavily dependent on drugs that are either sourced from China or include active pharmaceutical ingredients (APIs) imported from China.[35] It also raised concerns about America's reliance on imports of 'generic' drugs: that is, medicines that are no longer patented. 'The degree to which some of our own manufacturers rely on China to produce life-saving and life-sustaining medications is inexcusable,' said Josh Hawley, the Republican senator for Missouri, in February 2020.[36] That summer Donald Trump issued an executive order to reduce America's dependence on foreign manufacturers for essential medicines and to expand domestic production.[37] And Trump campaigned in 2024 saying he would 'phase out' pharmaceutical imports from China entirely.[38] Europe is a significant net exporter of pharmaceuticals but it too relies heavily on China and India for APIs and generics, importing around three-quarters of the total it uses.[39]

The extent of the US reliance on China for pharmaceuticals has been exaggerated. Some of the testimony in the bipartisan commission's report was mangled in the US media to suggest erroneously that 80 per cent of America's pharmaceutical ingredients come directly from China.[40] The true figure is estimated to be more like 17 per cent, and around 6 per cent for all pharmaceutical products.[41] But there is no question trade has been growing. The value of the global trade in pharmaceuticals was around $900 billion in 2022, representing a tenfold increase over the past thirty years and more than the value of the global semiconductor trade.

Intermediate inputs, including APIs, now account for half of that value, underlining the growing complexity of medicine supply chains.[42] There are few sectors that are as globalised as pharmaceuticals. China is estimated to supply around 40 per cent of the world's APIs.[43] India supplies around 20 per cent of all the world's generic drugs by volume, often using APIs imported from China.[44] Both countries have been able to leverage their cheaper local labour costs and have benefited from economies of scale. In 2023 America imported from China around $2 billion per year of essential medicines – defined as painkillers, anti-inflammatories, blood thinners, antibiotics etc – up from around $30 million per year at the turn of the millennium.[45]

However, the reliance goes both ways. China supplies the ingredients, but it needs to import finished drugs, including many cancer drugs, made in the United States and Europe.[46] In 2022 China imported $7 billion in pharmaceutical products from the US compared to $10 billion going the other way. From Germany in that year it imported $8 billion of pharmaceutical imports, with nothing going the other way. China also imports a considerable volume of APIs from other countries.[47] It is, then, a relationship of interdependence, not one-way dependence.

The US and Europe could attempt to reshore such API and generic drug manufacturing. It wouldn't be hugely difficult from a technical point of view given that most of these 'small molecule' drugs, like the generic painkiller paracetamol, are not particularly complex to manufacture. Yet it would come at both a direct cost in terms of building the new production facilities, which would be much more expensive to run in the US than in China or India, and a potential indirect cost by pulling US and European pharmaceutical firms away from their considerable comparative advantage in research. 'It would be like shifting manufacturing away from microchips and going back to producing T-shirts and sneakers,' cautions Monica de Bolle of the Peterson Institute.[48]

Despite fears at the time, there were no widespread or long-lasting shortages of pharmaceuticals during the pandemic. Yet that period did highlight the potential dangers of companies and governments relying on just-in-time deliveries for medicines.[49] And the temporary decision of the Indian government in March 2020 to halt exports of twenty-six pharmaceutical products – including paracetamol and various antibiotics – in response to its local wave of coronavirus infections was a warning.[50] A survey of European pharmaceutical firms in December 2020 identified China and India as countries from which a majority of companies expected raw material supply problems over the coming years.[51]

What the pandemic did not show, however, despite what some politicians have argued, is that the only logical answer is to establish pharmaceutical production units in each nation. Many experts argue governments and their allies would be better advised to invest in mapping global pharmaceutical supply chains to identify particular potential vulnerabilities, rather than rushing to expand domestic manufacturing across the board. Some of the confusion about the extent of America's reliance on China in recent years has stemmed from the fact that the US Food and Drug Administration does not itself provide clear data on the origin of pharmaceutical imports. To mitigate the risk of imports of pharmaceuticals (either APIs or generic drugs) potentially being cut off from China or India, either by accident or deliberately, states could formally commit to invest in shared production facilities. They might do the same for more complex vaccine production sites. That way they could considerably boost their security in health emergencies at a fraction of the cost of a comprehensive national pharmaceutical manufacturing reshoring effort.

There are wider dangers arising from countries trying to be self-sufficient in medicines, beyond the financial cost. To understand why, it's important to grasp that pharmaceutical nationalism is by no means a purely Western phenomenon.

Losing Face

A young Irish national called Ben Kavanagh was working as a teacher in Wuhan in January 2020 when the first citywide lockdown was imposed in China. He produced videos, shot on his phone for Channel 4 News in the UK, which featured eerie scenes of a city with a population of 11 million people with virtually no one in the streets. The alien and dystopian spectacle generated many millions of views on YouTube.[52] Little did most of the viewers realise that within months they would be living the same reality.

China's experience of the pandemic was unsynchronised with the rest of the world's. Beijing imposed that first lockdown when the virus had barely been heard of by most people in the West. But when Europe and America were suffering the second wave in late 2020 and their own lockdowns, life in large parts of China was relatively normal and Beijing was boasting about the effectiveness of its 'Zero Covid' policy, which involved onerous mass-testing and brutal pre-emptive quarantining of contacts of cases. Yet official hubris caused the country to fail to push the vaccination of its vulnerable elderly population adequately in 2021. Instead, Beijing allowed myths about the negative impact of vaccines on the health of older people to go unchallenged and tolerated nationalist media spreading falsehoods about the dangers of Western-developed mRNA vaccines.[53] So when the extremely transmissible omicron variant of Covid hit the country in 2022 the only way the Chinese authorities were able to prevent a lethal spike in infections was to impose ultra-draconian lockdowns. 'Use your soul to control the aspiration for freedom' was the message relayed by drones to Shanghai residents.[54] At this time most lockdowns in the West had largely ended.

It became clear in 2022 that the US had repeatedly offered its own mRNA vaccines and other assistance to President Xi Jinping's government through private channels. But Xi refused to accept them.[55] This stubbornness is likely to have cost many lives in China. It's impossible to say how many but when Xi was finally forced, by rare displays of spontaneous popular discontent, to scrap his Zero Covid lockdowns in December 2022, the number of excess deaths that followed was estimated to be between 1 and 2 million.[56] Had China accepted US mRNA vaccines – which data suggested were much more effective than China's vaccines, which used an inactivated virus instead to stimulate the immune system – and rolled them out determinedly among the country's vulnerable elderly in 2022, many of those lives might have been saved.[57] Why didn't it do so? The best guess from analysts is that Xi Jinping did not want to lose face by accepting and distributing an American invented vaccine.[58] There might have been a commercial obstacle too. Sources at Moderna, one of the makers of the mRNA vaccine, suggested Beijing had been demanding that the US firm hand over proprietary details of the technology as a prerequisite for selling into the country.[59] Either way, it's clear that when nationalism interferes with public health decisions the results can literally be deadly.

Vaccine Apartheid

So abundant were vaccines in Western countries in 2021 that people took to comparing which variety they had received for their boosters – Moderna, Pfizer, AstraZeneca – as they might compare varieties of coffee or favourite musical artists. 'Only hot people get the Pfizer vaccine' was a TikTok joke.[60] At one point the debate in some Western countries turned to whether the vaccine-hesitant should be punished for not taking up their free jabs. In many other parts of the world it was a very different story.

As we've seen, most final production of vaccines takes place in wealthier countries, a fact that enabled their populations to get them first during the Covid pandemic. By early 2021 rich nations had reserved some 5 billion doses of vaccines from manufacturers, more than they would ever need to fully vaccinate their entire populations.[61] 'The high-income countries have gotten to the front of the line and cleared the shelves,' observed Andrea Taylor of Duke University, who closely monitored government vaccine-purchase contracts.[62]

There was a multilateral scheme – the Covid-19 Vaccines Global Access (COVAX) initiative – to distribute vaccines to low-income countries too. This was supposed to involve governments paying into a fund that would then purchase Covid vaccines from manufacturers and distribute them to low-income countries.[63] COVAX did, ultimately, distribute some 1.9 billion doses to 146 countries and saved an estimated 7 million lives.[64] But many of them arrived only relatively late in the pandemic and the vaccination targets set by COVAX for low-income countries were missed.

By June 2022 around 70 per cent of people in high-income countries had been vaccinated with at least one dose, compared to fewer than 20 per cent in low-income states.[65] The World Health Organization's former chief scientist Soumya Swaminathan has described COVAX as a 'beautiful idea' on paper, but argues it ultimately did not deliver in the way envisaged because multinational pharmaceutical manufacturers and governments failed to prioritise it.[66] Some analysts calculate that if Indonesia and the Philippines had had a vaccination rate equivalent to that of the US, 19 per cent of its total deaths could have been averted; in Bolivia and El Salvador 29 and 53 per cent of deaths might not have happened. If Sri Lanka had enjoyed US vaccination rates 55 per cent of people who died of Covid would have lived, according to their estimates.[67]

Vaccine inequality likely led to hundreds of thousands of deaths

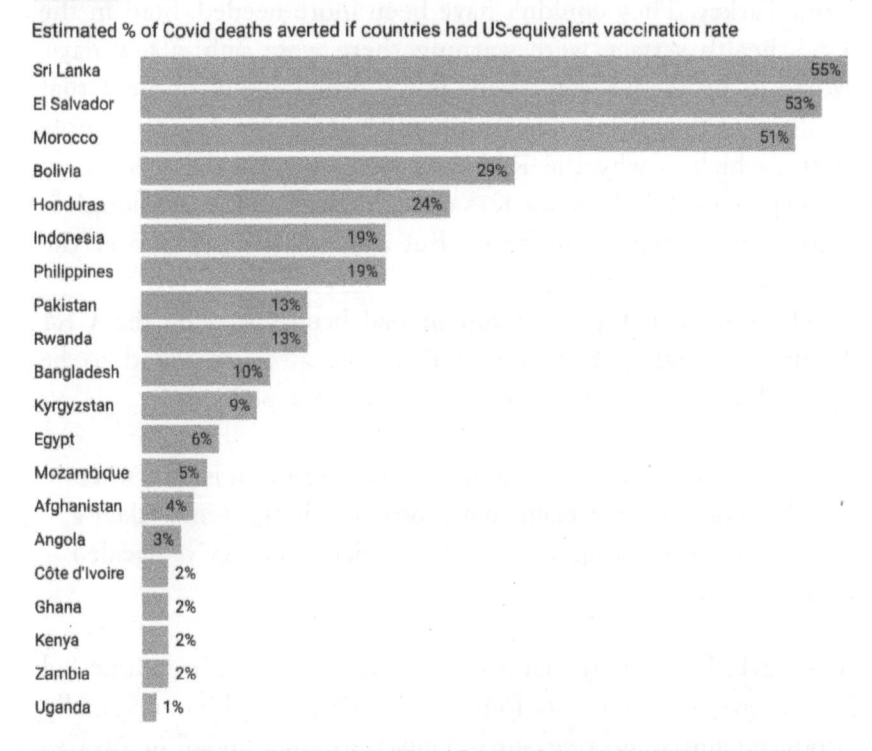

Estimated % of Covid deaths averted if countries had US-equivalent vaccination rate

Country	%
Sri Lanka	55%
El Salvador	53%
Morocco	51%
Bolivia	29%
Honduras	24%
Indonesia	19%
Philippines	19%
Pakistan	13%
Rwanda	13%
Bangladesh	10%
Kyrgyzstan	9%
Egypt	6%
Mozambique	5%
Afghanistan	4%
Angola	3%
Côte d'Ivoire	2%
Ghana	2%
Kenya	2%
Zambia	2%
Uganda	1%

Chart: Ben Chu • Source: Gozzi, N., Chinazzi, M., Dean, N.E. et al. Estimating the impact of COVID-19 vaccine inequities: a modeling study. Nat Commun 14, 3272 (2023). https://doi.org/10.1038/s41467-023-39098-w • Created with Datawrapper

Figure 16

One analysis suggests an equitable global distribution of vaccines would have averted 670,000 deaths in total.[68] This is in the context of a global excess death toll from the pandemic, estimated by *The Economist*, at between 19 and 36 million.[69] Such figures are why some, including the director-general of the World Health Organization, argue that the inevitable flipside of vaccine nationalism is a kind of vaccine apartheid.[70]

Turkish Drop

A gunmetal-grey Atlas A400M Royal Air Force (RAF) cargo plane touched down at Brize Norton airfield, near Oxford, in the early hours of 22 April 2020. In its hull were 67,000 surgical gowns from Turkey. They couldn't have been more needed. Staff in the UK's health service were warning there were only a few days' worth of protective equipment left – protective equipment that could save their lives. The shipment had been delayed multiple times, which is why the RAF was sent on a special mission to collect them. UK broadcasters covered the landing as though it were a humanitarian airdrop.[71] But around two weeks later the depressing reality emerged.

The gowns in the consignment had been tested by the UK's Health and Safety Executive and almost all were found to be unsuitable for use.[72] A government minister explained:

> There was a view that it was good enough PPE, it is only when it has got here that teams have looked at it again and taken a view that it is not up to the right standard and they've decided not to use it.[73]

The Turkish company that provided the gowns had been founded by the owner's sister only four months earlier and had originally produced shirts and tracksuits. They were impounded in a warehouse.

Around this time the UK government also purchased 250 ventilators from China that were subsequently deemed to be dangerous. Government accounts show that it ultimately had to write off around £15 billion of PPE, most of it purchased in haste during the pandemic.[74] It would be unreasonable to entirely blame UK ministers for this waste. There was a global rush to secure PPE, pushing up prices everywhere, and there was considerable public pressure to prioritise delivery over value for money. Reporting by the Organized Crime and Corruption Reporting Project found that in 2020 respirator face masks were being purchased at wildly different prices across Europe, ranging from 20 cents to 37 euros each.[75] But what episodes like the Turkish gowns fiasco underline is that a better way for countries to build resilience in the face of global health emergencies than onshoring production is to keep reasonable stockpiles.

Analysis suggests PPE stockpiles were simply too meagre in many countries in early 2020, or had been allowed to dwindle.[76] Australia had 9 million masks at the outset of the pandemic, down from 40 million a decade earlier. The US had only around 30 million surgical masks.[77] Finland, which had larger stockpiles than its Nordic neighbour Sweden, was notably better prepared.[78] Larger national stockpiles would reduce the likelihood of scrambles by multiple governments for orders in an emergency, which inevitably push up prices. It would also help if governments simply kept up-to-date inventories of stockpiles. The Canadian province of Alberta, which had made a significant investment in its planning and digital supply chain infrastructure in 2008, did notably better than other provinces in terms of sourcing PPE during the pandemic.[79] Governments could share data digitally with each other as a matter of course and in real time, and also mutually commit not to impose national export bans. The inevitable result of these beggar-thy-neighbour bans is that most states feel the need to follow suit or risk being disadvantaged; the entire world is then worse off as prices shoot up. The premier of the German state of Bavaria described the global medical supplies marketplace in April

2020 as the 'Wild West', as governments outbid each other for PPE supplies.[80] Major regional stockpiles – for example, pooled procurement in Europe, North and South America, Africa and Asia – would also defray the costs of national stockpiling for smaller countries.

Infrastructure for inspections of PPE at an earlier point in the supply chain might well have identified the problems with the Turkish-made gowns. Clearly defined international quality specifications for PPE would also have helped. Creating stockpiles and testing infrastructure involving different countries would not be cheap, but it would be considerably more efficient than the exile economics solution of reshoring.

Global mask sales in 2019 were around 12.5 billion. In 2020 that soared to 378 billion. By 2024, with the end of the pandemic, demand had fallen back to around 23 billion.[81] Around 70 per cent of the mask manufacturers established in the US during the pandemic were reported to have gone bust in 2024 due to the collapse in demand.[82] Would it be more effective for the US to subsidise those factories to remain open, or to invest in stockpiling? The OECD estimates that masks can be stored for at least a decade. Another sensible strategy, rather than keeping huge manufacturing spare capacity, would be government agreements with private-sector companies for rapid conversion of assembly lines to produce PPE during crises, ideally on a broad regional basis. Similarly, would it be a more effective use of public money to subsidise additional vaccine manufacturing in the US, or to invest more in early-stage research and development? The danger of onshoring production is that it tends to create companies that cannot compete in the global market and leads to pressure for trade protection, which is precisely what has been coming from the remaining US mask production sector.

Developed countries did step up mask production significantly in early 2020. But nowhere near on the scale of China, which went from producing 10 million face masks per day in 2019 to about 116 million per day at the end of February 2020, and as many as 200 million per day by the end of March. The car maker

BYD, which we met in Chapter 4, and the iPhone assembler Foxconn were among the firms that reconfigured their Chinese factories to produce 5 and 2 million masks per day, respectively.[83] While France tripled its daily production of masks, China ramped its own up by a factor of twenty. And it recommenced exports in March 2020.

The face mask shortage, like the silicon chip shortage outlined in Chapter 5, was primarily due to a surge in demand, rather than a shortfall in supply. And global supply responded pretty remarkably under the circumstances. The value of global trade declined by almost 8 per cent in 2020, yet trade in medical supplies grew by 16 per cent.[84] The successful European and US vaccine development programme also relied on cross-border scientific cooperation between researchers, as we saw in Chapter 6. Those who criticise global medical supply chains, like the US national security advisor Jake Sullivan in April 2023, should pause to consider how nation-states would have fared in their absence.[85] They might also consider what the price of medicines – already one of the biggest drivers of increases in household and government health spending in most countries – would be in the absence of global supply chains.

The pandemic gave us a taste of these costs. Polymerase chain reaction (PCR) tests, which detect the genetic material of the virus, were the gold standard for identifying whether people were infected or not. China was able to mass-produce these test kits early in the pandemic, and cheaply owing to its dominance in production of the necessary chemical reagents. Because China was producing more kits than it needed, the US and Europe imported them in large volumes in early 2020.[86] But as the US began to manufacture PCR test kits itself in 2021, its imports from China fell away. Europe also began to source its PCR kits from the US rather than China, perhaps influenced by a desire to be less dependent on Chinese imports. Whatever the motivation, analysts point out that this was an expensive choice for American and European taxpayers and patients. The median cost of a PCR test in the US was around $127.[87] In the UK they were £75 ($103).[88]

China's exports of masks collapsed early in the pandemic, but then soared in the following months

China masks and respirator exports, kg

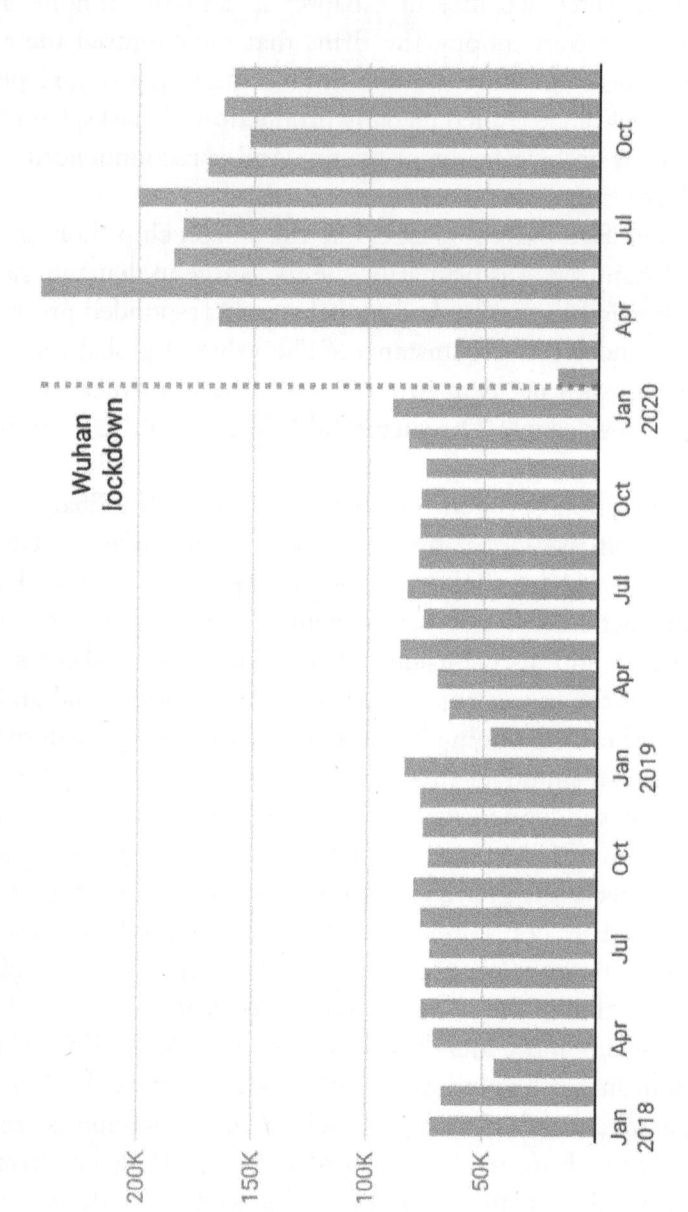

Chart: Ben Chu • Source: Peterson Institute • Created with Datawrapper

Figure 17

The estimated cost of a test in China was around $1.50 per person.[89] Much of that difference would have been due to the difference in local laboratory processing costs for the PCR swabs, but a considerable share would also have been due to the higher costs of production of the tests themselves in the US.

Global Public Goods

A rather strange moment in the pandemic came in July 2020 when the US, UK and Canadian intelligence services came together to accuse Russian hackers of attempting to steal their coronavirus research on behalf of their government – clearly presenting such work as a national commercial asset rather than a global public good.[90] They do not seem to have considered whether, given the circumstances of the pandemic, it might have been more beneficial for the planet for such research to be as broadly disseminated as possible.

The pandemic was riven with politicians engaging in nationalistic grandstanding. 'That doesn't surprise me at all, because we're a much better country than every single one of them,' UK education minister Gavin Williamson said when asked why the UK medical regulator had authorised Covid vaccines for use a few weeks before national regulators in Europe in December 2020.[91] 'I'm of course very pleased that it is a German company, a German research and development team, a German biotech enterprise that is among the first that we're negotiating with that can show these first research results,' said the German health minister Jens Spahn at a press conference in November 2020 when Uğur Şahin's BioNTech vaccine results were announced.[92] Never mind that it was based on work by a Turkish immigrant (Şahin) working with a Hungarian-born researcher residing in the US (Katalin Karikó) and that the trial had been conducted by an American multinational pharmaceutical company run by a Greek (Albert Bourla). The reality is that the coronavirus vaccines are global products, not truly belonging to any single nation. In July 2020 Donald Trump pulled the United

States out of the United Nations' public health arm, the World Health Organization (WHO), after claiming that China had 'total control' over the organisation and other countries were not paying in as much as the US.[93] Perhaps it seems naïve or idealistic to imagine that it could ever have been different – or that it could ever be different in the future given the growing distrust between China and Western governments. Yet history shows global co-operation in the face of a global public health threat is possible, even at times of high geopolitical tension.

In 1967 Donald Henderson of America's Communicable Disease Center (CDC) was appointed by the WHO to lead a global vaccination campaign against smallpox, which at that point was still killing 2 million people every year in Africa, Asia and South America, and exposing richer countries that had largely eradicated it to the risk of renewed outbreaks through international travel.[94] The funding for the global eradication campaign was $2.4 million per year, a sum too small to cover the costs of acquiring the vaccines, never mind the distributional logistics. So in May 1967 Henderson reached out to the Soviet deputy health minister, Dimitri Venediktov, on the sidelines of a WHO leadership meeting in Geneva and proposed that the two countries work together. Henderson was nervous. This was only five years after the Cuban Missile Crisis, the most perilous point of the Cold War, and he knew the Russians had lobbied against the appointment of an American to run the smallpox eradication initiative. But the answer was positive. 'I want you to know,' the Russian told Henderson, 'that we have checked you out and are now confident that you are honest and a good scientist, that your only objective is to eradicate smallpox. You will have our full support.'[95] The Soviets, seeing an opportunity to demonstrate their scientific and medical prowess to the world, agreed to collaborate. Over the following years both countries, under the auspices of the WHO, shared expertise, technology and resources.

More than a billion Soviet-manufactured doses of the vaccine were distributed, largely funded by American taxpayer dollars, across Africa and Asia. The last naturally occurring case of smallpox was a twenty-three-year-old Somalian cook in 1977.[96] The WHO officially declared smallpox eradicated in 1980. A disease that had ravaged humankind for 3,000 years – probably killing more people than any other pathogen – had finally been eradicated thanks to medical science and what the former WHO director-general Gro Harlem Brundtland described in 2010 as 'the quiet collaboration of the two superpowers during some of the hottest years of the Cold War'.[97] It is not easy to imagine today's exile economics producing such an outcome. What sort of world *will* exile economics create?

9
The Future

Travelling between the British colony of Hong Kong and Guangzhou in China in the middle years of the 1980s was like being sucked back in time. The roughly two-hour train journey on the old Kowloon–Canton Railway transported you from a land of neon-clad skyscrapers and roads full of modern Japanese cars to a universe of grey streets clogged with bicycles. It was a trip from abundance to privation. My first visit was in 1985.

My father left China as a child in the 1950s and emigrated with his parents to Sheffield, where he grewn up amid the terraced houses of northern England. But, by a twist of fate, he'd been sent by his employer, a now-defunct British engineering conglomerate called GEC, to work in Hong Kong and brought us, his young family, with him. We were taking the opportunity to visit the relatives my father had left behind in China, in the city of Guangzhou.

What we found was shocking to my young, naïve eyes. The family of my father's cousin – six people – lived in just three rooms of a crumbling, dank housing block built around a communal courtyard. At night, after we had returned to our hotel, they would pull out thin mattresses and sleep on the floor. There were no televisions, shopping malls, coffee shops or fast-food restaurants. The only place people could buy Western goods like modern kitchen appliances was in a government-controlled 'friendship store' and you had to pay with foreign currency. On 22 April 1986 we received a letter from my father's cousin, written on very thin paper, with a request. 'Dear cousin. Recently the China Travel Service Guangdong has opened a duty-free bazaar solely for overseas Chinese ethnic citizens of foreign nationality and the like. I wonder if you can take us there and buy a washing machine?' I hold that piece of paper in my hands now, forty years on, and marvel at how the living standards of my Chinese relations – and most other people in China – have been utterly transformed by their integration into the international economy by globalisation.

In 1990 the national income per person in China, adjusted for local purchasing power and inflation, was $1,641. In 2023 it was $22,000, a thirteenfold increase in just over thirty years. In 1990 the average Chinese income per head was just one-twentieth of America's. In 2023 it was almost a third.[1] In big coastal cities like Guangzhou, incomes are even higher. Our Chinese relatives can now buy washing machines, televisions and just about everything else by heading to the nearest shopping mall, or by clicking on a smartphone app. That journey from Hong Kong to Guangzhou – reduced to forty-five minutes thanks to the construction of a high-speed rail line – feels almost like any other intercity train connection in the developed world. Guangzhou now has a forest of skyscrapers of its own. So it's jarring to me, to put it mildly, to hear the apostles of exile economics suggest that Western economic integration with China was a great historic error, something that should never have taken place. 'The United States made a crucial mistake when it decided to treat China's non-market, Communist economy the same way as it treats the economies of our democratic, free market allies,' Robert Lighthizer, Donald Trump's official trade representative in his first term, wrote in 2023.[2] It certainly wasn't a mistake as far as my relatives in China are concerned. The same is true for the majority of people who live in Vietnam, Taiwan, Singapore, South Korea, Bangladesh, Poland, Brazil and the dozens of other countries around the world that were poor at the end of the Second World War and have seen their living standards shoot up.

So globalisation is, I admit, a personal issue for me. It wasn't just the opportunities afforded to my relatives in China but also to my father's family when they emigrated to England, just one particle of the great global flux of people described in Chapter 6. I likely wouldn't exist without globalisation. Perhaps there will be those who argue that makes me one of the privileged 'winners' of globalisation and therefore incapable of being objective. But, as we've seen, the popular idea that globalisation has inflicted only economic pain on Western workers is not supported by the evidence. It's true that the progressive interconnection of national economies since the 1970s has created some relative losers in rich nations, some blighted communities, not least in the North of England where I was born and mostly grew up. Yet the overall economic gains have been more than sufficient for the governments of those countries – whether America, Britain, France or Germany – to compensate those workers and communities and to give them opportunities to win. It's hard to argue that this redistribution and adjustment support was often lacking was the fault of China, Vietnam, Poland or Brazil, or the inexorable forces of globalisation. A more plausible culprit is the failures of the internal politics of developed countries – political failures that were far from inevitable. Moreover, turning the clock back on globalisation – something that Donald Trump has made clear he wants to accomplish – seems most unlikely to reverse the economic damage, but rather threatens to compound it. What we've learned in these pages is that exile economics is liable to make rich nations poorer, not more prosperous; less secure, not more so.

This is not a Panglossian diagnosis; the world created by globalisation is not the best of all possible worlds. The pandemic and the energy crisis shone a spotlight on potential vulnerabilities in the cross-border supply of vital goods and components. But arguably a better way to address these vulnerabilities is threefold: map, stockpile and diversify. First, firms and governments could adequately map critical supply chains – including the suppliers of their suppliers – and then stress-test them with scenario planning. What if the Strait of Hormuz in the Middle East were closed because of conflict? What if Taiwan were struck by a major earthquake? What if there were a failed harvest in Brazil? What if there were another pandemic, resulting in a surge in demand for certain goods? And so on. The next step could be to stockpile critical goods, components and materials, preferably on a regional rather than a national basis, as

European governments did in 2022 when they stockpiled natural gas to get the continent's energy system through the winter without Russian supplies. Why not learn from the success of Toyota which, as we saw in Chapter 5, shifted from an ultra-lean 'just-in-time' production model in the wake of the catastrophe of the 2011 Japanese earthquake to one that ran on larger inventories and with greater transparency up and down the supply chain? The approach could be through collaboration between governments and between the public and private sectors, not going it alone, or by instigating or participating in protectionist tariff wars. Third, countries could reduce the risk of important supply interruptions not by trying to bring production home, but by seeking and investing in a wider array of international suppliers – in other words, trade diversification. As Churchill is said to have remarked of the oil supplies needed to fuel the British Imperial Fleet in the First World War: 'Safety and certainty lie in variety and variety alone.'[3]

There is considerable scope for this. It's estimated by the McKinsey Global Institute that around 40 per cent of global trade value relies on three or fewer supplier states, pointing to a disconcertingly high level of geographic concentration and high potential vulnerability if those suppliers were to be cut off.[4] Yet only a quarter of this 40 per cent total (so around 10 per cent) is because there is only a small number of potential suppliers. The rest (30 per cent) is due to countries choosing to source from a small number of national suppliers, when they could import from a wider range of countries. Let's use agriculture to explain. As outlined in Chapter 3, Brazil and the United States account for about 90 per cent of the global traded supply of soybeans, and China, Japan and Thailand get around 90 per cent of their soybeans from these two countries. There's not realistically much scope for them to diversify away from Brazil and the US because of the huge natural advantages those two countries have in producing the crop. By contrast, global wheat production is much less geographically concentrated than soybean production, with the crop grown in a much wider range of countries. Nonetheless, some states have allowed a heavy reliance to develop on certain trade partners. For instance, around 90 per cent of Egypt's wheat imports are from Russia and Ukraine. Some 80 per cent of wheat imports to the Philippines come from the US and Australia. One relatively simple way for countries to reduce their trade vulnerabilities would be to ensure, where possible, that they were less reliant on single state suppliers. This would be much less potentially damaging than attempting reshoring – and certainly cheaper.

The Great Illusion

Yet the problem of China remains, a China whose ruling Communist regime has turned into a much more internally repressive and externally menacing force; which has failed to shift its national economic model away from household underconsumption and over-investment and which seems incapable of doing so – something that seems likely to bring on a protectionist backlash from the West and indeed other developing countries.

Again, this is personal for me. My relatives in China can buy things that they could not have dreamed of forty years ago. They can travel abroad. Yet they can't vote or speak or associate freely without fear of retaliation from the Communist Party. The liberal, freethinking Hong Kong where I lived in the 1980s is now an authoritarian Chinese city thanks to Xi Jinping and the Communist Party reneging on the 'one country, two systems' agreement with Britain, as part of its 1997 handover of the territory back to Beijing. It's that reneging that has prompted more than 144,000 Hong Kong citizens who qualify as 'British Nationals Overseas' to permanently emigrate to Britain since 2021.[5] I can understand the temptation for people to conclude that we are better off simply separating from a giant economy run by such a regime, no matter the economics.

Yet it's worth taking a step back to consider the counterfactual. What if the West had not traded with China after 1979, after the country opened itself up after the death of Mao Zedong? What if the United States had blocked China's entry into the World Trade Organization in 2001, as many US politicians now say would have been the right decision? Would the world today really be more secure? It's true that the ruling regime did not liberalise politically in the way that many hoped it would in the years after the turn of the millennium and that the Communist Party lurched in a violently authoritarian direction under Xi Jinping after 2013.

But would an alternative trade policy from the developed world after 1979 or 2001 have altered that dismal path? Would China be less of a threat today? Or might we have merely faced the same challenge today, but from a less prosperous China, in which the population was poorer and perhaps more ignorant of and hostile towards the West? And might China have made more political and social progress, under the surface, than it seems? The public protests that finally brought an end to Xi Jinping's Zero Covid policy in 2022, when young people held up blank pieces of paper to symbolise 'everything we want to say but cannot say', were breathtaking in their boldness.[6] We cannot know, but the idea that the world would today be safer is by no means a given. It seems fanciful to imagine that a world in which multilateral institutions such as the United Nations, the International Monetary Fund and the World Trade Organization – imperfect as they undoubtedly are – are wrecked by great power rivalry, or deliberately dismantled by a second Trump administration, would be more secure. It's possible that the free world today is in a superior position to face an authoritarian leadership in China *because of* globalisation.

In 1910 at the height of an arms race between imperial Britain and its fast-growing rival Germany, an English journalist called Norman Angell wrote a bestselling book called *The Great Illusion*. Angell's thesis was that, despite the sabre-rattling of politicians and popular jingoism of the era, a conflict between the great European powers was unlikely because of their economic and financial integration. In other words, because of globalisation. 'What is the real guarantee of the good behaviour of one state to another?' Angell asked. 'It is the elaborate interdependence which, not only in the economic sense, but in every sense, makes an unwarrantable aggression of one state upon another react upon the interests of the aggressor.'[7] Nevertheless, four years later, European states were at war with each other, with hundreds of thousands of soldiers being slaughtered on the Western Front in France and Belgium.

The idea that trade and interdependence guarantee peace is now seen as a fallacy. Yet it doesn't deserve to be entirely disregarded. The evidence of the years since the Second World War is that globalisation and positive-sum economic thinking have done a remarkable job in averting conflict between major powers.[8] Some research also shows that greater trade openness is associated with a lower probability of armed conflict between smaller states.[9] The case shouldn't be overstated. Causation is difficult to determine.

Yet the history of the 1930s does serve to demonstrate just what a dangerous accelerant deglobalisation can be for conflict. The Japanese decision to mount a surprise aerial attack on the US fleet in Hawaii in 1941 was a panicked response to the US government's decision a few weeks earlier to impose a de facto embargo on oil exports to Japan by freezing its American financial assets, itself a response to Japan's military incursions into south-east Asia. The US was the source of eight of every ten barrels of Japan's oil. Japan's commanders had stockpiled supplies but feared that the American embargo meant it was only a matter of time before their military machine broke down. 'If there were no supply of oil, battleships and any other warships would be nothing more than scarecrows,' one of its admirals warned.[10] The attack on Pearl Harbor was conceived as a way of crippling the US fleet and of buying Japan sufficient time to invade and seize the oil wells of the Dutch East Indies (now Indonesia). It was a spectacular and catastrophic miscalculation from the Japanese, since the attack brought America directly into the war with a vengeance. It was a miscalculation borne of imperial fanaticism – but also resource nationalism.

Similarly, Adolf Hitler's policy of autarky was shaped by Germany's experience in the First World War when German cities had been starved by a British naval blockade, which had crippled its war effort. One of the obstacles to autarky was the country's chronic reliance on imports of food, particularly edible fats. Nazi Germany explored multiple avenues to food self-sufficiency, including promoting soybeans, whose modern role we explored in Chapter 3, as a source of protein to German housewives. But the Nazis never bridged their national fat gap. That is one of the central reasons Hitler doubled down on the policy of pursuing *Lebensraum*, or 'living space', invading other countries in the conviction that it was entitled to their arable land to feed its domestic population. Documents used in evidence at the postwar Nuremberg Trials showed that the Nazi regime planned to plunder the food supplies of Russia and Ukraine and allow tens of millions there to starve. Thus did the Nazi obsession with food self-sufficiency ultimately reinforce the danger it posed to its neighbours and the entire world. To be clear, none of this is intended to somehow excuse the atrocities of imperial Japan or Nazi Germany, but it provides some important context for the nightmarish geopolitics of the 1930s and 1940s.

Global economic integration doesn't guarantee peace, but a world of economic and political fragmentation is likely to deliver a world of surging resource nationalism and a heightened danger of interstate aggression. History teaches us that those are the fruits of exile economics. Arguably a better way for Western countries to deal with China is to maintain and manage economic interconnections rather than dismantle them. On the specific issue of overproduction and dumping, they could appeal to Chinese economic self-interest and propose voluntary export curbs, as was achieved with Japan in the 1980s. If that fails, Western nations might then do better to impose capital controls to prevent China recycling its trade surpluses into Western currencies rather than opting for tariffs or import bans. Such a step would be profound and potentially destabilising, but it would address the origins of Chinese overproduction at source rather than risking an unravelling of the postwar trade order. If Xi Jinping wanted to avoid the kind of protectionist backlash that is otherwise coming, he would overhaul China's economic model without further delay.

It's crucial to recognise that we all have a stake in this. The Chinese novelist Yu Hua tells a joke about the anti-Japanese riots that happen from time to time in Chinese cities when nationalist fervour is whipped up over some perceived insult from Tokyo. A crowd, bent on destruction, surrounds a Japanese car. Then someone points out that the vehicle was made locally in a joint venture with a Chinese company. To which the answer comes: 'Let's smash half of it then.' Smashing up a globalised economy is smashing up our own joint property – it's an act of self-harm. Might hope, though, lie in some powerful countervailing forces?

Trade Finds a Way

In Chapter 4 we explored the story of the gas pipeline built between the Soviet Union and West Germany in 1984. The idea was that the Soviet Union would receive foreign currency and Western investment to build it and in return Europe would receive a cheap source of energy. The project was opposed by the administration of Ronald Reagan, which argued it would give the Soviets a potential 'energy weapon', and the row created a major split within NATO. The lesson that might be drawn is that energy interdependence between geopolitical adversaries is dangerous, especially given that Vladimir Putin significantly cut off Europe's gas supply, provided through similar pipes, in 2022. But another valid lesson is that trade, like water, tends to find a way through the cracks.

The Soviets had cheap gas and Western Europeans wanted to buy it. Cold War geopolitics was in the end trumped by economic interests. We might also point to the ability of Russia to work around the wide net of trade sanctions imposed on its regime by Western countries in the wake of the invasion of Ukraine, smuggling in industrial components for its military via neighbouring countries such as Kazakhstan and Georgia.[11] And the G7 and Australia explicitly carved out a route for Moscow to continue to sell its oil to the West in December 2022. Theoretically the price was capped at $60 per barrel, a $20 discount on the prevailing market price at the time, but the fact that Western firms were permitted to buy oil at all showed the limits to the domestic energy market pain their governments were prepared to tolerate.[12] On a less depressing note, we might look to the deal brokered by Turkey with Russia and

Ukraine, referenced in Chapter 3, to allow badly needed grain to flow out of Ukrainian ports in 2022, past the Russian Black Sea blockade that initially threatened to bring famine to parts of Africa and the Middle East.[13] Again, trade was able to find a way, despite the two nations being at war.

Evidence from Donald Trump's first term in office shows that tariffs sometimes merely divert trade rather than stop it. The Trump administration imposed 30 per cent tariffs on Chinese imported solar panels in 2018 but the US Commerce Department presented evidence in 2023 that Chinese solar panel manufacturers had shifted their assembly operations to countries such as Malaysia, Thailand, Cambodia and Vietnam and then sent the finished products to the US from them instead, thereby effectively evading the levies. This kind of adaptation is perhaps the most optimistic scenario for the years ahead if Trump's second term is as radically protectionist as he has pledged.

When I began researching this book I was sceptical of the case for dismantling global supply chains. Now my sense is that anyone who advocates it – whether in medicines, semiconductors, batteries or agriculture – has simply not examined these supply chains closely enough. It may be that the economic disruption in attempting to interfere with such expansive webs of interconnection simply proves too great for all sides and that the exile economic experiment is aborted. Or it could be bypassed by Chinese companies setting up factories in the West, much as Japan did in the 1980s. It is just about possible to envisage a narrow corridor down which the world could walk that involves a step-up in industrial strategy in developed nations and continued openness in trade. This industrial policy would involve heavy investment not in sectors such as steel, where global overproduction is a chronic problem, but in advanced manufacturing and cutting-edge clean technologies, such as industrial carbon emission capture and storage and hydrogen electrolysis using renewable power, in ways that drive national and also international productivity growth.

Advocates of industrial policy have a strong case when they argue that it has been too readily conflated with protectionism in the past. While it can certainly have protectionist dimensions when it is designed poorly, if the central thrust of industrial policy is to expand a nation's capabilities and deliver technological progress and broad-based growth it is just as legitimate in developed countries as in developing ones.[14] There's also a valid critique of what the Turkish-American economist Dani Rodrik termed 'hyper-globalisation' in the 2000s, where the concerns of multinational corporations in relation to protection of intellectual property were unduly privileged in trade negotiations and the domestic and democratic prerogatives of governments were undermined.[15] A downshift from this corporate-focused hyper-globalisation could be benign, especially if paired with a much more comprehensive programme focusing on helping those individuals and communities adversely impacted by global trade. This would be akin to what the World Trade Organization has called 'reglobalisation'.

In terms of cross-border trade measures, this could plausibly deliver a globalisation pause rather than an unravelling, something similar to what we saw in the early 1970s after President Nixon abruptly took America off the global currency gold standard established after the Second World War. Untethering global currencies from the dollar, which was itself attached to the price of gold, was destabilising but ultimately bearable, and the trend for trade liberalisation continued. Walking down this narrow path would also involve a strengthening of ties between allies and a wary maintenance of relations with others, rather than a degeneration into beggar-thy-neighbour. It would involve not wasteful national subsidy wars and tariffs, but subsidy 'clubs' between like-minded nations in areas such as EVs, semiconductors and critical materials. It would be natural for allies such as the US, Europe, Canada, Japan, South Korea, Australia and Mexico to combine in creating these.

It would see continued cooperation between the US and China in areas such as technology transfer for decarbonisation to developing countries, which would be carved out of other elements of the relationship. There are certainly times when what we might call the better angels of US policy under the Biden administration – or in the decisions taken in European capitals – have leaned in this direction and away from exile economics. It would be fanciful to suggest that Donald Trump's return to the White House makes it more, rather than less, likely that the world will be able to walk this narrow path – but it remains a viable route through the political, economic and environmental pressures of the coming decades.

The Future of Globalisation

Globalisation appears to be changing shape regardless of geopolitical revolutions. While the trade of physical goods – manufactured products, raw materials and agricultural produce – as a share of global economic output has been broadly stagnant for the past fifteen years, the share of services being traded across international borders has grown in that time, particularly in areas like offshoring corporate back-office administrative functions, including human resources and data processing. Cross-border data flows have been exploding, even as protectionism has been on the rise.[16] Countries such as India and Bangladesh have made considerable progress in exporting so-called 'Global Capability Centre' services to Western multinationals, leveraging their population's English language and information technology skills. Some argue that this trend is set to continue and accelerate thanks to improvements in communication technologies – and that it will be hard for the traditional protectionist tools to interfere with it. It's easy to slap tariffs on goods crossing borders, but not so easy to tax companies sending data via cloud computing servers for processing between two offices in different countries.

Others argue that exile economics could also intrude here in the form of national regulatory restrictions on cross-border corporate data flows such as requirements to keep and process data on servers located within a country. China's 'Great Firewall' to shield its domestic internet users from Western social media websites such as Facebook and to censor Western news media shows that states are far from impotent in the digital world. It's possible to imagine white-collar workers lobbying for such regulations if they fear their jobs are at risk of being offshored. The obstacle to professionals such as accountants, lawyers and medical general practitioners delivering their services in different countries today is already, some maintain, less to do with geographical distance and communication barriers than national regulatory barriers erected by those socially and politically powerful professionals in Western countries.[17] The World Trade Organization estimates that the cost of trading services overseas is five and a half times higher than selling domestically, compared to four times higher for merchandise. Alternatively, it's possible that advances in AI could lessen the need for white-collar workers in developed and developing countries alike. The future, as always with technology, is unclear.

Things can change more quickly than we anticipate. In 2016 the greatly respected trade economist Richard Baldwin published a book which argued the next great stage of globalisation was upon us and involved 'telerobotics' and 'holographic telepresence'. He speculated about hotel rooms in Oslo being cleaned by maids sitting in Manila and US security guard robots operated by security guards in Peru or German technicians fixing equipment in China through robots.[18] He also argued that a 1930s-style protectionist surge 'seems unlikely'. Later that year Donald Trump was elected. What this shows is just how hard it is, even for the most informed, to spot turning points in real time.

But while predicting the future with accuracy is impossible, we surely know enough to conclude that a substantially more closed global economy is likely to be a poorer one – and one that will find it harder, not easier, to deal with unexpected shocks and collective challenges. As outlined in Chapter 4, the largest collective challenge will be decarbonisation. From 2026 the EU is introducing a carbon border adjustment mechanism (CBAM) – essentially an import tax on cement, iron, steel, aluminium and fertilisers produced in countries with a higher share of fossil fuels in their production processes than Europe. This has already drawn accusations of 'green protectionism' from India.[19]

Yet there is a crucial distinction to be made here between these environmental tariffs and those of Donald Trump. The latter are intended to reduce trade. The former are intended to incentivise the exporter to reduce their emissions and to create a level playing field for domestic producers. The danger of a rush to exile economics is that it dismantles the rules-based system and institutions that enable mechanisms like CBAM to be implemented without risking a downward spiral of retaliation. The rules of the game matter as much as what the individual players do. The head of the World Trade Organization, Ngozi Okonjo-Iweala, argues that the natural solution is an international carbon pricing system, covering all trade, and says that the World Trade Organization is working with the United Nations, the OECD and the International Monetary Fund to explore what that would look like.[20] Yet it's hard to see such efforts ever being implemented in the hostile climate of exile economics.

Perhaps the central challenge is one of political communication. Defending open trade is difficult when the public mood has shifted into the historic grooves of a striving for self-sufficiency. Explaining why Chinese overproduction is a problem but one that should not be countered by cutting off trade, is hard. Explaining why it's important to tackle border security but maintain a degree of openness to migrants is difficult. Explaining why it's often safer to rely on food imports than to grow more produce at home is tricky. The peddlers of exile economics, on the other hand, seem to offer easy and intuitive answers.

There are, though, grounds for some hope for those convinced by the merits of openness. We began this book with the multilateral disintegration of 1933, the very depths of global economic despair and dysfunction. Yet the very next year, 1934, the Franklin Roosevelt administration signed into law the Reciprocal Trade Agreements Act. This empowered the president to negotiate tariff reduction deals with other nations, and greatly reduced the role of Congress and the influence of protectionist domestic industrial lobby groups. The new framework did not bear fruit until after 1945. But it laid the platform for the great expansion of postwar global free trade.

In Chapter Two we looked into the ancient Greek origins of 'autarky' – self-sufficiency – and discovered it was based, for ancient philosophers, on the idea that a solitary and self-sufficient life was more morally developed than a life of dependence. Yet even in that era there was a more nuanced interpretation. When the fifth-century BCE Athenian statesman Pericles spoke about the self-sufficiency of his democratic city-state he was referring to strength, not solitude. And strength was reflected in trade. 'Because of the greatness of our city the fruits of the whole earth flow in upon us; so that we enjoy the goods of other countries as freely as our own,' declared Pericles in his celebrated funeral oration for those Athenians who died during the Peloponnesian War. 'Our city is thrown open to the world and we never expel a foreigner and prevent him from seeing or learning anything of which the secret if revealed to an enemy might profit him.'[21] Under this reading, self-sufficiency moves from being one not of isolation but community, not of privation but abundance, not of closure to the world but a posture of openness – not exile economics but interconnection.

Acknowledgements

I owe a debt of gratitude to my longstanding agent Elly James of HHB Agency for chivvying me to come up with a strong idea which we could take to publishers and for giving me the motivation to persevere through the inevitable undulations of the pitching process. Thanks to Craig Templeton-Smith of Tempo & Talker who oversaw the BBC Radio 4 series *The New Age of Autarky* from which this project grew – and to Anouk Millet and Max Bower who produced the episodes. Also, my thanks go to my many excellent editors and colleagues on BBC *Newsnight* – much of the original reporting in this book was drawn from *Newsnight* 'sends' to places ranging from Newport, to Scunthorpe, to Sri Lanka! Thanks to Lindsay McCoy at BBC *Verify* for letting me take a decent chunk of time off as leave to write it up. My gratitude to Sarah Caro for initially commissioning this project while she was at Basic Books and to Joe Zigmond for picking it up with enthusiasm and for refining the concept through some imaginative and judicious editing. Thanks also to Siam Hatzaw at Basic for shepherding things over the line. I'm considerably indebted to John Springford, Jonathan Portes, Tim Lord and Ed Conway for kindly reading and commenting on some of the chapters although, of course, any errors are mine and mine alone. Finally, thanks to my wife Hattie for . . . everything. This book is dedicated to her.

Notes

Introduction

1. In the Great Depression of the early 1930s it's estimated that at least 1 million Mexicans in America – more than half of them US citizens – were deported to Mexico under the administration of the Republican president Herbert Hoover. See Francisco E. Balderrama and Raymond Rodríguez, *Decade of Betrayal: Mexican Repatriation in the 1930s*, revised edition, Albuquerque: University of New Mexico Press, 2006.
2. Quotes from a speech by Herbert Hoover given in Boston Massachusetts on 15 October 1928, https://archive.org/details/newdaycampaignspoooohoov/page/114
3. With these words President Herbert Hoover vetoed a bill passed by Congress to reduce US tariffs on 11 May 1932, https://www.presidency.ucsb.edu/documents/veto-bill-amend-the-tariff-act-1930
4. On 5 May 1930, 1,028 economists wrote to President Herbert Hoover urging him to veto a major increase in tariffs, saying, 'we are convinced that increased protective duties would be a mistake', https://econjwatch.org/file_download/162/2007-09-editorsfetter-char_issue.pdf
5. According to a telegram from the US ambassador in France to the US secretary of state on 19 January 1932, 'France probably would be prepared to undergo an economic war with the United States rather than surrender its quota policy because this policy has been extremely effective in the short time it has been in application in improving the French balance of trade', https://history.state.gov/historicaldocuments/frus1932v02/d115
6. On 19 September 1933 the US ambassador to Great Britain wrote a telegram to the US secretary of state recounting a meeting with the

British prime minister, Ramsay MacDonald, in which MacDonald said that the 'personal blow he had received in the lack of cooperation from the United States made him at one time almost despair', https://history.state.gov/historicaldocuments/frus1933v01/d565

7. This was how the Democrat president Franklin Roosevelt once described European statesmen in private according to his treasury secretary, Henry Morgenthau. See the Diary of Henry Morgenthau Jr, 9 May 1933, Farm Credit Diary, Book 9, https://www.fca.gov/template-fca/about/MorgenthauFarmCreditDiaryApril1933-Nov1933.pdf

8. This was how the League of Nations, the predecessor of the United Nations, described the events of the early 1930s. See the League of Nations' World Economic Survey 1931/32, p. 289.

9. In early 1933 a commission of experts was established by the League of Nations to set the agenda for the forthcoming World Economic Conference in London. The document they produced warned that a failure by the conference to stabilise currencies and reduce trade barriers 'threatens a world-wide adoption of ideals of national self-sufficiency which cut unmistakably athwart the lines of economic development. Such a choice would shake the whole system of international finance to its foundations, standards of living would be lowered and the social system as we know it could hardly survive.' See League of Nations, 'Monetary and Economic Conference: Draft Annotated Agenda' submitted by the Preparatory Commission of Experts, January 1933, https://deriv.nls.uk/dcn23/1916/8925/191689253.23.pdf

10. 'Let goods be homespun whenever it is reasonably and conveniently possible' was the argument of John Maynard Keynes in an essay published by the *Yale Review* in June 1933 called 'National Self-Sufficiency', https://jmaynardkeynes.ucc.ie/national-self-sufficiency.html

11. 3 May 2018, https://www.ntu.org/library/doclib/Embargoed-Economists-Letter-2018-1.pdf

12. Neville Chamberlain, House of Commons debate, 2 June 1933, *Hansard*, vol. 278, cc. 2243–71, https://api.parliament.uk/historic-hansard/commons/1933/jun/02/world-economic-conference

13. Charles Kindleberger, *The World in Depression 1929–1939*, London: Allen Lane, 1973, p. 292.

NOTES

14. Arthur W. Lewis, *Economic Survey, 1919–1939*, London: Allen & Unwin, 1949, pp. 200–1.

Chapter 1: The Creed

1. FAO/WFP Crop and Food Security Assessment Mission (CFSAM) to the Democratic Socialist Republic of Sri Lanka, World Food Programme, May 2024, https://www.wfp.org/publications/faowfp-crop-and-food-security-assessment-mission-cfsam-democratic-socialist-republic
2. Ben Chu, 'Can Sri Lanka Trade its Way Back to Prosperity?', *BBC News*, 2 February 2023, https://www.bbc.co.uk/news/business-64464220
3. Total tea production in 2021 was 300,000 tonnes but it fell to 250,000 tonnes in 2022 – a 16 per cent decline. See statistics from Sri Lanka's Tea Exports Association, https://teasrilanka.org/statistics#
4. Global Economic Prospects, World Bank, June 2024, https://www.worldbank.org/en/publication/global-economic-prospects
5. See Trump's interview at the Economic Club of Chicago on 15 October 2024, https://www.bloomberg.com/news/articles/2024-10-15/5-key-takeaways-from-trump-interview-on-tariffs-china-putin-fed
6. Office of the President of Sri Lanka, 22 April 2021, https://www.presidentsoffice.gov.lk/index.php/2021/04/22/importation-of-chemical-fertilizers-will-be-stopped-completely/
7. See Arthur Lewis, *Economic Survey 1919–1939*. Also see Alan de Bromhead, Alan Fernihough, Markus Lampe and Kevin Hjortshøj O'Rourke, 'When Britain Turned Inward: The Impact of Interwar British Protection', *American Economic Review*, 2019, 109 (2): 325–52. DOI: 10.1257/aer.20172020
8. G20 Leaders' Communiqué, G20 Argentina, 1 December 2018, https://cdn.gihub.org/umbraco/media/2568/g20-leaders-communique-12-18-argentina.pdf
9. Joseph E. Stiglitz, *Globalisation and its Discontents*, London: Penguin, 2002.
10. D. Acemoglu, D. Autor, D. Dorn, G.H. Hanson, and B. Price, 'Import Competition and the Great U.S. Employment Sag of the

NOTES

2000s' (NBER Working Paper No. 20395), 2014, National Bureau of Economic Research, https://doi.org/10.3386/w20395

11. 'The Inaugural Address', The White House, 20 January 2017, https://trumpwhitehouse.archives.gov/briefings-statements/the-inaugural-address/

12. Gordon Brown, 'The Key Lesson of Brexit Is That Globalisation Must Work for All of Britain', *Guardian*, 29 June 2016, https://www.theguardian.com/commentisfree/2016/jun/29/key-lesson-of-brexit-globalisation-must-work-for-all-of-britain

13. 'Majority of Americans Take a Dim View of Increased Trade with Other Countries', Pew Research Center, 29 July 2024, https://www.pewresearch.org/short-reads/2024/07/29/majority-of-americans-take-a-dim-view-of-increased-trade-with-other-countries/

14. David Steinberg and Yeling Tan, 'Public Responses to Foreign Protectionism: Evidence from the US–China Trade War', 2022 Working Papers 22-10, Peterson Institute for International Economics, https://www.piie.com/publications/working-papers/public-responses-foreign-protectionism-evidence-us-china-trade-war

15. 'Sentiment About Globalization Cooler Than Before the Pandemic across the World', *IPSOS*, 19 August 2021, https://www.ipsos.com/en/sentiment-about-globalization-cooler-pandemic-across-world

16. George W. Bush remarks at a Boeing plant, 17 May 2000, https://www.washingtonpost.com/wp-srv/world/foreignpolicy/bushchina.html

17. Bill Clinton speech on China Trade Bill at Johns Hopkins University, 8 March 2000, https://www.iatp.org/sites/default/files/Full_Text_of_Clintons_Speech_on_China_Trade_Bi.htm

18. 'Trump Again Raises Idea of Decoupling Economy from China', *Reuters*, 8 September 2020, https://www.reuters.com/article/world/asia-pacific/trump-again-raises-idea-of-decoupling-economy-from-china-idUSKBN25Z08T/

19. 'Remarks by National Security Advisor Jake Sullivan on Renewing American Economic Leadership at the Brookings Institution', The White House, 27 April 2023, https://www.whitehouse.gov/briefing-room/speeches-remarks/2023/04/27/remarks-by-national-security-advisor-jake-sullivan-on-renewing-american-economic-leadership-at-the-brookings-institution/

20. In 2007 China's then premier, Wen Jiabao, the second most

NOTES

powerful figure in the country, described China's growth as 'unstable, unbalanced, uncoordinated and unsustainable'. International Monetary Fund, 'IMF Survey: China's Difficult Rebalancing Act', *IMF Survey Online*, 12 September 2007, https://www.imf.org/en/News/Articles/2015/09/28/04/53/socar0912a

21. 'An Emboldened Donald Trump Puts Taiwan and Europe on Edge', *Bloomberg*, 17 July 2024, https://www.bloomberg.com/news/newsletters/2024-07-17/an-emboldened-donald-trump-puts-taiwan-and-europe-on-edge

22. Erica York, 'Trump's Tariff Proposals Would Raise Tariff Rates to Great Depression-Era Levels', Tax Foundation, 1 October 2024, https://taxfoundation.org/blog/trump-mckinley-tariffs-great-depression/

23. Robin Brooks, 'Big Changes Are Coming for Dollar and Emerging Markets', *Financial Times*, 12 November 2024, https://www.ft.com/content/c9617ae5-8b8d-450d-a45f-6e3b539225a9

24. 'Information Note on Trade in Intermediate Goods: Second Quarter 2023 WTO Statistics Division, https://www.wto.org/english/res_e/statis_e/miwi_e/info_note_2023q2_e.pdf

25. According to the OECD the US imported $2.5 trillion of goods and services in 2020, of which $1.2 trillion were intermediates. See OECD, Trade in Value Added (TiVA), 2023 edition.

26. International Study Group on Exports and Productivity, 'Exports and Productivity: Comparable Evidence for 14 Countries' (Policy Research Working Paper No. 4418), 2007, The World Bank, https://documents1.worldbank.org/curated/en/974171468143359663/pdf/wps4418.pdf

27. Veljko Fotak, Hye Seung (Grace) Lee, William L. Megginson and Jesus M. Salas, 'The Political Economy of Tariff Exemption Grants', *Journal of Financial and Quantitative Analysis*, 18 April 2023, http://dx.doi.org/10.2139/ssrn.3963039

28. See Trump's Mosinee, Wisconsin rally on 7 September 2024, when he claimed: 'We're going to be a tariff nation. It's not going to be a cost to you, it's going to be a cost to another country', https://x.com/acyn/status/1832508262316699871?s=46

29. P. Fajgelbaum and A. Khandelwal, 'The Economic Impacts of the US–China Trade War' (NBER Working Paper No. 29315), 2021, National Bureau of Economic Research, https://www.nber.org/papers/w29315

30. Kimberly A. Clausing and Mary E. Lovely, 'Why Trump's Tariff Proposals Would Harm Working Americans', Policy Brief No. 24-1, Washington, DC: Peterson Institute for International Economics, May 2024, https://www.piie.com/sites/default/files/2024-05/pb24-1.pdf
31. K.G. Abraham and M.S. Kearney, 'Explaining the Decline in the U.S. Employment-to-Population Ratio: A Review of the Evidence' (NBER Working Paper No. 24333), 2018, National Bureau of Economic Research, https://www.nber.org/system/files/working_papers/w24333/w24333.pdf#page=75
32. Lorenzo Caliendo and Fernando Parro, 'Lessons from US–China Trade Relations', *Annual Review of Economics*, 2023, 15: 513–47, https://doi.org/10.1146/annurev-economics-082222-082019
33. US Bureau of Labour Statistics, https://www.bls.gov/charts/job-openings-and-labor-turnover/opening-hire-seps-level.htm
34. Nicholas Bloom, Andre Kurmann, Kyle Handley and Philip Luck, 'The Impact of Chinese Trade on U.S. Employment: The Good, The Bad, and The Apocryphal', 2019 Meeting Papers 1433, Society for Economic Dynamics, https://red-files-public.s3.amazonaws.com/meetpapers/2019/paper_1433.pdf
35. P.D. Fajgelbaum and A.K. Khandelwal, 'Measuring the Unequal Gains from Trade' (NBER Working Paper No. 20331), 2014, National Bureau of Economic Research, https://www.nber.org/papers/w20331
36. 'America's Payoff from Engaging with World Markets since 1950 Was Almost $26 Trillion in 2022', Policy Brief, Washington, DC: Peterson Institute for International Economics, 2022, https://www.piie.com/publications/policy-briefs/americas-payoff-engaging-world-markets-1950-was-almost-26-trillion-2022
37. E. Helpman, 'Globalization and Wage Inequality' (Working Paper), 2016, Harvard University, https://scholar.harvard.edu/files/helpman/files/globalization_and_wage_inequality_120216_final_for_wp.pdf
38. Jagdish Bhagwati and T.N. Srinivasan, 'Trade and Poverty in the Poor Countries', *American Economic Review*, 2002, 92 (2): 180–3, DOI: 10.1257/000282802320189212
39. 'Could T-shirts Be the Way to Industrialise an African Nation?', *Financial Times*, 29 August 2024, https://www.ft.com/content/92b4f84d-229d-405b-85ec-7869529b7633

NOTES

40. Richard Baldwin, *The Globotics Upheaval: Globalization, Robotics, and the Future of Work*, London: Weidenfeld & Nicolson, 2019.
41. World Bank Data: Poverty Headcount Ratio at $1.90 a Day, World Bank, accessed 29 August 2024, https://data.worldbank.org/indicator/SI.POV.DDAY?locations=1W&start=1984&view=chart
42. P. Brenton and M. Maliszewska, 'Reshaping Global Value Chains in Light of COVID-19: Implications for Trade and Poverty Reduction in Developing Countries', World Bank, 2022, https://hdl.handle.net/10986/37032
43. Hunger and Food Insecurity, Food and Agriculture Organization of the United Nations, accessed 19 August 2024, https://www.fao.org/hunger/en/
44. International Monetary Fund, 'Geo-economic Fragmentation and the Future of Multilateralism' (Staff Discussion Note No. SDN/23/01), International Monetary Fund, 2023, https://www.imf.org/en/Publications/Staff-Discussion-Notes/Issues/2023/01/11/Geo-Economic-Fragmentation-and-the-Future-of-Multilateralism-527266?cid=bl-com-SDNEA2023001
45. The OECD model does not account for dynamic effects of lower trade connections on productivity growth via lower competition and investment, which would be expected to increase the overall losses. C. Arriola et al. (2023), 'Trade and Economic Impact of the COVID-19 Pandemic on the OECD Area', OECD iLibrary, July 2023, https://www.oecd-ilibrary.org/docserver/3e4b7ecf-en.pdf?expires=1724803293&id=id&accname=guest&checksum=278C64062A9470AC1B06163F449B514F
46. 'Statement from President Joe Biden on Historic Investment to Ensure Future of Auto Industry Is Made in America', The White House, 11 July 2024, https://www.whitehouse.gov/briefing-room/statements-releases/2024/07/11/statement-from-president-joe-biden-on-historic-investment-to-ensure-future-of-auto-industry-is-made-in-america/
47. 'Statement by President von der Leyen on the Inclusion of the Social Climate Fund in the Multiannual Financial Framework', European Commission, 28 August 2024, https://ec.europa.eu/commission/presscorner/detail/en/statement_24_3871; 'A Lift-Off Decade for India: How Modi Plans to Make Country a Global Manufacturing Powerhouse', *Economic Times*, 7 September 2024, https://economictimes.indiatimes.com/news/india/a-lift-

off-decade-for-india-how-modi-plans-to-make-country-a-global-manufacturing-powerhouse/articleshow/112974621.cms?from=mdr
48. 'What Will Happen If Donald Trump Wins the US Election 2024?', *The Times*, 25 April 2024, https://www.thetimes.com/world/us-world/article/what-will-happen-donald-trump-president-win-us-election-2024-xvc2qc0bv
49. 'Trump Would Not Weaken the Dollar, Says Adviser Scott Bessent', *Financial Times*, 13 October 2024, https://www.ft.com/content/fa08cc45-e6d1-4e19-b49b-047c5a23ca39
50. Rachel Reeves, Mais Lecture, 20 September 2023, https://labour.org.uk/updates/press-releases/rachel-reeves-mais-lecture/
51. Emmanuel Macron, Sorbonne speech, 25 April 2024, https://www.elysee.fr/en/emmanuel-macron/2024/04/24/europe-speech
52. See the calculations of Global Trade Alert, https://www.globaltradealert.org/reports/54
53. 'Global Trade Expected to Shrink by Nearly 5% in 2023 amid Geopolitical Strains and Shifting Trade', UNCTAD, 6 June 2023, https://unctad.org/news/global-trade-expected-shrink-nearly-5-2023-amid-geopolitical-strains-and-shifting-trade
54. 'Chinese Sanctions Hit US Drone Maker Supplying Ukraine', *Financial Times*, 31 October 2024, https://www.ft.com/content/b1104594-5da7-4b9a-b635-e7a80ab68fad
55. See Michael Pettis and Matthew Klein, *Trade Wars Are Class Wars: How Rising Inequality Distorts the Global Economy and Threatens International Peace*, New Haven: Yale University Press, 2020.
56. S.D. Cohen, 'The Route to Japan's Voluntary Export Restraints on Automobiles: An Analysis of the U.S. Government's Decision-making Process in 1981' (Working Paper No. 20), School of International Service, American University, https://nsarchive2.gwu.edu/japan/scohenwp.htm
57. Michael Pettis, 'The Case for Capital Controls to Rebalance Trade', Carnegie Endowment for International Peace, 14 February 2024, https://carnegieendowment.org/china-financial-markets/2024/02/can-trade-intervention-lead-to-freer-trade?lang=en
58. E. Boz, C. Casas, G. Georgiadis, G. Gopinath, H. Le Mezo, A. Mehl and T. Nguyen, 'Patterns of Invoicing Currency in Global Trade: New Evidence', *Journal of International Economics*, 2022, 135, 103–20, https://doi.org/10.1016/j.jinteco.2022.103120

NOTES

59. Adam Tooze, Chartbook 282, Substack, 14 May 2024, https://adamtooze.substack.com/p/chartbook-283-trump-trade-capital
60. Donald J. Trump @realDonaldTrump, 'When a country (USA) is losing many billions of dollars on trade with virtually every country it does business with, trade wars are good, and easy to win. Example, when we are down $100 billion with a certain country and they get cute, don't trade anymore-we win big. It's easy!', X, 2 March 2018, https://x.com/realDonaldTrump/status/969525362580484098.
61. Kristalina Georgieva, 'Price of Fragmentation: Global Economy in Shock', *Foreign Affairs*, 10 August 2024, https://www.foreignaffairs.com/world/price-fragmentation-global-economy-shock
62. 'WTO Chief Warns of Free-for-All Under Trump's Tariff Hike Plan', *Bloomberg*, 16 April 2024, https://www.bloomberg.com/news/articles/2024-04-16/wto-chief-warns-of-free-for-all-under-trump-s-tariff-hike-plan

Chapter 2: Origins

1. Plutarch, *Lives*, Volume VII, translation by Bernadotte Perrin, Cambridge, Mass. And London: Harvard University Press, 1958, p. 259, https://archive.org/details/liveswithenglishooplutuoft/page/258/mode/2up?q=diogenes
2. 'The partnership finally composed of several villages is the city-state; it has at last attained the limit of virtually complete self-sufficiency, and thus, while it comes into existence for the sake of life, it exists for the good life . . . And self-sufficiency is an end, and a chief good. From these things therefore it is clear that the city-state is a natural growth, and that man is by nature a political animal': Aristotle, *The Politics*, 1252b and 1.1253a, translated by H. Rackham, 1944, https://www.perseus.tufts.edu/hopper/text?doc=Perseus%3Atext%3A1999.01.0057%3Abook%3D1%3Asection%3D1252b
3. Interview with author, September 2022.
4. Peter Jones, 'How to Be Self-Sufficient', *Spectator*, 21 March 2022, https://www.spectator.co.uk/article/how-to-be-self-sufficient/
5. Thomas Aquinas, *De regno, ad regem Cypri*, Chapter 3, translated by Gerald B. Phelan, https://isidore.co/aquinas/DeRegno.htm

6. Daniel Defoe, *Robinson Crusoe* (orig. 1719), London: Penguin, 2019, Chapter 4.
7. Jean-Jacques Rousseau, *A Discourse on the Origin of Inequality* (orig. 1755), translation by G.D.H. Cole, Kansas: Digireads, 2006.
8. Jean-Jacques Rousseau, 'Considerations on the Government of Poland and on its Proposed Reformation', April 1772, Constitution Society, http://www.constitution.org/jjr/poland.htm, accessed 3 January 2008, https://www.files.ethz.ch/isn/125482/5016_Rousseau_Considerations_on_the_Government_of_Poland.pdf
9. Jean-Jacques Rousseau, 'Constitutional Project for Corsica', 1765, https://www.constitution.org/2-Authors/jjr/corsica.htm?utm_content=cmp-true
10. Thomas Carlyle, *The Works of Thomas Carlyle*, Vol. 4, New York: Charles Scribner's Sons, 1903, p. 272, https://archive.org/details/worksofthomascar29carl/page/272/mode/2up
11. John Hoyt Williams, 'Paraguayan Isolation under Dr. Francia: A Re-evaluation', *Hispanic American Historical Review*, 1 February 1972, vol. 52, no. 1, pp. 102–22.
12. Mario Pastore, 'Trade Contraction and Economic Regression: The Paraguayan Economy under Francia, 1814–1840', 1994, https://mpra.ub.uni-muenchen.de/27353/1/MPRA_paper_27353.pdf
13. Montesquieu, *Spirit of Laws* (orig. 1750), London: J. Nourse, 1752, Book 20, Chapters 1–8, translated by Thomas Nugent, https://press-pubs.uchicago.edu/founders/documents/v1ch4s2.html
14. 'The commercial spirit cannot co-exist with war, and sooner or later it takes possession of every nation . . . States find themselves compelled – not, it is true, exactly from motives of morality – to further the noble end of peace and to avert war': Immanuel Kant. *Perpetual Peace*, translated by Campbell Smith, George Allen & Unwin Ltd, London, 1917, p. 157, https://oll-resources.s3.us-east-2.amazonaws.com/oll3/store/titles/357/0075_Bk.pdf
15. Isaac Nakhimovsky, *The Closed Commercial State: Perpetual Peace and Commercial Society from Rousseau to Fichte*, Princeton and Oxford: Princeton University Press, 2011, p. 75.
16. Ibid., p. 83.
17. Theresa May, Conservative Party Conference Speech, 5 October 2016, https://www.independent.co.uk/news/uk/politics/

theresa-may-speech-tory-conference-2016-in-full-
transcript-a7346171.html
18. 'It is the purpose of the state first to give to each his own, first to
 establish him in his property, and then to protect him in it':
 Nakhimovsky, *The Closed Commercial State*, p. 158.
19. See John King Faribank and Merle Goldman, *China: A New History*,
 Cambridge, Mass. and London: Harvard University Press, 2006,
 p. 138. See also David Landes, *The Wealth and Poverty of Nations*,
 New York And London: W.W. Norton, 1998, p. 94.
20. Edward L. Dreyer, *Zheng He: China and the Oceans in the Early Ming
 Dynasty, 1405 1433*, New York: Longman, 2006. Also see Louis
 Levathes, *When China Ruled the Seas*, New York and Oxford: Oxford
 University Press, 1997.
21. David J. Lu, ed., *Japan: A Documentary History: The Dawn of History to
 the Late Tokugawa Period*, New York And London: M.E. Sharpe, 1997.
22. Kenichi Ohno, 'Meiji Japan: Progressive Learning of Western
 Technology', in Arkebe Oqubay and Kenichi Ohno, eds, *How
 Nations Learn: Technological Learning, Industrial Policy, and Catch-Up*,
 Oxford: Oxford University Press, 2019; online edn, Oxford
 Academic, 22 August 2019.
23. E. Backhouse and J.O.P. Bland, *Annals and Memoirs of the Court of
 Peking*, Boston: Houghton Mifflin, 1914, pp. 322–31.
24. Joanna Waley-Cohen, *The Sextants of Beijing*, New York and
 London: W.W. Norton, 1999.
25. M. Gandhi, *Harijan*, 10 November 1946, accessed from The
 Collected Works of Mahatma Gandhi, https://www.mkgandhi.org/
 cwmg.php
26. M. Gandhi, *Harijan*, 18 July 1946, accessed from The Collected
 Works of Mahatma Gandhi, https://www.mkgandhi.org/cwmg.php
27. M. Gandhi, *Khadi: Why and How*, Ahmedabad: Navajivan Publishing
 House, 1959, p. 166, https://www.gandhiashramsevagram.org/voice-
 of-truth/gandhiji-on-self-sufficiency.php
28. M. Gandhi, *The Collected Works of Mahatma Gandhi*, New Delhi:
 Government of India, 1971, p. 262.
29. 'Swadeshi is that spirit in us which restricts us to the use and
 service of our immediate surroundings to the exclusion of the more
 remote.' Address delivered before the Missionary Conference,

Madras, 14 February 1916. In *Speeches and Writings of M.K. Gandhi*, Madras: G.A. Nateson & Co, 1922, https://www.mkgandhi.org/ebks/speeches&writingsofmg.pdf

30. See Jawaharlal Nehru, *The Discovery of India*, Delhi: Oxford University Press, 1994, p. 298.
31. David Clingingsmith and Jeffrey G. Williamson, 'India's Deindustrialization in the 18th and 19th Centuries', Harvard University, August 2005, https://www.tcd.ie/Economics/staff/orourkek/Istanbul/JGWGEHNIndianDeind.pdf
32. Some historians suspect that the British protective tariffs against Indian imports might have slowed the British industrialisation of textile production. See Indrajit Ray, 'Identifying the Woes of the Cotton Textile Industry in Bengal: Tales of the Nineteenth Century', *Economic History Review*, vol. 62, no. 4, November 2009, pp. 857–92. Also see 'Tariff Protection of British Cotton 1774–1820s', *Pseudoerasmus*, 19 December 2016, available at: https://pseudoerasmus.com/2016/12/19/calico/
33. See for example Walter Rodney, *How Europe Underdeveloped Africa*, London: Bogle-L'Ouverture Publications, 1973. And see Frantz Fanon, *Les Damnés de la Terre*, Paris: Éditions Maspero, 1961.
34. Samir Amin, *Delinking: Towards a Polycentric World*, London: Zed Books, 1990.
35. Julius Nyerere, The Arusha Declaration, 5 February 1967.
36. Julius Nyerere, *Freedom and Socialism*, Oxford: Oxford University Press, 1968, p. 319, https://archive.org/details/freedomsocialismoooonyer/page/n7/mode/2up
37. Ibid., p. 321.
38. John Maynard Keynes, 'National Self-Sufficiency', *The Yale Review*, vol. 22, no. 4, June 1933, pp. 755–69, https://jmaynardkeynes.ucc.ie/national-self-sufficiency.html
39. Charles Fourier, *The Theory of the Four Movements*, translated by Ian Patterson, Cambridge: Cambridge University Press, 1996, p. 50, https://ia800702.us.archive.org/14/items/TheTheoryOfTheFourMovementsByCharlesFourier/The%20Theory%20of%20the%20Four%20Movements%20by%20Charles%20Fourier.pdf
40. Jonathan Beecher, *Charles Fourier: The Visionary and his World*, Los Angeles: University of California Press, 1986, p. 307.

41. Ibid., p. 264.
42. Ibid., p. 287.
43. Ibid., p. 242.
44. *Handbook of Texas*, La Réunion, https://www.tshaonline.org/handbook/entries/la-reunion
45. Jerry Mander and Edward Goldsmith, eds, *The Case against the Global Economy*, London: Routledge, 2001, p. 13, https://www.taylorfrancis.com/books/edit/10.4324/9781315071787/case-global-economy-edward-goldsmith-jerry-mander
46. Robert Lefevre, *A Way to Be Free: The Autobiography, Volume 1*, Culver City, CA: Pulpess, 1999, p. 117.
47. Robert Lefevre, 'Autarchy', *Rampart Journal of Individualist Thought*, vol. 2, no. 2, summer 1966, https://fair-use.org/rampart-journal/1966/06/autarchy.php
48. Mark Ames, 'Charles Koch's Brain', Not Safe for Work Corporation, 2013, https://archive.org/details/pdfy-qDYkCJZp968ltoLM
49. Free Society Project (FSP), available at: https://www.fsp.org/
50. BBC interview, 21 October 2022.
51. 'The Last Living Kibbutz', *Jerusalem Post*, 21 October 2022, https://www.jpost.com/magazine/the-last-living-kibbutz-378839
52. *Starter Guide to Intentional Communities*, International Communities, October 2021, available at: https://www.ic.org/wp-content/uploads/2021/10/Starter-Guide-to-Intentional-Communities.pdf
53. Adolf Hitler, *Mein Kampf*, translated by J. Murphy, London: Hurst and Blackett, 1942, Chapter IV, available at: https://gutenberg.net.au/ebooks02/0200601.txt
54. United States Holocaust Memorial Museum (USHMM), 'Lebensraum', *Encyclopedia of the Holocaust*, available at: https://encyclopedia.ushmm.org/content/en/article/lebensraum
55. Adolf Hitler, Nuremberg Speech, 12 September 1936, in *The Speeches of Adolf Hitler 1921-1941*, available at: https://identityhunters.files.wordpress.com/2017/07/the-speeches-of-adolf-hitler-1921-1941.pdf
56. The official Soviet economics newspaper, *Za Industrializatsiiu* ('For Industry'), summed up the logic: 'Economic independence means that the most important branches of the national economy are assured domestic raw materials and installations in a degree which makes them independent from individual nations of the capitalist

world [and] the impossibility of a country or a group of countries creating a monopoly situation in this or another mutual relations with the USSR', 15 February 1932, quoted in M.R. Dohan, 'The Economic Origins of Soviet Autarky 1927/28–1934', *Slavic Review*, vol. 35, no. 4, December 1976, pp. 603–35, doi:10.2307/2495654

57. See M. Fouquin and J. Hugot, 'Two Centuries of Bilateral Trade and Gravity Data: 1827–2014', 2016, CEPII Working Paper, N°2016-14, via Our World in Data, https://ourworldindata.org/grapher/merchandise-exports-gdp-cepii?time=1922..1960&country=R US~DE

58. Mao Zedong, speech in Shensi-Kansu-Ningsia Border Region, 10 January 1945, https://www.marxists.org/reference/archive/mao/selected-works/volume-3/mswv3_22.htm

59. Kim Il Sung, 'Talk to Instructors and Senior Officials of the Central Committee of the Workers Party of Korea', 17 December 1956, https://www.marxists.org/archive/kim-il-sung/cw/10.pdf

60. C. Hale, 'Multifunctional Juche: A Study of the Changing Dynamic Between Juche and the State Constitution in North Korea', *Korea Journal*, vol. 42, no. 3, autumn 2002, pp. 283–308, https://www.ekoreajournal.net/issue/view_pop3206.html

61. George Washington, 'First Annual Address to Congress, 8 January 1790', available at the American Presidency Project, https://www.presidency.ucsb.edu/documents/first-annual-address-congress-0

62. See Alexander Hamilton, 'Report on the Subject of Manufactures', 5 December 1791, Philadelphia, available at US National Archives, https://founders.archives.gov/documents/Hamilton/01-10-02-0001-0007

63. 'The system of protection, inasmuch as it forms the only means of placing those nations which are far behind in civilisation on equal terms with the one predominating nation ... appears to be the most efficient means of furthering the final union of nations, and hence also of promoting true freedom of trade': Friedrich List, *The National System of Political Economy*, translated by Sampson Lloyd, London, New York, Bombay and Calcutta: Longmans, Green & Co., 1909, https://oll.libertyfund.org/titles/lloyd-the-national-system-of-political-economy

64. Though it's worth noting that the British Whig historian Thomas

Babington Macaulay wryly lamented in 1824 that 'free trade, one of the greatest blessings which a government can confer on a people, is in almost every country unpopular'. *The Miscellaneous Writings of Lord Macaulay, vol. 1*, London: Longman, Green, Longman, and Roberts, 1860

65. There is a vigorous debate among economists over whether tariffs were a help or a hindrance to growth in this era. See D.A. Irwin, 'Interpreting the Tariff-Growth Correlation of the Late Nineteenth Century', National Bureau of Economic Research, 2002, https://www.nber.org/system/files/working_papers/w8739/w8739.pdf. Also see K.H. O'Rourke, 'Tariffs and Growth in the Late 19th Century', *The Economic Journal*, vol. 110, no. 463, April 2000, pp. 456–83.

66. S.H. Zebel, 'Joseph Chamberlain and the Genesis of Tariff Reform', *Journal of British Studies*, vol. 7, no. 1, 1967, pp. 131–57, http://www.jstor.org/stable/175383

67. E.H.H. Green, *The Crisis of Conservatism: The Politics, Economics and Ideology of the British Conservative Party, 1880–1914*, London: Routledge, 1997, p. 3.

68. J. Sullivan, 'Remarks by National Security Advisor Jake Sullivan on Renewing American Economic Leadership at the Brookings Institution', 27 April 2023, https://www.whitehouse.gov/briefing-room/speeches-remarks/2023/04/27/remarks-by-national-security-advisor-jake-sullivan-on-renewing-american-economic-leadership-at-the-brookings-institution/

69. A. Prokop, 'Curtis Yarvin Wants American Democracy Toppled. He Has Some Prominent Republican Fans', *Vox*, 24 October 2022, available at: https://www.vox.com/policy-and-politics/23373795/curtis-yarvin-neoreaction-redpill-moldbug

70. 'RIP Globalism, Dead of Coronavirus', *The American Mind*, 1 February 2020, https://americanmind.org/salvo/rip-globalism-dead-of-coronavirus/

71. Richard Potts et al., 'Environmental Dynamics during the Onset of the Middle Stone Age in Eastern Africa', *Science*, vol. 360, 2018, pp. 86–90.

72. See Joseph Henrich, *The Secret of our Success*, Princeton And Oxford: Princeton University Press, 2016.

73. A.G. Frank and B.K. Gills, *The World System: Five Hundred Years or Five Thousand?*, London and New York: Routledge, 1993.

NOTES

Chapter 3: Food

1. 'Tackling the Global Food Crisis: Impact, Policy Response, and the Role of the IMF', *IMF Notes*, 27 September 2022, https://www.imf.org/en/Publications/IMF-Notes/Issues/2022/09/27/Tackling-the-Global-Food-Crisis-Impact-Policy-Response-and-the-Role-of-the-IMF-523919?cid=bl-com-INSEA2022004
2. 'Security Council: 15032nd Meeting (AM)', Press Release, 26 October 2022, https://press.un.org/en/2022/sc15032.doc.htm
3. 'Food Is Part of Our National Security, Says Former MI5 Director General', *NFUonline*, 23 March 2023, https://www.nfuonline.com/updates-and-information/food-is-part-of-our-national-security-says-former-mi5-director-general/
4. Emmanuel Macron, Speech at the Sorbonne, 26 April 2024, https://www.elysee.fr/en/emmanuel-macron/2024/04/24/europe-speech
5. FAOSTAT: Food Security, https://www.fao.org/faostat/en/#data/FS
6. Import Dependence Ratio, Food Security Portal, facilitated by IFPRI, https://www.foodsecurityportal.org/node/2505/#_-import-dependence-ratio
7. 'Japan's Self-Sufficiency Ratio of Food', Ministry of Agriculture, Forestry and Fisheries of Japan, 2022, https://www.maff.go.jp/j/zyukyu/zikyu_ritu/attach/pdf/panfu1-12.pdf
8. UK Food Security Index 2024, UK Government, 2024, https://www.gov.uk/government/publications/uk-food-security-index-2024/uk-food-security-index-2024#:~=The%20production%20to%20supply%20ratio,roughly%2040%25%20of%20its%20food
9. Agricultural Production, *Our World In Data*, https://ourworldindata.org/agricultural-production
10. P. Kinnunen, J.H.A. Guillaume, M. Taka et al., 'Local Food Crop Production Can Fulfil Demand for Less Than One-Third of the Population', *Nature Food*, no. 1, 2020, pp. 229–37, https://doi.org/10.1038/s43016-020-0060-7
11. Christopher Bren d'Amour and Weston Anderson, 'International Trade and the Stability of Food Supplies in the Global South', *Environmental Research Letters*, vol. 15, no. 7, 2020, article 074005, https://doi.org/10.1088/1748-9326/ab832f
12. P. D'Odorico, J.A. Carr, F. Laio, L. Ridolfi and S. Vandoni, 'Feeding

Humanity through Global Food Trade', *Earth's Future*, 12 August 2014, https://doi.org/10.1002/2014EF000250

13. M. Fader, D. Gerten, M. Krause, W. Lucht and W. Cramer, 'Spatial Decoupling of Agricultural Production and Consumption: Quantifying Dependences of Countries on Food Imports due to Domestic Land and Water Constraints', *Environmental Research Letters*, vol. 8, no. 1, 2013, 014046, https://doi.org/10.1088/1748-9326/8/1/014046

14. OECD, 'Regional Contributions to Food Demand Growth, 2012–21 and 2022–31', 2023, OECD iLibrary, https://www.oecd-ilibrary.org/agriculture-and-food/regional-contributions-to-food-demand-growth-2012-21-and-2022-31_f10ab8de-en

15. 'Why Soyabeans Are the Crop of the Century', *Financial Times*, 5 June 2017, https://www.ft.com/content/35af007e-49f6-11e7-919a-1e14ce4af89b

16. Brian Lander and Thomas David DuBois, 'A History of Soy in China: From Weedy Bean to Global Commodity', *The Age of the Soybean: An Environmental History of Soy During the Great Acceleration*, edited by Claiton Marcio da Silva and Claudio de Majo, pp. 29–47, White Horse Press, 2022, http://www.jstor.org/stable/j.ctv309h1fx.8

17. Victoria Romanova, 'The Tiny Island of Russian Jews', *Jewish Communities of China*, 19 March 2012, https://www.jewsofchina.org/the-tiny-island-of-russian-jews

18. Ines Prodöhl, *Globalizing the Soybean: Fat, Feed, and Sometimes Food, c. 1900–1950*, Oxford And New York: Routledge, 2023, https://library.oapen.org/bitstream/id/22e39439-1cbe-45e5-8f23-f668c422738a/9781000877342.pdf

19. Soybean Car, The Henry Ford Museum, https://www.thehenryford.org/collections-and-research/digital-resources/popular-topics/soy-bean-car/

20. Carroll W. Pursell, 'The Farm Chemurgic Council and the United States Department of Agriculture, 1935–1939', *Isis*, vol. 60, no. 3, 1969, pp. 307–17, http://www.jstor.org/stable/229485

21. 'Meat Production by Type', *Our World in Data*, https://ourworldindata.org/meat-production

22. Niall Ferguson and Moritz Schularick, '"Chimerica" and the Global Asset Market Boom', *International Finance*, vol. 10, no. 1, December 2007, pp. 1–25, https://doi.org/10.1111/j.1468-2362.2007.00210.x

23. Cassiano Rocha, Ryan Nehring and Sandro Dutra e Silva, 'Soy without Borders: The Transnational Dynamics of Commodity Frontiers In South America (1971–2019)', *Global Environment*, vol. 15, 2022, pp. 423–55, 10.3197/ge.2022.150301
24. Claiton Marcio da Silva and Claudio de Majo, eds, *The Age of the Soybean: An Environmental History of Soy During the Great Acceleration*, Winwick: White Horse Press, 2022, http://www.jstor.org/stable/j.ctv309h1fx
25. UK Food Security Index 2024, UK Government, 2024, https://www.gov.uk/government/publications/uk-food-security-index-2024/uk-food-security-index-2024#:~=The%20production%20to%20supply%20ratio,roughly%2040%25%20of%20its%20food
26. Prodöhl, *Globalizing the Soybean*.
27. 'Rapid Response Report: Soy', Mighty Earth, March 2024, https://mightyearth.org/wp-content/uploads/2024/03/Mighty-Earth_Rapid-Response-Report-2_Soy_March2024.pdf
28. Xi Jinping, Speech at the Central Rural Work Conference, 23–24 December 2013, https://www.chinastory.cn/ywdbk/english/v1/detail/20190719/10127000004274156351738458029083 7_1.html
29. Wendy Wu, 'China Food Security: Beijing Doubles Down on Domestic Soybean Push amid Self-Sufficiency Drive', *South China Morning Post*, 9 May 2022, https://www.scmp.com/economy/china-economy/article/3177051/china-food-security-beijing-doubles-down-domestic-soybean
30. 'Arable Land (% of Land Area)', World Bank, https://data.worldbank.org/indicator/AG.LND.ARBL.ZS?locations=CN-US
31. H. Yao, X. Zuo, D. Zuo, H. Lin, X. Huang and C. Zang, 'Study on Soybean Potential Productivity and Food Security in China under the Influence of COVID-19 Outbreak', *Geoscience Frontiers*, 2020, https://doi.org/10.1016/j.geosus.2020.06.002
32. Rishi Sunak, X (formerly Twitter), 10 March 2024, https://x.com/RishiSunak/status/1803018993118101771
33. P. D'Odorico, K.F. Davis, L. Rosa, J.A. Carr, D. Chiarelli, J. Dell'Angelo et al., 'The Global Food-Energy-Water Nexus', *Reviews of Geophysics*, vol. 56, 2018, pp. 456–531, https://doi.org/10.1029/2017RG000591
34. Henry Dimbleby, National Food Strategy, July 2021, https://www.nationalfoodstrategy.org/

35. Rishi Sunak, Speech on Net Zero, 20 September 2023, https://www.gov.uk/government/speeches/pm-speech-on-net-zero-20-september-2023
36. UK Diet Trends: Stats & Facts, *Finder*, accessed 29 August 2024, https://www.finder.com/uk/stats-facts/uk-diet-trends
37. 'Land Use for Different Foods', *Our World in Data*, https://ourworldindata.org/grapher/land-use-protein-poore
38. Statista Global Consumer Survey, April 2018 to September 2022, https://www.statista.com/chart/28584/gcs-vegetarianism-countries-timeline/
39. Food Security Index, Economist Impact, 2024, https://impact.economist.com/sustainability/project/food-security-index
40. The government in Tokyo, rightly or wrongly, regards the situation very differently. Having been shocked by the spike in global food prices in the wake of Russia's invasion of Ukraine in 2022 and also developing a growing appreciation of the potential knock-on impacts of Chinese aggression towards Taiwan on global supply chains, Tokyo, like Beijing, is now trying to increase domestic production in everything from wheat to soybeans.
41. 'Global Trade Explorer: What Are the Most Important Trade Corridors?', McKinsey & Company, 2022, https://www.mckinsey.com/mgi/our-research/global-trade-explorer-what-are-the-most-important-trade-corridors?sector=06m&toggle=e&year=2022&sub-sector=T6M
42. World Food Programme, 2024, https://www.wfp.org/countries/ukraine#:~=Cash%20assistance%20gives%20people%20the,million%20people%20since%20April%202022
43. 'Agricultural Employment (% of Total Employment)', World Bank, https://data.worldbank.org/indicator/SL.AGR.EMPL.ZS?locations=KE-ZM-MU
44. 'LDCs and Multilateral Trade: Key Issues and Challenges', World Trade Organization, 3 November 2023, https://www.wto.org/library/events/event_resources/devel_03112023l0/ldc_and_multilateral_trade_digital.pdf
45. Xi Jinping, Speech at Central Rural Work Conference, 23-24 December 2013, https://www.chinastory.cn/ywdbk/english/v1/detail/20190719/1012700000042741563517384580290837_1.html

NOTES

Chapter 4: Energy

1. 'Uniper Has Received Gazprom's Force Majeure Letter on Gas Supplies', *Reuters*, 18 July 2022, https://www.reuters.com/article/idUSL8N2YZ3VA/
2. 'Nord Stream by Numbers', Nord Stream, 28 November 2013, https://www.nord-stream.com/download/file/documents/pdf/en/2013/11/nord-stream-by-the-numbers_177_20131128.pdf
3. Nord Stream, 7 February 2022, https://www.nord-stream.com/press-info/press-releases/the-nord-stream-pipeline-transported-a-volume-of-592-billion-cubic-metres-of-natural-gas-in-2021-522/
4. European Council, 'Where Does the EU's Gas Come From?', Consilium.europa.eu, accessed 31 December 2024, https://www.consilium.europa.eu/en/infographics/eu-gas-supply/
5. 'Pipeline Politics between Europe and Russia: A Historical Review from the Cold War to the Post-Cold War', *The Korean Journal of International Studies*, vol. 14, no. 1, pp. 105–29, https://doi.org/10.14731/kjis.2016.4.14.1.105
6. 'USSR–Western Europe: Implications of the Siberia-to-Europe Gas Pipeline', CIA report, March 1981, https://www.cia.gov/readingroom/docs/DOC_0000500594.pdf
7. 'Europe's Search for Energy amid a War Recalls Reagan's 1980s Battle', *New York Times*, 23 March 2022, https://www.nytimes.com/2022/03/23/climate/europe-russia-gas-reagan.html
8. Wes Vernon, 'The Inside Story of the Soviet Downfall', *RenewAmerica*, 23 April 2007, https://web.archive.org/web/20110719170642/http://www.renewamerica.com/columns/vernon/070423
9. 'The Ghost of Blinken Past', *Foreign Policy*, 3 December 2020, https://foreignpolicy.com/2020/12/03/blinken-secretary-state-alliances-nato-ally-versus-ally/
10. In July 2024 German state prosecutors issued an arrest warrant for a Ukrainian diving instructor in relation to the Nord Stream sabotage but in the summer of 2024 there was still no confirmation of who ordered it. 'German Arrest Warrant over Nord Stream Blast Mystery', *BBC News*, 14 August 2024, https://www.bbc.co.uk/news/articles/cnvyz1472rpo
11. 'Don't Heat the Pool, Germans Told as Putin's Gas Crisis Bites',

NOTES

The Times, 22 July 2022, https://www.thetimes.com/world/europe/article/don-t-heat-the-pool-germans-told-as-putin-s-gas-crisis-bites-q6dsfd3x8

12. 'Gas Crisis Hits Dutch Greenhouses', *Reuters*, 8 September 2022, https://www.reuters.com/world/europe/no-tulips-amsterdam-gas-crisis-hits-dutch-greenhouses-2022-09-07/

13. 'REPowerEU: Joint European Action for More Affordable, Secure and Sustainable Energy', European Commission, 8 March 2022, https://ec.europa.eu/commission/presscorner/detail/en/ip_22_1511

14. 'Commission Staff Working Document: Implementing the REPowerEU Action Plan', SWD(2022) 230 final, Brussels, 18 May 2022, https://eur-lex.europa.eu/legal-content/EN/TXT/PDF/?uri=CELEX:52022SC0230&from=EN

15. 'Statement by President von der Leyen on Energy', European Commission, 7 September 2022, https://ec.europa.eu/commission/presscorner/detail/en/speech_22_5389

16. 'Germany Mulls Extending Coal Phaseout to Wean Off Russian Gas', *Bloomberg*, 28 February 2022, https://www.bloomberg.com/news/articles/2022-02-28/germany-mulls-extending-coal-phaseout-to-wean-off-russian-gas

17. 'Germany Aims to Get 100% Energy from Renewable Sources by 2035', *Reuters*, 28 February 2022, https://www.reuters.com/business/sustainable-business/germany-aims-get-100-energy-renewable-sources-by-2035-2022-02-28/

18. BBC Newsnight interview, 21 September 2022.

19. Liz Truss, 'Bills Are High and People Are Scared But Trust Me – the Government Is on your Side', *Sun*, 30 October 2022, https://www.thesun.co.uk/news/19972195/liz-truss-bills-government-on-your-side/

20. 'UK Labour Party Pledges to Set Up Public Energy Company If Elected,' *Reuters*, 27 September 2022, https://www.reuters.com/world/uk/uk-labour-party-pledges-set-up-public-energy-company-if-elected-2022-09-27/

21. 'U.S. Energy Facts: Imports and Exports', EIA, https://www.eia.gov/energyexplained/us-energy-facts/imports-and-exports.php

22. In August 2022 European gas prices peaked at $70 per million British thermal units compared to $8.8 in the US.

23. 'Remarks by President Biden on Actions to Strengthen Energy Security and Lower Costs', White House, 19 October 2022, https://www.whitehouse.gov/briefing-room/speeches-remarks/2022/10/19/remarks-by-president-biden-on-actions-to-strengthen-energy-security-and-lower-costs/
24. US Secretary of Energy Jennifer M. Granholm, 24 August 2023, https://www.energy.gov/articles/us-department-energy-projects-strong-growth-us-wind-power-sector
25. 'Excerpts from the Science and Technology Section of the Prime Minister's 76th Independence Day Speech', Public Services Agency, 15 August 2022, https://www.psa.gov.in/article/excerpts-science-and-technology-prime-ministers-76th-independence-day-speech/4035
26. 'China's Stronger Ability to Ensure Energy, Food Security Injects Confidence to World', *Global Times*, 17 October 2022, https://www.globaltimes.cn/page/202210/1277295.shtml
27. 'Full Text of Xi Jinping's Speech at China's 20th Party Congress', *Bloomberg*, 18 October 2022, https://www.bloomberg.com/news/articles/2022-10-18/full-text-of-xi-jinping-s-speech-at-china-20th-party-congress-2022
28. In 2022 crude petroleum made up 6.1 per cent of the value of global trade, refined petroleum 4.6 per cent, petroleum gas 3.5 per cent and coal briquettes 1.2 per cent, according to the Organisation of Economics Complexity, https://oec.world/en/profile/world/wld
29. 'Germany Mulls Extending Coal Phaseout to Wean Off Russian Gas', *Bloomberg*, 28 February, 2022, https://www.bloomberg.com/news/articles/2022-02-28/germany-mulls-extending-coal-phaseout-to-wean-off-russian-gas..
30. Kennedy Maize, 'Sunburned: The Solyndra Story', Medium, 2 June 2014, https://medium.com/@kennedymaize/sunburned-18e9d17d238
31. In September 2011 the FBI joined the US Department of Energy's investigation into Solyndra. In 2015 the Department of Justice decided to not pursue criminal prosecution of Solyndra officials.
32. The Department of Energy's Loan Guarantee to Solyndra, Inc. Special Report 11-0078-I, US Department of Energy, Office of Inspector General, 24 August 2015, https://www.energy.gov/ig/articles/special-report-11-0078-i
33. 'Solyndra Tubes Used in Calif. Art Installation', *Associated Press*, 14

September 2012, https://www.youtube.com/watch?v=J-gv54bU1E0&t=20s&ab_channel=AssociatedPress
34. 'How Solar Developed from the Bottom Up in China', University of California Institute on Global Conflict and Cooperation, 14 March 2023, https://ucigcc.org/blog/how-solar-developed-from-the-bottom-up-in-china/
35. Daoyuan Wen, Weijun Gao, Fanyue Qian, Qunyin Gu and Jianxing Ren, 'Development of Solar Photovoltaic Industry and Market in China, Germany, Japan and the United States of America Using Incentive Policies', *Energy Exploration & Exploitation*, vol. 39, 2021, 01445987209792 5, 10.1177/01445987209792 56.
36. 'China's Solar Production Costs Fall by 42% in Last Year', Wood Mackenzie, August 2023, https://www.woodmac.com/press-releases/chinas-solar-production-costs-fall-by-42-in-last-year/
37. 'Solar Exports from China Increase by a Third', Ember, May 2024, https://ember-climate.org/insights/research/china-solar-exports/
38. 'U.S. Solar Panel Makers Seek New Tariffs to Protect Domestic Factories', *Reuters*, 24 April 2024, https://www.reuters.com/business/energy/us-solar-panel-makers-seek-new-tariffs-protect-domestic-factories-2024-04-24/
39. Quillan Robinson, 'The True Cost of Chinese Solar Panels', *Time*, 18 January 2024, https://time.com/6564184/chinese-solar-panels-cost/
40. '22 MW Offshore Wind Turbine in the Works for 2024-25', *Offshore Wind*, 23 October 2023, https://www.offshorewind.biz/2023/10/23/22-mw-offshore-wind-turbine-in-the-works-for-2024-25/
41. 'Moment Giant Wind Turbine Blade Carried through Hawick', *BBC News*, 12 December 2023, https://www.bbc.co.uk/news/av/uk-scotland-67696665
42. 'China Wind Turbine Exports Surged 60% in 2023', *Caixin Global*, 23 April 2024, https://www.caixinglobal.com/2024-04-23/charts-of-the-day-china-wind-turbine-exports-surged-60-in-2023-102189309.html
43. 'Wind Market Share 2024', Enerdata, 22 April 2024, https://www.enerdata.net/publications/executive-briefing/wind-market-share.html
44. 'Wind Turbine Technology Evolution Is Diverging Quickly between China and the Rest of the World', Wood Mackenzie, 18 May 2024, https://www.woodmac.com/news/opinion/wind-turbine-technology-evolution-is-diverging-quickly-between-china-and-the-rest-of-the-world/

45. 'Speech by Executive Vice President Vestager on Technology and Politics at the Institute for Advanced Study', 9 April 2024, https://ec.europa.eu/commission/presscorner/detail/en/speech_24_1927
46. 'Global Renewables and Energy Efficiency Pledge', COP28 UAE, 2 December 2023, https://www.cop28.com/en/global-renewables-and-energy-efficiency-pledge
47. 'Renewables 2023', IEA, 2024, Paris, https://www.iea.org/reports/renewables-2023#
48. 'World Energy Outlook 2023 Free Dataset', IEA, Paris, 2023, https://www.iea.org/data-and-statistics/data-product/world-energy-outlook-2023-extended-dataset
49. 'Europe Must Rely Less on Chinese Technology, Danish PM Says', *Financial Times*, 2 September 2024, https://www.ft.com/content/fb5d678f-d828-460b-b683-caade2b04fe3
50. 'Gina Raimondo and Margrethe Vestager on Future of US–EU Economic Ties', Atlantic Council, streamed live 30 January 2024, https://www.youtube.com/watch?v=-gVloP_MyTY&ab_channel=AtlanticCouncil
51. 'Biden Administration Will Investigate National Security Risks Posed by China's Semiconductor Industry', *NBC News*, 28 August 2024, https://www.nbcnews.com/politics/national-security/biden-administration-will-investigate-national-security-risks-posed-ch-rcna141099
52. Chinese state subsidies for electric and hybrid vehicles totalled $57 billion between 2016 and 2022, consultants AlixPartners have estimated.
53. 'How Did China Come to Dominate Electric Cars?', *Technology Review*, 21 February 2023, https://www.technologyreview.com/2023/02/21/1068880/how-did-china-dominate-electric-cars-policy/
54. 'BYD's Growing Market Share in China's EV Market', EV Markets Reports, 5 August 2024, https://evmarketsreports.com/byds-growing-market-share-in-chinas-ev-market/
55. 'EV Price Gap: A Divide in the Global Automotive Industry', JATO Dynamics, May 2024, https://info.jato.com/ev-price-gap-report
56. Office of Sherrod Brown, 11 April 2024, https://www.brown.senate.gov/imo/media/doc/04112024evlettertopresidentbiden1.pdf
57. European Commission, 4 July 2024, https://ec.europa.eu/commission/presscorner/detail/en/ip_24_3630
58. 'Canada Hits China-Made Electric Cars with 100% Tariff', *BBC*

News, 27 August 2024, https://www.bbc.co.uk/news/articles/cm2no91v4m50
59. 'Türkiye Slaps 40% Extra Tax on EV Imports from China', *Daily Sabah*, 31 August 2023, https://www.dailysabah.com/business/automotive/turkiye-slaps-40-extra-tax-on-ev-imports-from-china
60. 'Gov't Announces Progressive Tax for Imported Electric Vehicles in Brazil', *Datamar News*, 2 January 2024, https://www.datamarnews.com/noticias/govt-announces-progressive-tax-for-imported-electric-vehicles-in-brazil/
61. 'China–Japan Row Reveals Deep-Seated Differences', *BBC News*, 21 September 2010, https://www.bbc.co.uk/news/world-asia-pacific-11380373
62. 'Hybrid Threats: The 2010 Senkaku Crisis', in S. Aday, M. Andžāns, U. Bērziņa-Čerenkova, F. Granelli, J. Gravelines, M. Hills, M. Holmstrom, A. Klus, I. Martinez-Sanchez, M. Mattiisen, H. Molder, Y. Morakabati, J. Pamment, A. Sari, V. Sazonov, G. Simons and J. Terra, *Hybrid Threats. A Strategic Communications Perspective*, Riga: NATO Strategic Communications Centre of Excellence, 2019, https://stratcomcoe.org/publications/hybrid-threats-the-2010-senkaku-crisis/82
63. 'Amid Tension, China Blocks Vital Exports to Japan', *New York Times*, 22 September 2010, https://www.nytimes.com/2010/09/23/business/global/23rare.html?pagewanted=all&_r=0
64. 'Critical Minerals Data Explorer', IEA, Paris, 2024, https://www.iea.org/data-and-statistics/data-tools/critical-minerals-data-explorer
65. 'Global Critical Minerals Outlook 2024', IEA, Paris, 2024, https://www.iea.org/reports/global-critical-minerals-outlook-2024
66. 'China's Clean Tech Supply Chain', *Technology Review*, 13 September 2023, https://www.technologyreview.com/2023/09/13/1079377/china-clean-tech-supply-chain/#:~=They%20are%20trying%20to%20%5Bhave,times%20but%20it%20would%20survive
67. 'The Future of Copper', IHS Markit, 14 July 2022, https://cdn.ihsmarkit.com/www/pdf/0722/The-Future-of-Copper_Full-Report_14July2022.pdf
68. 'Congo Seeks Outside Advice on Imposing Cobalt Export Curbs', *Bloomberg*, 11 April 2024, https://www.bloomberg.com/news/articles/2024-04-11/congo-seeks-outside-advice-on-imposing-cobalt-export-curbs

69. 'China to Restrict Exports of Chipmaking Materials as US Mulls New Curbs', *Reuters*, 4 July 2023, https://www.reuters.com/markets/commodities/china-restrict-exports-chipmaking-materials-us-mulls-new-curbs-2023-07-04/
70. 'China, World's Top Graphite Producer, Tightens Exports of Key Battery Material', *Reuters*, 20 October 2023, https://www.reuters.com/world/china/china-require-export-permits-some-graphite-products-dec-1-2023-10-20/
71. Shuang-Liang Liu, Hong-Rui Fan, Xuan Liu, Jianyin Meng, Alan R. Butcher, Lahaye Yann, Kui-Feng Yang and Xiao-Chun Li, 'Global Rare Earth Elements Projects: New Developments and Supply Chains', *Ore Geology Reviews*, vol. 152, article 105428, 2023, https://doi.org/10.1016/j.oregeorev.2023.105428
72. 'USAID Graphite Report', Land Links, November 2021, https://www.land-links.org/wp-content/uploads/2021/11/USAID_GM_Graphite.pdf
73. 'How Sodium Could Change the Game for Batteries', *Technology Review*, 11 May 2023, https://www.technologyreview.com/2023/05/11/1072865/how-sodium-could-change-the-game-for-batteries/
74. 'The Future of Copper', IHS Markit, 14 July 2022, https://cdn.ihsmarkit.com/www/pdf/0722/The-Future-of-Copper_Full-Report_14July2022.pdf
75. 'Remarks by Secretary of the Treasury Janet L. Yellen at American Chamber of Commerce Event in Guangzhou, the People's Republic of China', US Department of the Treasury, 5 April 2024, https://home.treasury.gov/news/press-releases/jy2227
76. 'China's Solar and EV Battery Overcapacity Risks', *Economist Intelligence Unit*, May 2024, https://www.eiu.com/n/solar-and-ev-battery-overcapacity-are-risks-to-china/
77. Expected global demand for lithium-ion battery manufacturing capacity in 2025 is 1.6 terawatt hours. China's expected capacity then will be around 6 terawatt hours. 'China Already Makes as Many Batteries as the Entire World Wants', *BloombergNEF*, 16 October 2023, https://about.bnef.com/blog/china-already-makes-as-many-batteries-as-the-entire-world-wants/
78. 'Chinese Car Executive Calls West's Claim of Overcapacity a "Fake Concept"', *Financial Times*, 14 May 2024, https://www.ft.com/content/436d9af7-f86c-429e-8f94-03067d043ef7

NOTES

79. Europe and the US's combined solar generating capacity in 2023 was 426 gigawatts compared to 610 gigawatts in China: Online Data Query Tool, International Renewable Energy Agency, https://pxweb.irena.org/pxweb/en/IRENASTAT
80. In 2023 the rest of the world, excluding China, added 130 gigawatts of solar power, according to the International Renewable Energy Agency, https://pxweb.irena.org/pxweb/en/
81. 'China Added More Solar Panels in 2023 Than US Did in its Entire History', *Bloomberg*, 26 January 2024, https://www.bloomberg.com/news/articles/2024-01-26/china-added-more-solar-panels-in-2023-than-us-did-in-its-entire-history?srnd=green&sref=O79Q3OZU
82. 'China's Solar Power Capacity Soared 55% in 2023 and Wind Capacity 21%', *Enerdata*, 29 January 2024, https://www.enerdata.net/publications/daily-energy-news/chinas-solar-power-capacity-soared-55-2023-and-wind-capacity-21.html
83. Based on estimates supplied by Carbon Brief to the author, 2024.
84. Solar PV prices, Our World in Data, https://ourworldindata.org/grapher/solar-pv-prices
85. 'Why Did Renewables Become So Cheap So Fast?', *Our World in Data*, https://ourworldindata.org/cheap-renewables-growth
86. EV Price Gap Report, JATO Dynamics, Q4 2023, https://info.jato.com/ev-price-gap-report
87. 'Making Solar Panels Is "Horrible" Business. The U.S. Still Wants It', *Bloomberg*, 20 July 2023, https://www.bloomberg.com/news/articles/2023-07-20/making-solar-panels-is-horrible-business-the-us-still-wants-it
88. 'UK Fails to Clear Any Offshore Wind in Renewable Energy Auction', *Bloomberg*, 8 September 2023, https://www.bloomberg.com/news/articles/2023-09-08/uk-fails-to-clear-any-offshore-wind-in-renewable-energy-auction
89. 'U.S. Offshore Wind Sector "Fundamentally Broken" – BP Exec', *Reuters*, 2 November 2023, https://www.reuters.com/business/energy/bp-low-carbon-boss-calls-us-offshore-wind-industry-fundamentally-broken-2023-11-01/#:~:text=%22Ultimately%2C%20offshore%20wind%20in%20the,permitting%2C%20etc...%22
90. 'Germany Installs 17 GW of Renewables in 2023', *Renewables Now*, 8 January 2024, https://renewablesnow.com/news/germany-installs-17-gw-of-renewables-in-2023-845103/

NOTES

91. 'I Went to China And Drove a Dozen Electric Cars. Western Automakers Are Cooked', *InsideEVs*, 15 April 2024, https://insideevs.com/features/719015/china-is-ahead-of-west/
92. Michael Liebreich, 11 May 2024, https://x.com/MLiebreich/status/1789217326098776384
93. The IEA says global solar PV manufacturing capacity needs to reach 650 gigawatts per year by 2030 for the world to be on course for net zero by 2050. But it projects global manufacturing capacity to reach almost 1,000 gigawatts as soon as the end of 2024 – well ahead of schedule: 'Renewable Energy Market Update – June 2023', IEA, Paris, 2023, https://www.iea.org/reports/renewable-energy-market-update-june-2023
94. 'Renewables 2024', IEA, Paris, 2024, https://www.iea.org/reports/renewables-2024
95. 'The State of Clean Technology Manufacturing – November 2023 Update', IEA, Paris, 2023, https://www.iea.org/reports/the-state-of-clean-technology-manufacturing-november-2023-update
96. 'Global Wind Report 2024', Global Wind Energy Council (GWEC), April 2024, https://gwec.net/wp-content/uploads/2024/04/GWR-2024_digital-version_final-1.pdf
97. J.P. Helveston, G. He and M.R. Davidson, 'Quantifying the Cost Savings of Global Solar Photovoltaic Supply Chains', *Nature*, vol. 612, no. 7938, pp. 83–7, 2022, doi: 10.1038/s41586-022-05316-6. https://www.jhelvy.com/research/2022-nature/
98. 'India to Stick with Plan to Tax Imports of Solar Equipment', *Bloomberg*, 1 February 2022, https://www.bloomberg.com/news/articles/2022-02-01/india-to-stick-with-plan-to-tax-imports-of-solar-equipment
99. 'Indian Solar PV Additions Down 28% in 2023 as Utility-Scale Segment Lags', *PV Tech*, 10 January 2024, https://www.pv-tech.org/indian-solar-pv-additions-down-28-in-2023-as-utility-scale-segment-lags/
100. See the Observatory of Economic Complexity, https://oec.world/en/profile/country/chn
101. 'How Margaret Thatcher Brought Nissan to the UK', Motorious blog, 11 March 2019, https://www.motorious.com/articles/highlights/margaret-thatcher-nissan-sunderland/
102. 'Top 10: Best-Selling EVs in the UK', *EV Magazine*, 16 August

2024, https://evmagazine.com/top10/top-10-best-selling-evs-in-the-uk

103. 'The Contributions of Japanese-Brand Automakers to the United States Economy: Updated Study', Japan Automobile Manufacturers Association, 21 May 2019, https://www.jama.org/wp-content/uploads/2019/05/prusa-jama-usa-employment-study-2019-2018-data-5-21-19-final.pdf

104. 'Europe Taking a Constructive Approach to the Influx of Chinese Electric Vehicles', Peterson Institute for International Economics (PIIE), 23 August 2024, https://www.piie.com/blogs/realtime-economics/2024/europe-taking-constructive-approach-influx-chinese-electric-vehicles

105. 'Developing Economies Counter Beijing's Export Boom with Tariffs', *Financial Times*, 11 September 2024, https://www.ft.com/content/1196fab7-3f7e-469c-83df-f0c51361687c

106. 'Ford to Build $3.5B LFP Battery Factory Using China Tech', *TechCrunch*, 13 February 2023, https://techcrunch.com/2023/02/13/ford-to-build-3-5b-factory-catl/

107. 'To Avoid Hefty Tariffs, China's BYD Eyes U.S. Car Market Via Mexico', *Wall Street Journal*, 16 February 2024, https://www.wsj.com/business/autos/chinese-ev-maker-byd-exploring-mexico-factory-as-entry-to-u-s-market-41136ofa

108. 'Trump Suggests Tariffs Higher Than 200% on Vehicles from Mexico', *Reuters*, 13 October 2024, https://www.reuters.com/world/us/trump-suggests-tariffs-higher-than-200-vehicles-mexico-2024-10-13/

109. 'Trump Invites Chinese to Build US Auto Plants: Sign of Possible Thaw as GOP Candidate Offers China the Same Deal Reagan Gave Japan in the 1980s', *Asia Times*, 20 March 2024, https://asiatimes.com/2024/03/trump-invites-chinese-to-build-us-auto-plants/

110. 'Tesla's Shanghai Plant Delivers 947,000 Vehicles in 2023', *Xinhua News*, 3 January 2024, https://english.news.cn/20240103/ee7a313aa02141358c9f241f0db6034a/c.html#:~:text=SHANGHAI%2C%20Jan.,and%20deliveries%20report%20for%202023

111. 'China New Three Export Indices', Capital Economics, https://www.capitaleconomics.com/data-and-charts/china-new-three-export-indices

112. 'Visualization: How Much Do EV Batteries Cost?', *Visual Capitalist*, 12 June 2024, https://www.visualcapitalist.com/visualized-how-much-do-ev-batteries-cost/
113. 'Solar Panel Company Stops Production at Its German Factory', *Yahoo Finance*, 29 April 2024, https://finance.yahoo.com/news/solar-panel-company-stops-production-170001868.html

Chapter 5: Silicon

1. 'How the Global Chip Shortage Might Affect People Who Just Want to Wash their Dogs', *Washington Post*, 2 May 2021, https://www.washingtonpost.com/technology/2021/05/02/chip-semiconductor-shortage-impact/
2. 'Ford, Other Auto Makers Cut Output on Chip Shortage', *Wall Street Journal*, 19 October 2021, https://www.wsj.com/articles/ford-other-auto-makers-cut-output-on-chip-shortage-11610280001
3. 'How Many Semiconductor Chips Are in a Car', *Polar Semiconductor*, 22 September 2021, https://polarsemi.com/blog/blog-semiconductor-chips-in-a-car/#:~:text=So%2C%'ohere's%20the%20typical%20orang',That's%20a%20lot!
4. 'Shortages Related to Semiconductors to Cost the Auto Industry $210 Billion in Revenues This Year, Says New AlixPartners Forecast', *AlixPartners*, 15 March 2021, https://www.alixpartners.com/newsroom/press-release-shortages-related-to-semiconductors-to-cost-the-auto-industry-210-billion-in-revenues-this-year-says-new-alixpartners-forecast/
5. 'Next Victim of Chip Shortage Will Be Your Home Internet Router', *Bloomberg*, 8 April 2021, https://www.bloomberg.com/news/articles/2021-04-08/next-victim-of-chip-shortage-will-be-your-home-internet-router?sref=eeq6exxF
6. 'How the Chip Shortage Is Affecting the World', *BBC News*, 22 February 2021, https://www.bbc.co.uk/news/technology-56433082
7. 'Semiconductor Shortage: What You Need to Know', *BBC News*, 7 October 2020, https://www.bbc.co.uk/news/technology-54894801
8. Spencer Hill, 'Goldman Sachs – A Semi-Troubling Shortage', 21 April 2021, https://www.scribd.com/document/506814229/Goldman-Sachs-A-Semi-Troubling-Shortage

9. 'The Semiconductor Decade: A Trillion-Dollar Industry', McKinsey & Company, 10 June 2021, https://www.mckinsey.com/industries/semiconductors/our-insights/the-semiconductor-decade-a-trillion-dollar-industry
10. 'The Emergence of Smart Bombs', *Air & Space Forces Magazine*, 1 March 2010, https://www.airandspaceforces.com/article/0310bombs/
11. Chris Miller, *Chip War*, London: Simon & Schuster, 2022, pp. 57–61.
12. 'Surface-to-Air Missiles Need Chips, Too, Pentagon Tells Congress', *Bloomberg*, 22 July 2022, https://www.bloomberg.com/news/articles/2022-07-22/surface-to-air-missiles-need-chips-too-pentagon-tells-congress. 'The Story of Saint Javelin', *NATO Review*, 22 February 2024, https://www.nato.int/docu/review/articles/2024/02/22/the-story-of-saint-javelin/index.html
13. 'Final Report', National Security Commission on Artificial Intelligence, March 2021, https://cybercemetery.unt.edu/nscai/20211005231038mp_/https://www.nscai.gov/wp-content/uploads/2021/03/Full-Report-Digital-1.pdf
14. 'Fact Sheet: CHIPS and Science Act Will Lower Costs, Create Jobs, Strengthen Supply Chains, and Counter China', The White House, 9 August 2022, https://www.whitehouse.gov/briefing-room/statements-releases/2022/08/09/fact-sheet-chips-and-science-act-will-lower-costs-create-jobs-strengthen-supply-chains-and-counter-china/
15. Miller, *Chip War*, p. 78.
16. 'CHIPS: Driving Innovation in the Semiconductor Industry', Semiconductor Industry Association, 1 October 2022, https://www.semiconductors.org/chips/
17. 'Remarks by President Biden on the CHIPS and Science Act', The White House, 4 November 2022, https://www.whitehouse.gov/briefing-room/speeches-remarks/2022/11/04/remarks-by-president-biden-on-the-chips-and-science-act/
18. 'Remarks by National Security Advisor Jake Sullivan at the Special Competitive Studies Project Global Emerging Technologies Summit', The White House, 16 September 2022, https://www.whitehouse.gov/briefing-room/speeches-remarks/2022/09/16/remarks-by-national-security-advisor-jake-sullivan-at-the-special-competitive-studies-project-global-emerging-technologies-summit/
19. 'Commerce Implements New Export Controls on Advanced

Computing and Semiconductor Manufacturing Items to the People's Republic of China (PRC) Bureau of Industry and Security', US Department of Commerce, 7 October 2022, https://www.bis.doc.gov/index.php/documents/about-bis/newsroom/press-releases/3158-2022-10-07-bis-press-release-advanced-computing-and-semiconductor-manufacturing-controls-final/file

20. 'Commerce Strengthens Restrictions on Advanced Computing Semiconductors', Bureau of Industry and Security, US Department of Commerce, 17 October 2023, https://www.bis.doc.gov/index.php/documents/about-bis/newsroom/press-releases/3355-2023-10-17-bis-press-release-acs-and-sme-rules-final-js/file#

21. 'Statement Regarding Dutch Government's Export Control Regulations Announcement', ASML, 30 June 2023, https://www.asml.com/en/news/press-releases/2023/statement-regarding-export-control-regulations-dutch-government. 'Dutch Export Controls: Semiconductor Technology Regulation', *Official Government Gazette*, 17 August 2023, https://zoek.officielebekendmakingen.nl/stcrt-2023-18212.html

22. 'Japan Restricts Chipmaking Equipment Exports to Align with US Curbs', *Reuters*, 31 March 2023, https://www.reuters.com/technology/japan-restrict-chipmaking-equipment-exports-aligning-it-with-us-china-curbs-2023-03-31/

23. 'Remarks by National Security Advisor Jake Sullivan on Renewing American Economic Leadership at the Brookings Institution', The White House, 27 April 2023, https://www.whitehouse.gov/briefing-room/speeches-remarks/2023/04/27/remarks-by-national-security-advisor-jake-sullivan-on-renewing-american-economic-leadership-at-the-brookings-institution/

24. 'US Urges Allies to Further Squeeze China on Chip Technology', *Bloomberg*, 6 March 2024, https://www.bloomberg.com/news/articles/2024-03-06/us-urges-allies-to-further-squeeze-china-on-chip-technology

25. 'US Pushing Netherlands, Japan to Restrict More Chipmaking Equipment to China', *Reuters*, 18 June 2024, https://www.reuters.com/world/us-pushing-netherlands-japan-restrict-more-chipmaking-equipment-china-source-2024-06-18/

26. 'Germany in Talks to Limit the Export of Chip Chemicals to China', *Bloomberg*, 27 April 2023, https://www.bloomberg.com/news/

NOTES

articles/2023-04-27/germany-in-talks-to-limit-the-export-of-chip-chemicals-to-china

27. 'China's Semiconductor Industry Faces New Challenges', *Yonhap News Agency*, 24 October 2023, https://en.yna.co.kr/view/AEN20231024002800320

28. According to UN Comtrade data, China spent $350 billion importing integrated circuits in 2023 and $338 billion on importing crude oil, https://comtradeplus.un.org/TradeFlow

29. 'Global Semiconductor Sales, Units Shipped Reach All-Time Highs in 2021 as Industry Ramps Up Production Amid Shortage', IC Insights, January 2022, https://www.icinsights.com/files/data/articles/documents/1347.pdf

30. The production of a Huawei phone with 7 nanometre node chips in September 2023 was seen as something of a breakthrough. But this was not achieved with the most advanced lithography technology and these chips are still some way off the most cutting edge. See 'Huawei Mate 60 Pro: A Breakthrough in Semiconductor Technology', *Bloomberg*, 4 September 2023, https://www.bloomberg.com/news/features/2023-09-04/look-inside-huawei-mate-60-pro-phone-powered-by-made-in-china-chip

31. 'The Semiconductor Supply Chain', Center for Security and Emerging Technologies, June 2022, https://cset.georgetown.edu/publication/the-semiconductor-supply-chain/

32. 'Cabinet Approves Programme for Development of Semiconductors and Display Manufacturing Ecosystem in India', Press Information Bureau, 15 December 2021, https://pib.gov.in/PressReleasePage.aspx?PRID=1781723

33. 'Chip Supremacy Gives South Korea More Geopolitical Freedom: Lawmaker', *Korea Herald*, 2 January 2023, https://www.koreaherald.com/view.php?ud=20230102000494

34. EUV Lithography: A European Joint Project', Zeiss, 15 May 2024, https://www.zeiss.com/semiconductor-manufacturing-technology/smt-magazine/euv-lithography-as-an-european-joint-project.html

35. 'EUV Chipmaking: How the U.S. Lost Control of Cutting-Edge Semiconductor Tech', *Bloomberg*, 11 April 2024, https://www.bloomberg.com/news/articles/2024-04-11/euv-chipmaking-how-us-lost-control-of-cutting-edge-semiconductor-tech

36. 'How Our Suppliers Make Us Strong', Zeiss, 16 March 2022,

https://www.zeiss.com/semiconductor-manufacturing-technology/smt-magazine/how-our-suppliers-make-us-strong.html#:~:text=Even%20though%20we%20have%20no,as%20if%20we%20had%20competitors

37. They are Shin-Etsu Chemical, Tokyo Ohka Kogyo, JSR and Fujifilm Electronic Materials. See 'High Purity Quartz Market Report', *Research in China*, August 2021, http://www.researchinchina.com/Htmls/Report/2021/71712.html

38. These machines are called in-line coaters/developers for extreme ultraviolet lithography. The CEO of Tokyo Electron, Toshiki Kawai, wrote in September 2023 that one of its strengths was 'a 100% share in EUV coater/lithography developers, which are necessary for semiconductor evolution'. See Tokyo Electron Limited Integrated Report 2023, September 2023, https://www.tel.com/ir/library/ar/f3gfkt000000003v-att/ir2023_all_en.pdf

39. 'The Semiconductor Supply Chain Issue Brief', Center for Security and Emerging Technologies, September 2022, https://cset.georgetown.edu/wp-content/uploads/The-Semiconductor-Supply-Chain-Issue-Brief.pdf

40. 'Visualizing the Abundance of Elements in the Earth's Crust', World Economic Forum, 14 December 2021, https://www.weforum.org/agenda/2021/12/abundance-elements-earth-crust/

41. 'Know the Source: The Polysilicon Supply Chain', *Minespider*, 2 February 2022, https://www.minespider.com/blog/know-the-source-the-polysilicon-supply-chain

42. 'The Ultra-Pure, Super-Secret Sand That Makes Your Phone Possible', *Wired*, 7 August 2018, https://www.wired.com/story/book-excerpt-science-of-ultra-pure-silicon/

43. 'Rare Form of Quartz Key to Xinjiang's Solar Boom', *South China Morning Post*, 15 October 2021, https://www.scmp.com/news/china/article/3153656/rare-form-quartz-key-xinjiangs-solar-boom-and-almost-all-it-us

44. A rival mining project for high-purity quartz in Australia – Ultra High Purity Quartz – has stopped making updates to its website. A Norwegian company called Norwegian Crystallites was also named as being a supplier of high-purity quartz, but in relatively small values, https://siliconmountain.wordpress.com/

45. Ed Conway, *Material World*, London: WH Allen, 2022, p. 107.

46. 'Solar Panel Recycling: What the Future Holds', *EnergyTrend*, 7 April 2024, https://www.energytrend.com/news/20240407-46330.html
47. Saif M. Khan, Alexander Mann and Dahlia Peterson, 'The Semiconductor Supply Chain: Assessing National Competitiveness', Center for Security and Emerging Technology, January 2021, https://doi.org/10.51593/20190016
48. 'Chips Are the New Oil and America Is Spending Billions to Safeguard Its Supply: Recent Shortages and Fears of China's Ambitions to Dominate the Industry Have Led to a Frenetic Effort to Rev Up U.S. Production', *Wall Street Journal*, 14 January 2023, https://www.wsj.com/articles/chips-semiconductors-manufacturing-china-taiwan-11673650917
49. 'Strengthening the Global Semiconductor Value Chain', Semiconductor Industry Association, April 2021, https://www.semiconductors.org/wp-content/uploads/2021/05/BCG-x-SIA-Strengthening-the-Global-Semiconductor-Value-Chain-April-2021_1.pdf
50. 'The Resilience Myth: Fatal Flaws in the Push to Secure Chip Supply Chains', *Financial Times*, 27 August 2024, https://www.ft.com/content/f76534bf-b501-4cbf-9a46-80be9feb670c
51. 'Chips Are the New Oil and America Is Spending Billions to Safeguard its Supply', *Wall Street Journal*, 14 January 2023, https://www.wsj.com/articles/chips-semiconductors-manufacturing-china-taiwan-11673650917
52. 'What's Happening with the U.S. Semiconductor Market: Intel CEO Patrick Gelsinger on Why the Chips Act Was So Crucial to the Global Supply Chain', *Wall Street Journal*, 30 October 2022, https://www.wsj.com/articles/intel-gelsinger-u-s-semiconductor-market-11666989610
53. 'Geopolitical Spotlight Shifts to Semiconductors: The New Oil', TS Lombard, May 2023, https://blogs.tslombard.com/geopolitical-spotlight-shifts-to-semiconductors-the-new-oil
54. 'Strengthening the Global Semiconductor Value Chain', Semiconductor Industry Association, April 2021, https://www.semiconductors.org/wp-content/uploads/2021/05/BCG-x-SIA-Strengthening-the-Global-Semiconductor-Value-Chain-April-2021_1.pdf

NOTES

55. TSMC website, https://www.tsmc.com/static/abouttsmcaz/index.htm
56. 'Preliminary Terms for Samsung Semiconductor Facility', US Department of Commerce, 24 April 2024, https://www.commerce.gov/news/press-releases/2024/04/biden-harris-administration-announces-preliminary-terms-samsung
57. 'Semiconductor Ecosystem Overview', Semiconductor Industry Association, 15 July 2023, https://www.semiconductors.org/ecosystem/
58. 'Fact Sheet: The Manufacturing Renaissance That Will Drive the Economy of the Future', Joint Economic Committee Democrats, 24 April 2024, https://www.jec.senate.gov/public/index.cfm/democrats/2024/4/fact-sheet-the-manufacturing-renaissance-that-will-drive-the-economy-of-the-future
59. 'Strengthening the Global Semiconductor Value Chain', Boston Consulting Group and Semiconductor Industry Association, April 2021, https://www.semiconductors.org/wp-content/uploads/2021/05/BCG-x-SIA-Strengthening-the-Global-Semiconductor-Value-Chain-April-2021_1.pdf
60. 'Vying for Talent: Morris Chang', Brookings Institution, 14 April 2022, https://www.brookings.edu/wp-content/uploads/2022/04/Vying-for-Talent-Morris-Chang-20220414.pdf
61. 'National Semiconductor Strategy', UK Government, 30 March 2023, https://www.gov.uk/government/publications/national-semiconductor-strategy/national-semiconductor-strategy
62. 'Vishay Intertechnology Acquires Nexperia's Newport Wafer Fab for $177 Million', Vishay Intertechnology, 23 August 2023, https://ir.vishay.com/news-releases/news-release-details/vishay-intertechnology-acquires-nexperias-newport-wafer-fab-177.
63. 'Why the World Relies On ASML for Machines That Print Chips', *CNBC*, 23 March 2022, https://www.youtube.com/watch?v=iSVHp6CAyQ8
64. Boston Consulting Group (BCG) & Semiconductor Industry Association (SIA), 'Emerging Resilience in the Semiconductor Supply Chain, 2024, https://www.semiconductors.org/wp-content/uploads/2024/05/Report_Emerging-Resilience-in-the-Semiconductor-Supply-Chain.pdf
65. 'Trump Attacks Bipartisan Semiconductor Law, a Key Policy Achievement for Biden', *New York Times*, 26 October 2024, https://

www.nytimes.com/2024/10/26/us/politics/trump-joe-rogan-chips-science-act.html,
66. 'Trump Likely to Uphold CHIPS Act Despite his Campaign Rhetoric, Policy Experts Say', *CNBC*, 7 November 2024, https://www.cnbc.com/2024/11/07/trump-likely-to-uphold-chips-act-despite-his-campaign-rhetoric-experts-say.html
67. 'Is the EU Chips Act the Right Approach?', Bruegel, 2 June 2022, https://www.bruegel.org/blog-post/eu-chips-act-right-approach
68. 'China's Semiconductor Push Falters as Major Chipmakers Go Bankrupt', Tekedia, 18 June 2024, https://www.tekedia.com/chinas-semiconductor-push-falters-as-major-chipmakers-go-bankrupt/. 'China Is Said to Be Raising Up to $31.5 Billion to Fuel Chip Vision', *Bloomberg*, 1 March 2018, https://www.bloomberg.com/news/articles/2018-03-01/china-is-said-raising-up-to-31-5-billion-to-fuel-chip-vision
69. 'Made in China 2025: Semiconductor Goals', Center for Security and Emerging Technologies, December 2021, https://cset.georgetown.edu/wp-content/uploads/t0432_made_in_china_2025_EN.pdf
70. 'Semiconductor Market Report', *IC Insights*, December 2021, https://www.icinsights.com/files/data/articles/documents/1330.pdf
71. 'Huawei's Advanced Chip Sparks US Concerns', *Register*, 19 September 2023, https://www.theregister.com/2023/09/19/huaweis_advanced_chip_sparks_us/
72. David von Seggern, 'Measured Energy in Japan Quake', *Physics Today*, vol. 65, no. 7, 1 July 2012, p. 10, https://doi.org/10.1063/PT.3.1619
73. Hirofumi Matsuo, 'Implications of the Tohoku Earthquake for Toyota's Coordination Mechanism: Supply Chain Disruption of Automotive Semiconductors', *International Journal of Production Economics*, vol. 161, 2015, pp. 217–27, https://da.lib.kobe-u.ac.jp/da/kernel/90003501/90003501.pdf
74. 'Auto Makers Retreat from 50 Years of "Just-in-Time" Manufacturing', *Wall Street Journal*, 3 May 2021, https://www.wsj.com/articles/auto-makers-retreat-from-50-years-of-just-in-time-manufacturing-11620051251
75. Taiichi Ohno, *Toyota Production System*, 1st edn, Portland, OR: Productivity Press, 1988.

76. 'What Is Just-In-Time?', *Toyota UK Magazine*, accessed 26 September 2024, https://mag.toyota.co.uk/just-in-time/
77. 'Toyota, Citing Lessons Learned from 2011 Earthquake, Expects No Major Semiconductor Impact', *Supply Chain Dive*, 14 May 2021, https://www.supplychaindive.com/news/toyota-semiconductor-shortage-earthquake-inventory-ihs-gartner-forecast-2022/600193/
78. 'Who Won the Automotive Global Sales Race in 2021?', *Carexpert*, accessed 26 September 2024, https://www.carexpert.com.au/car-news/who-won-the-automotive-global-sales-race-in-2021
79. 'Understanding the Global Chip Shortage', British Computer Society, 15 October 2023, https://www.bcs.org/articles-opinion-and-research/understanding-the-global-chip-shortage/
80. 'Semiconductor Sales and Production Trends', Semiconductor Industry Association, 15 June 2021, https://www.semiconductors.org/global-semiconductor-sales-units-shipped-reach-all-time-highs-in-2021-as-industry-ramps-up-production-amid-shortage/
81. Tech Insights, data supplied to author in September 2024.
82. 'Renesas Semiconductor Overview', Renesas, July 2022, https://www.renesas.com/us/en/node/1498021
83. 'How Climate Change Affected Semiconductor Production', *MSCI*, 5 April 2023, https://www.msci.com/www/blog-posts/how-climate-change-affected/02841370014
84. 'Texas Freeze Shuts Chip Factories amid Shortages', *BBC News*, 9 March 2021, https://www.bbc.co.uk/news/technology-56114503

Chapter 6: People

1. 'Covid-19: Vaccine Rollout Gets Under Way in UK', *BBC News*, 8 December 2020, https://www.bbc.co.uk/news/uk-55227325
2. 'Meet the Couple Who Helped Make the Pfizer Vaccine Possible', *New York Times*, 10 November 2020, https://www.nytimes.com/2020/11/10/business/biontech-covid-vaccine.html
3. See Pfizer website, https://www.pfizer.com/science/coronavirus/vaccine/working-to-reach-everyone-everywhere
4. 'Scientist behind BioNTech/Pfizer Coronavirus Vaccine Says It Can End Pandemic', *Guardian*, 12 November 2020, https://www.

theguardian.com/world/2020/nov/12/scientist-behind-biontech-pfizer-coronavirus-vaccine-says-it-can-end-pandemic

5. 'Here's to the Immigrant Heroes behind the BioNTech-Pfizer Vaccine', *Bloomberg*, 13 November 2020, https://www.bloomberg.com/view/articles/2020-11-13/here-s-to-the-immigrant-heroes-behind-the-biontech-pfizer-vaccine

6. 'Immigrant Ingenuity behind a Vaccine', *Christian Science Monitor*, 17 December 2020, https://www.csmonitor.com/Daily/2020/20201217/Immigrant-ingenuity-behind-a-vaccine

7. 'Donald Trump Presidential Campaign Announcement Full Speech', *C-SPAN*, 16 June 2015, https://www.youtube.com/watch?v=qI4Hb3FvD5Y

8. 'Donald Trump Urges Ban on Muslims Coming to US', *BBC News*, 8 December 2015, https://www.bbc.co.uk/news/world-us-canada-35035190

9. 'Trump Repeats "Poisoning the Blood" Anti-Immigrant Remark', *Reuters*, 16 December 2023, https://www.reuters.com/world/us/trump-repeats-poisoning-blood-anti-immigrant-remark-2023-12-16/

10. 'Trump's Poisoning the Blood: Racism and Rhetoric', *Axios*, 30 December 2023, https://www.axios.com/2023/12/30/trump-poisoning-the-blood-racism

11. 'What We Know About Unauthorized Immigrants Living in the U.S.', Pew Research Center, 22 July 2024, https://www.pewresearch.org/short-reads/2024/07/22/what-we-know-about-unauthorized-immigrants-living-in-the-us/. Also see M.M. Fazel-Zarandi, J.S. Feinstein and E.H. Kaplan, 'The Number of Undocumented Immigrants in the United States: Estimates Based on Demographic Modelling with Data from 1990 to 2016', *PLoS ONE*, vol. 13, no. 9, 2018, e0201193, https://doi.org/10.1371/journal.pone.0201193

12. 'Hungarian Prime Minister Says Migrants Are "Poison" and "Not Needed"', *Guardian*, 27 July 2016, accessed 17 November 2024, https://www.theguardian.com/world/2016/jul/26/hungarian-prime-minister-viktor-orban-praises-donald-trump

13. 'Austria Far Right Calls for EU "Remigration" Commissioner', *Euractiv*, 12 June 2024, https://www.euractiv.com/section/migration/news/austria-far-right-calls-for-eu-remigration-commissioner/

14. 'Geert Wilders: Who Is He and What Does He Want?', *BBC News*,

23 November 2023, accessed 17 November 2024, https://www.bbc.co.uk/news/world-europe-67506583
15. International Migration Outlook 2024, OECD Publishing, Paris, 2024, https://doi.org/10.1787/50b0353e-en
16. 'Ipsos Global Trends Report 2023', Ipsos, 2023, https://www.ipsos.com/sites/default/files/2023-Ipsos-Global-Trends-Report.pdf
17. 'Ipsos Global Trends 2017', Ipsos, 2017, https://www.ipsos.com/sites/default/files/2017-05/global_trends.pdf
18. 'What Worries the World', Ipsos, 25 July 2024, https://www.ipsos.com/en-nl/what-worries-world-july-2024
19. 'Democracy Perception Index 2024', May 2024, https://www.allianceofdemocracies.org/wp-content/uploads/2024/05/DPI-2024.pdf
20. 'Immigration', Gallup, accessed 29 August 2024, https://news.gallup.com/poll/1660/immigration.aspx
21. Immigration tracker, YouGov, September 2024, https://yougov.co.uk/topics/politics/trackers/has-immigration-in-the-past-10-years-been-good-for-britain
22. Laura Fermi, *Atoms in the Family*, Chicago And London: University of Chicago, 1934, p. 120.
23. 'Enrico Fermi Saves his Jewish Family from the Holocaust', *Jewish Press*, 10 August 2016, https://www.jewishpress.com/sections/features/features-on-jewish-world/enrico-fermi-saves-his-jewish-family-from-the-holocaust/2016/08/10/.
24. 'Enrico Fermi Dies at 53; Pioneer in Atomic Energy', *New York Times*, 29 November 1954, https://www.nytimes.com/1954/11/29/archives/enrico-fermi.html
25. Paul Johnson, 'One Man and his Dogma', *Spectator*, 8 August 2009, review of *The Storm of War: A New History of the Second World War* by Andrew Roberts, https://www.spectator.co.uk/article/one-man-and-his-dogma/
26. 'Immigrants and Nobel Prizes: 1901–2023', National Foundation for American Policy, https://nfap.com/research/immigrants-and-nobel-prizes-1901-2023/
27. 'Oral History Interview: Morris Chang', SEMI, 24 August 2007, https://www.semi.org/en/Oral-History-Interview-Morris-Chang
28. 'Tech Pioneer Channels Hard Lessons into Silicon Valley Success', *NPR*, 20 February 2012, https://www.npr.org/sections/

alltechconsidered/2012/02/20/147162496/tech-pioneer-channels-hard-lessons-into-silicon-valley-success
29. 'How Jensen Huang's Nvidia Is Powering the AI Revolution', *New Yorker*, 4 December 2023, https://www.newyorker.com/magazine/2023/12/04/how-jensen-huangs-nvidia-is-powering-the-ai-revolution
30. 'The Geopolitical Gamble of Taiwan's TSMC', *New York Times*, 24 January 2024, https://www.nytimes.com/2024/01/24/opinion/tsmc-taiwan-china.html
31. Pierre Azoulay, Benjamin F. Jones, J. Daniel Kim and Javier Miranda, 'Immigration and Entrepreneurship in the United States', *American Economic Review: Insights*, vol. 4, no. 1, 2022, pp. 71–88.
32. 'International Migration Outlook 2024', OECD Publishing, Paris, 2024, https://doi.org/10.1787/50b0353e-en
33. 'International Migration Outlook 2011', OECD Publishing, Paris, 2011, https://doi.org/10.1787/migr_outlook-2011-en
34. G. Peri, K.Y. Shih and C. Sparber, 'Foreign STEM Workers and Native Wages and Employment in U.S. Cities', NBER Working Paper No. w20093, National Bureau of Economic Research, 2014, https://www.nber.org/papers/w20093
35. See UNESCO Institute for Statistics, https://data.uis.unesco.org/
36. Tom Tugendhat, 'China Links Pose a Threat to Academic Freedom in Britain', *Financial Times*, 19 June 2021, https://www.ft.com/content/f96e158c-a7ce-489d-846a-3445114752dd
37. 'UCL Professor Warns Academic Freedom at Risk as Module Removed after Student Complaints', *Sky News*, 20 October 2023, https://news.sky.com/story/ucl-professor-warns-academic-freedom-at-risk-as-module-removed-after-student-complaints-13091493
38. 'China', Intelligence and Security Committee of Parliament, July 2023, https://isc.independent.gov.uk/wp-content/uploads/2023/07/ISC-China.pdf
39. 'Joint Address by MI5 and FBI Heads', MI5, 6 July 2022, https://www.mi5.gov.uk/joint-address-by-mi5-and-fbi-heads
40. 'UK University Crackdown on Chinese Students Harms Country's Tech Ambitions', *Bloomberg*, 1 August 2024, https://www.bloomberg.com/news/articles/2024-08-01/uk-university-crackdown-on-chinese-students-harms-country-s-tech-ambitions
41. 'Demand for Study Abroad Rising in China, but Students

NOTES

Considering More Destinations in 2024', ICEF Monitor, February 2024, https://monitor.icef.com/2024/02/demand-for-study-abroad-rising-in-china-but-students-considering-more-destinations-in-2024/

42. 'Rubio Warns Florida Universities and State Leadership of Threat of CCP Espionage in Higher Education', US Senator for Florida, 17 March 2022, https://www.rubio.senate.gov/rubio-warns-florida-universities-and-state-leadership-of-threat-of-ccp-espionage-in-higher-education/

43. Christopher Wray, 'The Threat Posed by the Chinese Government and the Chinese Communist Party to the Economic and National Security of the United States', Federal Bureau of Investigation, 7 July 2022, https://www.fbi.gov/news/speeches/the-threat-posed-by-the-chinese-government-and-the-chinese-communist-party-to-the-economic-and-national-security-of-the-united-states

44. 'DoJ China Initiative to Catch Spies Prompts FBI Misconduct, Racism Claims', *Bloomberg*, 14 December 2021, https://www.bloomberg.com/news/features/2021-12-14/doj-china-initiative-to-catch-spies-prompts-fbi-misconduct-racism-claims

45. 'Trump's Suspension of Entry of Chinese Students and Researchers with Military-Civil Fusion Links', *Law and Border*, 15 October 2023, https://lawandborder.com/trumps-suspension-of-entry-of-chinese-students-and-researchers-with-military-civil-fusion-links/#:~:text=The%20Biden%20administration%20has%20continued,according%20to%20State%20Department%20statistics

46. 'Chinese on Campus', BBC Radio 4, 16 February 2022, produced by Leeanne Coyle and Mark Rickards, a Whistledown Scotland production, https://www.bbc.co.uk/programmes/m0014gbk

47. 'Xi's Student Spy Army and How They Can Be Outsmarted', *The Times*, 23 June 2024, https://www.thetimes.com/world/asia/article/xis-student-spy-army-and-how-they-can-be-outsmarted-g3k6txc82

48. 'China's Government Threats to Academic Freedom Abroad', Human Rights Watch, 21 March 2019, https://www.hrw.org/news/2019/03/21/china-government-threats-academic-freedom-abroad

49. Amy Gadsden, 'Vying for Talent: Competition for High-Skilled Labor in the U.S. and China', Brookings Institution, 15 September 2022, https://www.brookings.edu/wp-content/uploads/2022/09/Vying-for-Talent-Amy-Gadsden-20220915.pdf

NOTES

50. Steven Chu, 'Vying for Talent: High-Skilled Immigration in U.S.-China Competition', Brookings Institution, 9 June 2022, https://www.brookings.edu/wp-content/uploads/2022/06/Vying-for-Talent-Steven-Chu-20220609.pdf
51. 'British Universities Are in a Global Competition – Government Must Step Up', *Financial Times*, 3 June 2024, https://www.ft.com/content/371122db-c169-4fa3-90a4-ff4c12dc6141
52. 'What does the US get wrong about China? With Adam Posen', *Financial Times*, 22 July 2024, https://www.ft.com/content/dbbaaa6d-ed07-4706-8fce-70d202e15d1f
53. 'The Chipmakers: U.S. Strengths and Priorities for the High-End Semiconductor Workforce', Center for Security and Emerging Technology, September 2020, https://cset.georgetown.edu/publication/the-chipmakers-u-s-strengths-and-priorities-for-the-high-end-semiconductor-workforce/
54. 'Chipping Away: July 2023', Semiconductor Industry Association, July 2023, https://www.semiconductors.org/wp-content/uploads/2023/07/SIA_July2023_ChippingAway_website.pdf
55. National Security STEM Talent Letter to Chuck Schumer, Nancy Pelosi et al., 9 May 2022, https://s3.documentcloud.org/documents/21947011/national-security-stem-talent-letter.pdf
56. 'China Is Fast Outpacing U.S. STEM PhD Growth', Center for Security and Emerging Technology, August 2021, https://cset.georgetown.edu/publication/china-is-fast-outpacing-u-s-stem-phd-growth/#:~:text=Since%20the%20mid%2D2000s%2C%20China,future%20competitiveness%20in%20STEM%20ofields
57. Includes home-purchase subsidies and typical signing bonuses of 3 to 5 million yuan, or $420,000 to $700,000.
58. C. Cao, J. Baas, C.S. Wagner and K. Jonkers, 'Returning Scientists and the Emergence of China's Science System', *Science and Public Policy*, vol. 47, no. 2, 2020, pp. 172–83, https://doi.org/10.1093/scipol/scz056
59. 'AI and Immigrants', National Foundation for American Policy, June 2023, https://nfap.com/wp-content/uploads/2023/06/AI-AND-IMMIGRANTS.NFAP-Policy-Brief.2023.pdf
60. Mariel Larzellere, *The 1980 Cuban Boatlift*, Washington, DC: National Defence University Press, 1988, https://media.defense.gov/2020/Apr/23/2002287258/-1/-1/0/LARZELERE_MARIEL_BOATLIFT.PDF

61. David Card, 'The Impact of the Mariel Boatlift on the Miami Labor Market', October 1990, University of California, Berkeley, https://davidcard.berkeley.edu/papers/mariel-impact.pdf
62. Matthew Yglesias, 'The Mariel Boatlift: What It Tells Us about the Effects of Immigration on Wages', *Vox*, 23 June 2017, https://www.vox.com/the-big-idea/2017/6/23/15855342/immigrants-wages-trump-economics-mariel-boatlift-hispanic-cuban
63. National Academies of Sciences, Engineering, and Medicine, *The Economic and Fiscal Consequences of Immigration*, Washington, DC: The National Academies Press, 2016, https://nap.nationalacademies.org/catalog/23550/the-economic-and-fiscal-consequences-of-immigration
64. Bank of England, 'The Impact of Immigration on Occupational Wages: Evidence from Britain', Working Paper No. 560, October 2015, https://www.bankofengland.co.uk/-/media/boe/files/working-paper/2015/the-impact-of-immigration-on-occupational-wages-evidence-from-britain.pdf
65. Migration Advisory Committee, 'EEA Migration in the UK: Final Report', September 2018, https://assets.publishing.service.gov.uk/government/uploads/system/uploads/attachment_data/file/741926/Final_EEA_report.PDF
66. Guglielmo Barone and Sauro Mocetti, 'With a Little Help from Abroad: The Effect of Low-Skilled Immigration on the Female Labor Supply', May 2010, https://eml.berkeley.edu/~webfac/card/laborlunch/mocetti.pdf
67. Brian Bell, 'Crime and Immigration', *IZA World of Labor*, vol. 33, 2019, https://doi.org/10.15185/izawol.33.v2
68. Michael Tonry, 'Why Crime Rates Are Falling throughout the Western World', *Crime and Justice*, vol. 43, 2014, pp. 1–63, https://www.journals.uchicago.edu/doi/10.1086/678181
69. Brian Bell, Anna Fasani and Stephen Machin, 'Crime and Immigration', London School of Economics, 2013, https://eprints.lse.ac.uk/59323/1/CEP_Bell_Fasani_Machin_Crime-and-immigration_2013.pdf
70. 'World Migration Report 2024', International Organization for Migration, https://worldmigrationreport.iom.int/msite/wmr-2024-interactive/
71. 'International Migration Outlook 2024', OECD Publishing, Paris, 2024, https://doi.org/10.1787/50b0353e-en

72. Alberto Alesina, Armando Miano and Stefanie Stantcheva, 'Immigration and Redistribution', National Bureau of Economic Research, Working Paper No. 24733, June 2018, revised March 2022, http://www.nber.org/papers/w24733
73. 'Nearly 900 Million Worldwide Wanted to Migrate in 2021', Gallup, 25 January 2022, https://news.gallup.com/poll/468218/nearly-900-million-worldwide-wanted-migrate-2021.aspx
74. Abhijit Banerjee and Esther Duflo, *Good Economics for Hard Times*, London: Allen Lane, 2019.
75. Lant Pritchett and Farah Hani, 'The Economics of International Migrations', for *Oxford Research Encyclopedia of Economics and Finance*, December 2019, https://lantpritchett.org/wp-content/uploads/2019/12/Encyclopedia-economics-of-international-migration_final_v2.pdf.
76. See ODA trends and statistics, OECD, https://www.oecd.org/en/topics/sub-issues/oda-trends-and-statistics.html
77. Michael A. Clemens, 'Economics and Emigration: Trillion-Dollar Bills on the Sidewalk?', *Journal of Economic Perspectives*, vol. 25, no. 3, summer 2011, pp. 83–106, https://doi.org/10.1257/jep.25.3.83
78. 'World Migration Report 2024', International Organization for Migration, August 2024, https://worldmigrationreport.iom.int/msite/wmr-2024-interactive/
79. Keith E. Maskus, 'A Benefit-Cost Analysis of Increased International Migration of Skilled Labor in Africa and the World', *Journal of Benefit-Cost Analysis*, vol. 14, no. 2, 2023, pp. 246–69, published online 22 June 2023, https://www.cambridge.org/core/journals/journal-of-benefit-cost-analysis/article/benefitcost-analysis-of-increased-international-migration-of-skilled-labor-in-africa-and-the-world/D11396C36829F0DD3B43B1DE8BED78EC
80. S.O. Becker and T. Fetzer, 'Does Migration Cause Extreme Voting?', Centre for Competitive Advantage in the Global Economy (CAGE) Working Paper No. 306. October 2016, https://warwick.ac.uk/fac/soc/economics/research/centres/cage/manage/publications/306-2016_becker_fetzer.pdf
81. 'How Trump Won the 2024 Election – CBS News Exit Poll Results', *CBS News*, last modified 8 November 2024, https://www.cbsnews.com/news/exit-polls-2024-presidential-election/
82. Environics Institute, *Canadian Public Opinion about Immigration and*

NOTES

Refugees – Fall 2024, 17 October 2024, https://www.environicsinstitute.org/projects/project-details/canadian-public-opinion-about-immigration-and-refugees---fall-2024

83. European Parliament, EU Post-electoral Survey 2024, conducted by Verian, 13 June–8 July 2024, survey of 26,349 respondents, with results weighted by population size and national election turnout, accessed 12 November 2024, https://europa.eu/eurobarometer/surveys/detail/3292

84. 'World Population Prospects 2022: Summary of Results', United Nations, https://www.un.org/development/desa/pd/sites/www.un.org.development.desa.pd/files/wpp2022_summary_of_results.pdf

85. 'Global Trends Report 2023', United Nations High Commissioner for Refugees,' https://www.unhcr.org/global-trends-report-2023

86. 'International Migration Outlook 2023', OECD Publishing, Paris, 2023, https://doi.org/10.1787/b0f40584-en

87. 'Trump Says Foreign College Graduates Should Automatically Get Green Cards', *Reuters*, 20 June 2024, https://www.reuters.com/world/us/trump-says-foreign-college-graduates-should-automatically-get-green-cards-2024-06-20/#:~:text=June%2020%20(Reuters)%20%2D%20Republican,to%20his%20hardline%20immigration%20stance

88. 'Turkish Guest Workers Transformed German Society', *Deutsche Welle*, 27 December 2012, https://www.dw.com/en/turkish-guest-workers-transformed-german-society/a-15489210

Chapter 7: Steel

1. 'Andrew Carnegie Net Worth', Celebrity Net Worth, 1 March 2024, https://www.celebritynetworth.com/richest-businessmen/richest-billionaires/andrew-carnegie-net-worth/

2. 'Elon Musk Profile', Bloomberg Billionaires Index, accessed 12 November 2024, https://www.bloomberg.com/billionaires/profiles/elon-r-musk/

3. Andrew Carnegie, 'Wealth', *North American Review*, vol. 391, June 1889, https://www1.swarthmore.edu/SocSci/rbannis1/AIH19th/Carnegie.html

4. 'Elon Musk's Twitter Revolution: White Supremacy and Nazi

Content', *Vice*, 20 August 2023, https://www.vice.com/en/article/n7zm9q/elon-musk-twitter-nazis-white-supremacy
5. 'Labor Force and Employment, 1800–1960', National Bureau of Economic Research, January 1966, http://www.nber.org/chapters/c1567
6. 'Number of Nvidia Employees (2024)', Exploding Topics, last modified 19 August 2024, https://explodingtopics.com/blog/nvidia-employees
7. 'No Inventions, No Innovations: A History of U.S. Steel', Construction Physics substack, 29 December 2023, https://www.construction-physics.com/p/no-inventions-no-innovations-a-history
8. Marvin B. Lieberman and Douglas R. Johnson, 'Comparative productivity of Japanese and U.S. Steel Producers, 1958–1993', *Japan and the World Economy*, Elsevier, vol. 11, no. 1, January 1999, pp. 1–27, https://ideas.repec.org/a/eee/japwor/v11y1999i1p1-27.html
9. 'U.S. Steel Explores Options after Rejecting $7.3 Bln Offer from Cleveland-Cliffs', *Reuters*, 14 August 2023, https://www.reuters.com/markets/commodities/us-steel-explore-strategic-alternatives-company-2023-08-13/
10. 'Japan's Nippon Steel to Acquire U.S. Steel for $14.9 Billion', *Reuters*, 19 December 2023, https://www.reuters.com/markets/deals/japans-nippon-steel-plans-acquire-us-steel-7-bln-nikkei-2023-12-18/
11. Office of Senator John Fetterman, 15 December 2023, https://www.fetterman.senate.gov/press-releases/fetterman-blasts-u-s-steel-sale-vows-to-take-all-possible-actions-to-block-acquisition/
12. Office of Senator Marco Rubio, 19 December 2023, https://www.rubio.senate.gov/wp-content/uploads/2023/12/CFIUS_USX_Letter_Vance-2.pdf
13. 'Trump Says He Will Absolutely Block Nippon US Steel Deal', *Bloomberg*, 31 January 2024, https://www.bloomberg.com/news/articles/2024-01-31/trump-says-he-will-absolutely-block-nippon-us-steel-deal
14. 'Statement from President Biden on US Steel', The White House, 14 March 2024, https://www.whitehouse.gov/briefing-room/statements-releases/2024/03/14/statement-from-president-biden-on-us-steel/
15. Sir Henry Bessemer, *An Autobiography*, London: Macmillan, 1905.
16. 'All the Metals We Mined in One Chart', Visual Capitalist,

September 2021, https://elements.visualcapitalist.com/wp-content/uploads/2021/09/all-of-the-metals-one-visualization.html
17. 'Iron and Steel Technology Roadmap', IEA, Paris, 2020, https://www.iea.org/reports/iron-and-steel-technology-roadmap
18. 'World Steel in Figures 2024', World Steel Association, https://worldsteel.org/data/world-steel-in-figures-2024/
19. Around 2.6 billion tonnes of carbon dioxide emissions annually.
20. 'Presidential Proclamation Adjusting Imports of Steel into the United States', The White House, 8 March 2018, https://trumpwhitehouse.archives.gov/presidential-actions/presidential-proclamation-adjusting-imports-steel-united-states/
21. Donald Trump, Twitter, 2 March 2018, https://twitter.com/realDonaldTrump/status/969558431802806272?ref_src=twsrc%5Etfw
22. 'POSCO Gwangyang Steel Plant', Global Energy Monitor, accessed 4 September 2024, https://www.gem.wiki/POSCO_Gwangyang_steel_plant
23. Gwangyang's 23 million tonne capacity was overtaken by the 30 million tonnes of a plant operated by China's Jiangsu Shagang Group in Zhangjiagang in the early 2020s. 'Zhangjiagang Hongchang Steel Co Ltd', Global Energy Monitor, accessed 4 September 2024, https://www.gem.wiki/Zhangjiagang_Hongchang_Steel_Co_Ltd#cite_note-6.
24. According to the World Bank, Kenya's GDP per capita in constant 2015 US$ in 1960 was $793, while South Korea's was $1,027. 'GDP per Capita (Constant 2015 US$)', World Bank, accessed 4 September 2024, https://data.worldbank.org/indicator/NY.GDP.PCAP.KD?locations=KE-KR
25. Ha-Joon Chang, *23 Things They Don't Tell You about Capitalism*, London: Penguin, 2011, p. 126.
26. Joe Studwell, *How Asia Works*, London: Profile Books, 2014, pp. 94–5.
27. According to the World Bank, Kenya's GDP per capita in constant 2015 US$ in 2023 was $1,813, while South Korea's was $34,121.
28. BBC Newsnight interview, 15 September 2023.
29. 'UK Steel Key Statistics Guide, May 2023', https://www.makeuk.org/about/uk-steel/new-uk-steel-key-statistics; 'UK Steel Production at Lowest Level Since the Great Depression', *The Times*, 27 January 2023, https://www.thetimes.co.uk/article/uk-steel-production-at-lowest-level-since-the-great-depression-dqsmfnwgz

NOTES

30. 'British Steel Set to Cut up to 2,000 Jobs in Furnace Closure Plan', *BBC News*, 6 November 2023, https://www.bbc.co.uk/news/business-67332093
31. 'Blast Furnace Closure Leaves UK Woefully Underprepared for War', GMB, 24 January 2024, https://www.gmb.org.uk/news/blast-furnace-closure-leaves-uk-woefully-underprepared-for-war
32. 'UK Government to Acquire Sheffield Forgemasters International Limited', UK Government, 28 July 2021, https://www.gov.uk/government/news/uk-government-to-acquire-sheffield-forgemasters-international-limited
33. 'The Future of the European Steel Industry', McKinsey & Company, accessed 4 September 2024, https://www.mckinsey.com/~/media/mckinsey/industries/metals%20and%20mining/our%20insights/the%20future%20of%20the%20european%20steel%20industry/the-future-of-the-european-steel-industry_vf.pdf
34. 'French Workers Vandalise Factory Office over Job Cuts', *France24*, 4 April 2008, https://www.france24.com/en/20080404-french-workers-vandalise-factory-office-over-job-cuts-steel-jobs; 'Thyssenkrupp to Scrap 3000 Steel Jobs as Part of Coronavirus Crisis Package', *EURACTIV*, 22 June 2020, https://www.euractiv.com/section/economy-jobs/news/thyssenkrupp-to-scrap-3000-steel-jobs-as-part-of-coronavirus-crisis-package/; 'French Steelworkers Blockade Industry', *Guardian*, 5 October 2012, https://www.theguardian.com/business/2012/oct/05/french-steelworkers-blockade-industry; 'Germany's Broken Heartland: The Mighty Mills of the Ruhr Are Running Down', *Independent*, 9 October 2012, https://www.independent.co.uk/news/business/germany-s-broken-heartland-the-mighty-mills-of-the-ruhr-are-running-down-and-tens-of-thousands-of-steel-jobs-are-being-lost-can-the-foundry-of-the-reich-recast-itself-in-a-new-mould-john-eisenhammer-reports-from-1497650.html
35. Chad P. Bown, 'Trump's Steel and Aluminum Tariffs Are Counterproductive: Here Are 5 More Things You Need to Know', Peterson Institute for International Economics, 7 March 2018, https://www.piie.com/blogs/trade-and-investment-policy-watch/trumps-steel-and-aluminum-tariffs-are-counterproductive-here
36. 'U.S. Industrial Production: Iron and Steel Mills', Federal Reserve Economic Data, 2023, https://fred.stlouisfed.org/series/IPN3311A2RSQ#0

37. David H. Autor, David Dorn and Gordon H. Hanson, 'The China Shock: Learning from Labor Market Adjustment to Large Changes in Trade', January 2016, NBER Working Paper No. w21906, available at SSRN: https://ssrn.com/abstract=2721747
38. West Virginia Encyclopedia, accessed 29 August 2024, https://www.wvencyclopedia.org/articles/973
39. 'Inside the West Virginia Steel Town Destroyed by NAFTA', *Independent*, 22 March 2018, https://www.independent.co.uk/news/world/americas/us-politics/inside-the-west-virginia-steel-town-destroyed-by-nafta-where-94-of-jobs-have-disappeared-and-donald-trump-is-king-weirton-a738984
40. 'Pittsburgh's Population Problem', *Pittsburgh Quarterly*, spring 2023, https://pittsburghquarterly.com/articles/pittsburghs-population-problem/
41. 'State of Aging, Disability, and Family Caregiving in Allegheny County', University of Pittsburgh, December 2022, https://ucsur.pitt.edu/files/center/soa/2022/Allegheny_County_State_of_Aging_2022%20Exec_Summary_FINAL.pdf
42. 'Steve Bannon Plans New Political Movement', *Hollywood Reporter*, 8 August 2017, https://www.hollywoodreporter.com/news/general-news/steve-bannon-trump-tower-interview-trumps-strategist-plots-new-political-movement-948747/
43. Robert E. Lipsey, 'U.S. Foreign Trade and the Balance of Payments, 1800–1913', in Stanley L. Engerman and Robert E. Gallman, eds, *The Cambridge Economic History of the United States*, Cambridge: Cambridge University Press, 2000, pp. 685–732.
44. David H. Autor, David Dorn, Gordon H. Hanson and Kaveh Majlesi, 'Importing Political Polarization? The Electoral Consequences of Rising Trade Exposure', *American Economic Review*, vol. 110, no. 10, 2020, pp. 3139–83.
45. 'Iron and Steel Technology Roadmap', IEA, Paris, 2020, https://www.iea.org/reports/iron-and-steel-technology-roadmap
46. 'How Are Roads Changing Lives in Madagascar?', World Bank, 10 February 2023, https://www.worldbank.org/en/results/2023/02/10/how-are-roads-changing-lives-in-madagascar
47. Stefan Pauliuk, Tao Wang and Daniel B. Müller, 'Steel All over the World: Estimating In-Use Stocks of Iron for 200 Countries',

Resources, Conservation and Recycling, vol. 71, 2013, pp. 22–30, https://doi.org/10.1016/j.resconrec.2012.11.008

48. Ed Conway, *Material World: A Substantial Story of our Past and Future*, London: WH Allen, 2023.
49. Ed Conway, 'The Best Datapoint of All Steel', Substack, 3 July 2023, https://edconway.substack.com/p/the-best-datapoint-of-all-steel
50. According to the World Steel Association, seventy-one countries accounted for approximately 98 per cent of total world crude steel production in 2022: 'World Crude Steel Production 2022', World Steel Association, December 2023, https://worldsteel.org/media/press-releases/2024/december-2023-crude-steel-production-and-2023-global-totals/
51. 'Latest Developments in Steelmaking Capacity 2024', OECD, 2024, https://one.oecd.org/document/DSTI/SC(2024)3/FINAL/en/pdf
52. 'The Future of the European Steel Industry', McKinsey & Company, March 2021, https://www.mckinsey.com/~/media/mckinsey/industries/metals%20and%20mining/our%20insights/the%20future%20of%20the%20european%20steel%20industry/the-future-of-the-european-steel-industry_vf.pdf
53. 'Latest Developments in Steelmaking Capacity 2023', OECD, 2023. https://one.oecd.org/document/DSTI/SC(2024)3/FINAL/en/pdf#:~:text=World%20crude%20steelmaking%20capacity%20in,steel%20production%20by%20543%20mmt.
54. 'World Steel in Figures 2023', World Steel Association, 2023, https://unesid.org/descargas_files/World-Steel-in-Figures-2023.pdf
55. Kenneth Rogoff and Yuanchen Yang, 'Rethinking China's Growth', Draft for Economic Policy Conference, 19–20 October 2023, https://www.economic-policy.org/wp-content/uploads/2023/10/Rogoff-Yang.pdf
56. 'A Comprehensive Assessment of America's Infrastructure', American Society of Civil Engineers, 2021, https://infrastructurereportcard.org/wp-content/uploads/2020/12/2021-IRC-Executive-Summary-1.pdf
57. Marian Moszoro, 'The Direct Employment Impact of Public Investment', IMF Working Papers No. 2021/131, Washington, DC: International Monetary Fund, 6 May 2021, https://www.imf.org/en/

Publications/WP/Issues/2021/05/06/The-Direct-Employment-Impact-of-Public-Investment-50251

58. China produced 1,018 million tonnes of steel in 2022 according to the World Steel Association. But the OECD estimates its capacity at 1,150 million tonnes, giving an excess capacity of 132 million tones. The World Steel Association estimates US steel production in 2022 at 81 million tonnes, the UK at 6 million tonnes, France at 12 million tonnes, Canada at 12 million tonnes, the Netherlands at 6 million tonnes and Austria at 8 million tonnes, giving a total of 125 million tonnes. 'Steelmaking Capacity', OECD, 2023, https://stats.oecd.org/Index.aspx?DataSetCode=STI_STEEL_MAKINGCAPACITY

59. For total steel production in EU27 in 2022, see 'European Steel in Figures', Eurofer, 2023, https://www.eurofer.eu/assets/publications/brochures-booklets-and-factsheets/european-steel-in-figures-2023/FINAL_EUROFER_Steel-in-Figures_2023.pdf; for China, India and US steel production in 2022, see 'Total Production of Crude Steel', World Steel Association, https://worldsteel.org/data/annual-production-steel-data/?ind=P1_crude_steel_total_pub/CHN/IND

60. 'Steel Trade and Trade Policy Developments (Jan.–Jun. 2023)', OECD, https://one.oecd.org/document/DSTI/SC(2023)15/FINAL/en/pdf

61. Author's calculations based on 'World Steel in Figures 2024', https://worldsteel.org/data/world-steel-in-figures-2024/

62. Gianpiero Mattera, 'Steel Production Capacity and Trade Dynamics', OECD Directorate for Science, Technology and Innovation, 2021, https://web-archive.oecd.org/2021-04-13/584858-steel-production-capacity-and-trade-dynamics.pdf

63. 'Fact Sheet: Scrap Use in the Steel Industry', World Steel Association, 2021, https://worldsteel.org/wp-content/uploads/Fact-sheet-on-scrap_2021.pdf

64. 'Scrap and Recycling', ArcelorMittal, accessed 4 September 2024, https://corporate.arcelormittal.com/sustainability/by-products-scrap-and-the-circular-economy#:~:text=Scrap%20and%20recycling&text=Nearly%20all%20steel%20is%20recycled,the%20projected%20demand%20for%20steel

65. J. Allwood, C. Dunant, R. Lupton and A. Serrenho, 'Steel Arising: Opportunities for the UK in a Transforming Global Steel Industry,

NOTES

2019, Apollo – University of Cambridge Repository, https://doi.org/10.17863/CAM.40835

66. 'Circular Economy', World Steel Association, accessed 4 September 2024, https://worldsteel.org/circular-economy/
67. 'The Circular Economy: A Powerful Force for Climate Mitigation', Sitra, 2018, https://www.sitra.fi/app/uploads/2018/06/the-circular-economy-a-powerful-force-for-climate-mitigation.pdf
68. 'World Steel Recycling in Figures 2018–2022', Bureau of International Recycling, 2023, https://www.bir.org/component/flexicontent/download/996/175/36?method=view
69. 'Iron and Steel Technology Roadmap', IEA, Paris, 2020, https://www.iea.org/reports/iron-and-steel-technology-roadmap
70. 'Visualizing the Abundance of Elements in the Earth's Crust', Visual Capitalist, 7 December 2021, https://www.visualcapitalist.com/visualizing-the-abundance-of-elements-in-the-earths-crust/
71. 'Iron Ore Facts', Natural Resources Canada, https://natural-resources.canada.ca/our-natural-resources/minerals-mining/mining-data-statistics-and-analysis/minerals-metals-facts/iron-ore-facts/20517
72. Allan Collard-Wexler and Jan De Loecker, 'Reallocation and Technology: Evidence from the US Steel Industry', *The American Economic Review*, vol. 105, no. 1, 2015, pp. 131–71, http://www.jstor.org/stable/43497056
73. D. Autor, A. Beck, D. Dorn and G.H. Hanson, 'Help for the Heartland? The Employment and Electoral Effects of the Trump Tariffs in the United States', 2024, NBER Working Paper No. w32082, National Bureau of Economic Research, https://www.nber.org/papers/w32082
74. 'Tracking the Economic Impact of the Trump Tariffs', Tax Foundation, 26 June 2024, https://taxfoundation.org/research/all/federal/trump-tariffs-biden-tariffs/
75. Adam Posen, 'America's Zero-Sum Economics Doesn't Add Up', *Foreign Policy*, 24 March 2023, https://foreignpolicy.com/2023/03/24/economy-trade-united-states-china-industry-manufacturing-supply-chains-biden/
76. 'Global Blast Furnace Tracker', Global Energy Monitor, June 2023, https://docs.google.com/spreadsheets/d/1hSyy-fVDCKowvpad2ql2P_GxCzWG7T_-rwkSs1rmBM8/edit#gid=1152851148
77. 'Pedal to the Metal 2022', Global Energy Monitor, 2022, https://

globalenergymonitor.org/wp-content/uploads/2022/06/GEM_SteelPlants2022.pdf
78. 'Brazil Launches China Anti-Dumping Probes After Imports Soar', *Financial Times*, 17 March 2024, https://www.ft.com/content/8703874e-44cb-4197-8dca-c7b555da8aef
79. 'Commission Imposes Definitive Safeguard Measures on Imports of Steel Products', European Commission, 1 February 2019, https://ec.europa.eu/commission/presscorner/detail/en/IP_19_821
80. 'The Race across Europe to Build Green Steel Plants', *BBC News*, 17 February 2023, https://www.bbc.co.uk/news/business-64538296
81. Healthcare, finance, education and information services account for 37.5 per cent of all employment in Pittsburgh: Andrew Schwab, 'The Collapse of Pittsburgh Steel: A Spatial Analysis of the Steel Industry Collapse in Pittsburgh and its Effects', 25 April 2023, https://storymaps.arcgis.com/stories/193c7822ffbf42e1bc3be7a463f69054
82. 'Economy at a Glance: Pittsburgh, PA', U.S. Bureau of Labor Statistics, accessed 29 August 2024, https://www.bls.gov/eag/eag.pa_pittsburgh_msa.htm
83. 'Rustbelt Renaissance: Pittsburgh Becomes an FDI Standout', *Financial Times*, 10 May 2023, https://www.ft.com/content/2da8f284-59f6-42a6-a154-aa58caf7e4b6
84. 'Pittsburgh Ranked 3rd Best City in America to Live', *CBS News*, 26 July 2017, https://www.cbsnews.com/pittsburgh/news/pittsburgh-ranked-3rd-best-city-to-live/

Chapter 8: Medicine

1. 'Nurse Fails Hilariously at Making Face Mask from her Giant Bra', *New York Post*, 14 April 2020, https://nypost.com/2020/04/14/nurse-fails-hilariously-at-making-face-mask-from-her-giant-bra/
2. 'A Grapefruit a Day Keeps the Coronavirus Away! Desperate Chinese Resort to Using FRUIT and BRAS as Face Masks', *Daily Mail*, 7 December 2020, https://www.dailymail.co.uk/news/article-7947709/A-grapefruit-day-keeps-coronavirus-away-Desperate-Chinese-resort-using-FRUIT-face-masks.html

NOTES

3. N95 means it filters 95 per cent of particles smaller than 300 nanometres.
4. In 2019 the Chinese government stated it produced 4.2 billion masks, implying production of around 11.5 million per day.
5. 'The Face Mask Global Value Chain in the COVID-19 Outbreak: Evidence and Policy Lessons', OECD Policy Responses to Coronavirus (COVID-19), OECD Publishing, Paris, 2020, https://doi.org/10.1787/a4df866d-en. It was not just masks. According to the World Bank, between January and August 2020, sixty-seven countries imposed 152 measures to restrict exports of medical goods more broadly. See Paul Brenton and Maryla Maliszewska, *Reshaping Global Value Chains in Light of COVID-19: Implications for Trade and Poverty Reduction in Developing Countries*, Washington, DC: World Bank, 2022, http://hdl.handle.net/10986/37032
6. 'Coronavirus Sparks a "War for Masks" as Accusations Fly', *CNN*, 3 April 2020, https://edition.cnn.com/2020/04/03/europe/coronavirus-masks-war-intl/index.html
7. 'Scramble for Virus Supplies Strains Global Solidarity', *Associated Press*, 15 April 2020, https://apnews.com/article/health-ap-top-news-international-news-global-trade-virus-outbreak-b37eadbf9885767d01270117820f4b37
8. 'Burberry Contributes to Fight against COVID-19', Burberry, April 2020, https://www.burberryplc.com/news/corporate/2020/burberry-contributes-to-fight-against-covid-19
9. 'Louis Vuitton to Make Free Masks for Frontline Health Workers', *Retail Gazette*, April 2020, https://www.retailgazette.co.uk/blog/2020/04/louis-vuitton-to-make-free-masks-for-frontline-health-workers/
10. 'Amid Criticism, Macron Vows to Raise Medical Gear Output to Tackle Coronavirus', *Reuters*, 31 March 2020, https://www.reuters.com/article/idUSKBN21I1PT/
11. Chad P. Bown, 'How COVID-19 Medical Supply Shortages Led to Extraordinary Trade and Industrial Policy', Working Paper 21-12, Peterson Institute for International Economics, 2021, https://www.piie.com/publications/working-papers/2021/how-covid-19-medical-supply-shortages-led-extraordinary-trade-and
12. 'United States Invokes Defense Production Act to Limit Exports of

NOTES

Critical U.S. Medical Supplies', Baker McKenzie, April 2020, https://sanctionsnews.bakermckenzie.com/united-states-invokes-defense-production-act-to-limit-exports-of-critical-us-medical-supplies/

13. 'Remarks by President Biden at Signing of an Executive Order on Supply Chains', The White House, 24 February 2021, https://www.whitehouse.gov/briefing-room/speeches-remarks/2021/02/24/remarks-by-president-biden-at-signing-of-an-executive-order-on-supply-chains/

14. 'Exclusive: AstraZeneca to Supply 31 Million COVID-19 Shots to EU in First Quarter, 60% Cut for EU', *Reuters*, 22 January 2021, https://www.reuters.com/business/healthcare-pharmaceuticals/exclusive-astrazeneca-supply-31-mln-covid-19-shots-eu-first-quarter-60-cut-eu-2021-01-22/

15. 'EU Vaccine Export Row: Bloc Backtracks on Controls for NI', *BBC News*, 30 January 2021, https://www.bbc.co.uk/news/uk-55865539

16. 'You're Like a Piece of Soap! MEP Blasts AstraZeneca's CEO: How Do You Have No Clue?', YouTube, uploaded by Publicae, 25 February 2021, https://www.youtube.com/watch?v=PQJvJoHBa4c

17. 'Covid Vaccine: Why Did EU Take AstraZeneca to Court?', *BBC News*, 18 June 2021, https://www.bbc.co.uk/news/56483766

18. 'Biden Uses Trump's America-First Vaccine Plan to Corner Market', *Bloomberg*, 24 March 2021, https://www.bloomberg.com/news/articles/2021-03-24/biden-uses-trump-s-america-first-vaccine-plan-to-corner-market

19. '15 Million Covid Vaccine Doses Thrown Away in the U.S. since March, New Data Shows', *NBC News*, 1 September 2021, https://www.nbcnews.com/news/us-news/america-has-wasted-least-15-million-covid-vaccine-doses-march-n1278211

20. 'How Trump's "America First" Edict Delayed the Global Covid Fight', *Politico*, 1 December 2021, https://www.politico.com/news/2021/12/01/trump-america-first-covid-523604

21. 'Fact Sheet: President Biden to Launch a National Biotechnology and Biomanufacturing Initiative', The White House, 12 September 2022, https://www.whitehouse.gov/briefing-room/statements-releases/2022/09/12/fact-sheet-president-biden-to-launch-a-national-biotechnology-and-biomanufacturing-initiative/

NOTES

22. 'Pfizer Expands its Major Manufacturing Network in Kalamazoo, Michigan', Pfizer, 12 October 2021, https://www.pfizercentreone.com/insights-resources/news-updates/pfizer-expands-its-major-manufacturing-network-kalamazoo-michigan
23. 'Moderna Announces Expansion of its Manufacturing Technology Center in Massachusetts', Moderna, 11 March 2021, https://investors.modernatx.com/news/news-details/2021/Moderna-Announces-Expansion-of-its-Manufacturing-Technology-Center-in-Massachusetts/default.aspx
24. 'BioNTech Provides Update on Vaccine Production Status', BioNTech, 26 March 2021, https://investors.biontech.de/news-releases/news-release-details/biontech-provides-update-vaccine-production-status-marburg
25. 'AstraZeneca Plans £650 Million Investment in UK', UK Government, 6 March 2021, https://www.gov.uk/government/news/astrazeneca-plans-650-million-investment-in-uk
26. 'Coronavirus Vaccine Makers Are Not Mass-Slaughtering Sharks', *New York Times*, 13 October 2020, https://www.nytimes.com/2020/10/13/science/sharks-vaccines-covid-squalene.html
27. 'Why Grandparents Can't Find Vaccines: Scarcity of Niche Biotech Ingredients', *Washington Post*, 18 February 2021, https://www.washingtonpost.com/business/2021/02/18/vaccine-fat-lipids-supply/
28. 'Lipids: The Unsung Heroes of the Pfizer and Moderna Vaccine', *Chemical & Engineering News*, 2 February 2021, https://cen.acs.org/business/outsourcing/Lipids-unsung-COVID-19-vaccine/99/web/2021/02
29. 'Covid: EU Approves AstraZeneca Vaccine Amid Supply Row', *BBC News*, 29 January 2021, https://www.bbc.co.uk/news/world-europe-55862233
30. 'COVID-19 Vaccines: How Important Is the Vial?', *European Pharmaceutical Review*, 8 February 2021, https://www.europeanpharmaceuticalreview.com/article/142130/covid-19-vaccines-how-important-is-the-glass-vial/
31. 'Waiving IP Rules Will Not Deliver More COVID Vaccines', International Federation of Pharmaceutical Manufacturers & Associations, 29 April 2021, https://www.ifpma.org/insights/waiving-ip-rules-will-not-deliver-more-covid-vaccines/
32. 'Transforming vaccine manufacturing CEPI', accessed 18 September 2024, https://cepi.net/manufacturing-and-supply-chain

33. Simon J. Evenett, Bernard Hoekman, Nadia Rocha and Michele Ruta, 'The COVID-19 Vaccine Production Club: Will Value Chains Temper Nationalism?', Policy Research Working Paper No. 9565, Washington, DC: World Bank, 2021, http://hdl.handle.net/10986/35244
34. 'China Threat to Halt U.S. Antibiotics Supply', *The Times*, 11 March 2019, https://www.thetimes.com/article/china-threat-to-halt-us-antibiotics-supply-36tm2v2xp
35. 'Annual Report to Congress', U.S.-China Economic and Security Review Commission, 2019, https://www.uscc.gov/annual-report/2019-annual-report-congress
36. Senator Josh Hawley's Office, 24 February 2020, https://www.hawley.senate.gov/senator-hawley-demands-answers-fda-coronavirus-threatens-drug-shortage/
37. 'Executive Order Ensuring Essential Medicines, Medical Countermeasures, and Critical Inputs Are Made in the United States', The White House, 6 August 2020, https://trumpwhitehouse.archives.gov/presidential-actions/executive-order-ensuring-essential-medicines-medical-countermeasures-critical-inputs-made-united-states/
38. 'Agenda47: President Trump Announces America First Trade Platform for Second Term That Takes Sledgehammer to Globalism', Donald J. Trump, 27 February 2023, https://www.donaldjtrump.com/news/6966e7ae-3dfa-445f-b570-69c6c72a882f
39. 'A Strong European API Industry Can Achieve Strategic Autonomy of the EU Health System', Medicines for Europe, November 2022, https://www.medicinesforeurope.com/wp-content/uploads/2022/11/A-Strong-European-API-Industry-Can-Achieve-Strategic-Autonomy-of-the-EU-Health-System-1.pdf
40. 'Why You Shouldn't Trust Anyone Who Claims 80 Percent of America's Drugs Come from China', *Reason*, 6 April 2020, https://reason.com/2020/04/06/why-you-shouldnt-trust-anyone-who-claims-80-percent-of-americas-drugs-come-from-china/
41. 'The U.S. Is Relying More on China for Pharmaceuticals, and Vice Versa', Atlantic Council, 20 April 2023, https://www.atlanticcouncil.org/blogs/econographics/the-us-is-relying-more-on-china-for-pharmaceuticals-and-vice-versa/
42. 'Securing Medical Supply Chains in a Post-Pandemic World', OECD Health Policy Studies, OECD Publishing, Paris, 2024, https://doi.org/10.1787/119c59d9-en

43. 'China API Market Report', Optima Insights, February 2019, https://www.optimainsights.org/reports/69-china-api-market
44. J. Cherian, S. Sarkar, M. Rahi, S. Selvaraj and B. Bhargava, 'India's Road to Independence in Manufacturing Active Pharmaceutical Ingredients: Focus on Essential Medicines', *Economies*, vol. 9, no. 2, article 71, 2021, https://doi.org/10.3390/economies9020071
45. Monica de Bolle, 'Barring Pharmaceutical Imports from China Would Hurt the United States and the World', Peterson Institute for International Economics, 22 February 2024, https://www.piie.com/blogs/realtime-economics/2024/barring-pharmaceutical-imports-china-would-hurt-united-states-and
46. 'China's Removal of Imported Drug Tariffs: Implications for Foreign and Domestic Companies', *Pharmaceutical Executive*, 19 June 2018, https://www.pharmexec.com/view/chinas-removal-imported-drug-tariffs-implications-foreign-and-domestic-companies
47. See McKinsey's Global Trade Explorer, https://www.mckinsey.com/mgi/our-research/global-trade-explorer-what-are-the-most-important-trade-corridors?sector=09m&eco=wld&toggle=i&year=2022&sub-sector=M78
48. 'Barring Pharmaceutical Imports, China Would Hurt the United States and the World', Peterson Institute for International Economics, 22 February 2024, https://www.piie.com/blogs/realtime-economics/2024/barring-pharmaceutical-imports-china-would-hurt-united-states-and
49. K. Callaway Kim, S.D. Rothenberger, M. Tadrous et al., 'Drug Shortages prior to and during the COVID-19 Pandemic', JAMA Network Open, 2024;7(4):e244246, doi:10.1001/jamanetworkopen.2024.4246
50. 'Global Supplier India Curbs Drug Exports as Coronavirus Fears Grow', *Reuters*, 3 March 2020, https://www.reuters.com/article/world/global-supplier-india-curbs-drug-exports-as-coronavirus-fears-grow-idUSKBN20Q0ZQ
51. 'Global Pharmaceuticals and the COVID-19 Pandemic: Insights and Impacts', European Fine Chemicals Group (EFCG), 11 December 2020, https://efcg.cefic.org/wp-content/uploads/2021/06/20201211_IQVIA-for-EFCG_Executive-summary.pdf
52. 'Inside Wuhan: Q&A from China Coronavirus Lockdown', *Channel*

4 News, 23 January 2020, https://www.channel4.com/news/inside-wuhan-qa-from-china-coronavirus-lockdown

53. 'China Turbocharges Bid to Discredit Western Vaccines, Spread Virus Conspiracy Theories', *Washington Post*, 20 January 2021, https://www.washingtonpost.com/world/asia_pacific/vaccines-coronavirus-china-conspiracy-theories/2021/01/20/89bd3d2a-5a2d-11eb-a849-6f9423a75ffd_story.html
54. X, April 6, 2022, https://x.com/aliceysu/status/1511558828802068481
55. 'The US Keeps Offering China its COVID Vaccines. China Keeps Saying No', *Bloomberg*, 6 January 2023, https://www.bloomberg.com/news/articles/2023-01-06/the-us-keeps-offering-china-its-covid-vaccines-china-keeps-saying-no
56. H. Xiao, Z. Wang, F. Liu, J.M. Unger, 'Excess All-Cause Mortality in China after Ending the Zero COVID Policy', JAMA Network Open, 2023;6(8):e2330877. doi:10.1001/jamanetworkopen.2023.30877
57. 'How China's Sinovac Compares with BioNTech's mRNA Vaccine', *Economist*, 19 April 2022, https://www.economist.com/graphic-detail/2022/04/19/how-chinas-sinovac-compares-with-biontechs-mrna-vaccine
58. 'China's COVID Situation Worsened by Lack of Local mRNA Vaccine', *Bloomberg*, 26 April 2022, https://www.bloomberg.com/news/articles/2022-04-26/china-covid-situation-worsened-by-lack-of-local-mrna-vaccine
59. 'Moderna Refused China Request to Reveal Vaccine Technology', *Financial Times*, 25 April 2022, https://www.ft.com/content/a481c129-c5aa-4972-84a8-3a45bb000098
60. 'Only Hot People Get the Pfizer Vaccine', TikTok, 12 August 2021, https://www.tiktok.com/search?q=only%20hot%20people%20get%20the%20Pfizer&t=1723462925701
61. See Duke Global Health Innovation Center's vaccine 'Launch and Scale Speedometer', https://launchandscalefaster.org/covid-19/vaccinepurchases
62. 'With First Dibs on Vaccines, Rich Countries Have "Cleared the Shelves"', *New York Times*, 15 December 2020, https://www.nytimes.com/2020/12/15/us/coronavirus-vaccine-doses-reserved.html
63. 'COVID-19 Vaccines: The COVAX Initiative', World Health Organization, https://www.who.int/initiatives/act-accelerator/covax

NOTES

64. Oliver J. Watson et al., 'Global Impact of the First Year of COVID-19 Vaccination: A Mathematical Modelling Study', *The Lancet Infectious Diseases*, vol. 22, issue 9, September 2022, pp. 1293–1302.
65. 'UN Expert Urges States to End Vaccine Apartheid', Office of the High Commissioner for Human Rights, 14 June 2022, https://www.ohchr.org/en/press-releases/2022/06/un-expert-urges-states-end-vaccine-apartheid
66. 'In Conversation with Soumya Swaminathan, Doctor of Science Honoris Causa', McGill University, 8 September 2022, https://healthenews.mcgill.ca/in-conversation-with-soumya-swaminathan-doctor-of-science-honoris-causa/
67. N. Gozzi, M. Chinazzi, N.E. Dean et al., 'Estimating the Impact of COVID-19 Vaccine Inequities: A Modeling Study', *Nature Communications*, vol. 14, article 3272, 2023, https://doi.org/10.1038/s41467-023-39098-w
68. Virat Agrawal, Neeraj Sood and Christopher M. Whaley, 'The Impact of the Global COVID-19 Vaccination Campaign on All-Cause Mortality', NBER Working Paper No. 31812, October 2023, National Bureau of Economic Research, http://www.nber.org/papers/w31812
69. 'Coronavirus Excess Deaths Estimates', *Economist*, 12 June 2021, https://www.economist.com/graphic-detail/coronavirus-excess-deaths-estimates
70. 'World Has Entered Stage of Vaccine Apartheid, WHO Head Says', *Reuters*, 17 May 2021, https://www.reuters.com/business/healthcare-pharmaceuticals/world-has-entered-stage-vaccine-apartheid-who-head-2021-05-17/
71. 'Coronavirus Plane Carrying PPE Arrives from Turkey', *Sky News*, 22 April 2020, https://news.sky.com/video/coronavirus-plane-carrying-ppe-arrives-from-turkey-11976949
72. 'Exclusive: Gowns Delayed as PPE Shipment from Turkey Impounded for Failing Inspection', *Telegraph*, 6 May 2020, https://www.telegraph.co.uk/news/2020/05/06/exclusive-gowns-delayed-ppe-shipment-turkey-impounded-failing/
73. 'Government Confirms 400,000 Turkish Gowns Are "Useless" for NHS', *Guardian*, 7 May 2020, https://www.theguardian.com/world/2020/may/07/government-confirms-400000-turkish-gowns-are-useless-for-nhs

74. 'DHSC Annual Report and Accounts 2021–22', National Audit Office, 26 January 2023, https://www.nao.org.uk/press-releases/dhsc-annual-report-and-accounts-2021-22/
75. 'Europe's COVID-19 Spending Spree Unmasked', Organized Crime and Corruption Reporting Project, 21 October 2020, https://www.occrp.org/en/coronavirus/europes-covid-19-spending-spree-unmasked
76. S. Bhaskar, J. Tan, M.L.A.M. Bogers, T. Minssen, H. Badaruddin, S. Israeli-Korn and H. Chesbrough, 'At the Epicenter of COVID-19 – the Tragic Failure of the Global Supply Chain for Medical Supplies', *Front Public Health*, November 2020, 24:8:562882, doi: 10.3389/fpubh.2020.562882, PMID: 33335876, PMCID: PMC7737425.
77. 'HHS Clarifies US Has About 1% of Face Masks Needed for Full-Blown Pandemic', *CNBC*, 4 March 2020, https://www.cnbc.com/2020/03/04/hhs-clarifies-us-has-about-1percent-of-face-masks-needed-for-full-blown-pandemic.html
78. 'Finland: Prepper Nation', *New York Times*, 5 April 2020, https://www.nytimes.com/2020/04/05/world/europe/coronavirus-finland-masks.html
79. A. Snowdon and A. Wright, 'Digitally Enabled Supply Chain as a Strategic Asset for the COVID-19 Response in Alberta', *Healthcare Management Forum*, vol. 35, no. 2, pp. 90–8, 2022, doi:10.1177/08404704211057525
80. 'U.S. Big Bucks Turn Global Face Mask Hunt into Wild West', *Reuters*, 3 April 2020, https://www.reuters.com/article/health-coronavirus-masks/u-s-big-bucks-turn-global-face-mask-hunt-into-wild-west-idUSL8N2BR410/
81. 'Global Face Mask Sales', Statista, 12 January 2020, https://www.statista.com/chart/29100/global-face-mask-sales/
82. 'The U.S. Invested Millions to Produce Masks at Home. Now Nobody's Buying', *Wall Street Journal*, 4 February 2024, https://www.wsj.com/health/healthcare/the-u-s-invested-millions-to-produce-masks-at-home-now-nobodys-buying-fee1c49f
83. 'China Pushes All-Out Production of Face Masks in Virus Fight', *Nikkei Asia*, 19 February 2020, https://asia.nikkei.com/Spotlight/Coronavirus/China-pushes-all-out-production-of-face-masks-in-virus-fight

NOTES

84. 'World Trade Report 2021', World Trade Organization, https://www.wto.org/english/res_e/booksp_e/wtr21_e/01_wtr21_e.pdf
85. 'Remarks by National Security Advisor Jake Sullivan on Renewing American Economic Leadership at the Brookings Institution', The White House, 27 April 2023, https://www.whitehouse.gov/briefing-room/speeches-remarks/2023/04/27/remarks-by-national-security-advisor-jake-sullivan-on-renewing-american-economic-leadership-at-the-brookings-institution/
86. 'COVID-19 Originated in China. So Did Diagnostic Tests That Saved Lives', Peterson Institute for International Economics, 3 January 2024, https://www.piie.com/blogs/realtime-economics/2024/covid-19-originated-china-so-did-diagnostic-tests-saved-lives
87. 'How Much Does It Cost to Get a COVID-19 Test? It Depends', Johns Hopkins University, https://coronavirus.jhu.edu/from-our-experts/q-and-a-how-much-does-it-cost-to-get-a-covid-19-test-it-depends
88. 'Covid: Watchdog to Immediately Investigate Covid PCR Test Cost', 12 August 2021, https://www.bbc.co.uk/news/uk-58191963
89. Z. Li, F. Liu, J. Cui et al., 'Comprehensive Large-Scale Nucleic Acid-Testing Strategies Support China's Sustained Containment of COVID-19', *Nature Medicine*, vol. 27, 2021, pp. 740–2, https://doi.org/10.1038/s41591-021-01308-7
90. 'Coronavirus: Russian Spies Target Covid-19 Vaccine Research', *BBC News*, 16 July 2020, https://www.bbc.co.uk/news/technology-53429506
91. 'Coronavirus: UK Got Vaccine First Because It's "a Better Country," Says Gavin Williamson', *BBC News*, 4 December 2020, https://www.bbc.co.uk/news/uk-politics-55175162
92. 'COVID Vaccine Leader Started with Wild Idea in Cancer Research', *Bloomberg*, 10 November 2020, https://www.bloomberg.com/news/articles/2020-11-10/covid-vaccine-leader-started-with-wild-idea-in-cancer-research
93. 'Coronavirus: Trump Moves to Pull US Out of World Health Organization', *BBC News*, 7 July 2020, https://www.bbc.co.uk/news/world-us-canada-53327906
94. 'Smallpox Eradication Model: Global Cooperation', Center for Strategic and International Studies, 17 May 2023, https://www.csis.org/analysis/smallpox-eradication-model-global-cooperation
95. Erez Manela, 'A Pox on Your Narrative: Writing Disease Control

into Cold War History', *Diplomatic History*, vol. 34, issue 2, April 2010, pp. 299–323, https://doi.org/10.1111/j.1467-7709.2009.00850.x
96. 'How COVID-19 Vaccination Campaigns Can Learn from Smallpox', Gavi, 10 February 2021, https://www.gavi.org/vaccineswork/how-covid-19-world-can-learn-last-person-get-smallpox
97. 'Commemorating the 30th Anniversary of Smallpox Eradication', World Health Organization, 17 May 2010, https://www.who.int/director-general/speeches/detail/commemorating-the-30th-anniversary-of-smallpox-eradication

Chapter 9: The Future

1. In the US, the EU and the UK, GDP per capita has increased around 1.5 times over that period. 'GDP per Capita, PPP (Current International $), World Bank, https://data.worldbank.org/indicator/NY.GDP.PCAP.PP.CD
2. Robert Lighthizer, *No Trade Is Free: Changing Course, Taking on China, and Helping America's Workers*, New York: Broadside Books, 2023, p. 36.
3. Daniel Yergin, 'Ensuring Energy Security', *Foreign Affairs*, vol. 85, no. 2, March/April 2006, pp. 69–82, accessed 3 September 2024, https://www.foreignaffairs.com/world/ensuring-energy-security
4. 'The Complication of Concentration in Global Trade', McKinsey & Company, March 2023, https://www.mckinsey.com/~/media/mckinsey/mckinsey%20global%20institute/our%20research/the%20complication%20of%20concentration%20in%20global%20trade/the-complication-of-concentration-in-global-trade_vf.pdf
5. 'Safe and Legal Humanitarian Routes to the UK', UK Government, March 2024, https://www.gov.uk/government/statistics/immigration-system-statistics-year-ending-march-2024/safe-and-legal-humanitarian-routes-to-the-uk
6. 'China's Protests: Blank Paper Becomes the Symbol of Rare Demonstrations', *BBC News*, 28 November 2022, https://www.bbc.co.uk/news/world-asia-china-63778871
7. Norman Angell, *Europe's Optical Illusion*, London: Simpkin, Marshall, Hamilton, Kent, 1909.
8. Q. Huang and Z. Li, 'Trade and Peace: The WTO Case', *China*

Economic Review, vol. 83, 102072, 2024, https://doi.org/10.1016/j.chieco.2023.102072

9. J.-W. Lee and J.H. Pyun, 'Does Trade Integration Contribute to Peace?', *Review of Development Economics*, vol. 20, no. 3, 2016, pp. 590–603, https://doi.org/10.1111/rode.12222
10. 'Blood and Oil: Why Japan Attacked Pearl Harbor', *Washington Post*, 1 December 1991, https://www.washingtonpost.com/archive/opinions/1991/12/01/blood-and-oil-why-japan-attacked-pearl/1238a2e3-6055-4d73-817d-baf67d3a9db8/
11. 'Russia Evading Sanctions Thanks to Shadow Trade Deals', King's College London, 19 September 2023, https://www.kcl.ac.uk/news/russia-evading-sanctions-thanks-to-shadow-trade-deals
12. 'G7 Australia Price Cap on Seaborne Russian-Origin Crude Oil', Federal Foreign Office of Germany, 5 December 2022, https://www.auswaertiges-amt.de/en/newsroom/news/g7-australia-price-cap-seaborne-russian-origin-crude-oil/2567026
13. 'Black Sea Grain Initiative', United Nations, August 2023, https://www.un.org/en/black-sea-grain-initiative
14. See Réka Juhász, Nathan J. Lane and Dani Rodrik, 'The New Economics of Industrial Policy', Working Paper No. 31538, Cambridge, MA: National Bureau of Economic Research, August 2023, https://www.nber.org/papers/w31538
15. See Dani Rodrik, *The Globalization Paradox: Democracy and the Future of the World Economy*, Oxford: W.W. Norton, 2011.
16. Between 2010 and 2019, cross-border data flows grew at a 45 per cent annual rate, from around 45 to 1,500 terabits per second: see 'Global Flows: The Ties That Bind in an Interconnected World', McKinsey & Company, July 2021, https://www.mckinsey.com/capabilities/strategy-and-corporate-finance/our-insights/global-flows-the-ties-that-bind-in-an-interconnected-world#/
17. 'Professional Protectionists', Centre for Economic Policy Research, October 2021, https://www.cepr.net/documents/publications/professional_protectionists.htm
18. See Richard Baldwin, *The Great Convergence: Information Technology and the New World Economy*, London: Harvard University Press, 2016, p. 297.
19. 'A Green Protectionism Wave', *Deccan Herald*, 10 July 2023, https://www.deccanherald.com/opinion/a-green-protectionism-wave-2813520

20. 'Global Carbon Pricing Needed to Avert Trade Friction, Says WTO Chief', *Financial Times*, 16 September 2023, https://www.ft.com/content/b2de8c00-a46b-41e3-ba8b-a1e9e0c8b975
21. 'Pericles' Funeral Oration' by Thucydides, translated by Benjamin Jowett, 1881, https://en.wikisource.org/wiki/Pericles%27s_Funeral_Oration_(Jowett)

Index

academic exchange, immigration and, 148–53
Academic Technology Approval Scheme (ATAS), 149
active pharmaceutical ingredients (APIs), 196–8
Advanced Semiconductor Materials Lithography (ASML), 121–2, 124, 129
Africa, 7, 44, 80, 103, 159–60
   and invasion of Ukraine, 57–8
   South Africa, 2, 33, 48, 64, 100, 183
   Sub-Saharan Africa, 27, 80
   West Africa, 27
AI *see* artificial intelligence
alarmist picture, painting (objection to warnings), 28–30
Alexander the Great, 35
Ally versus Ally (Blinken), 85
American Society of Civil Engineers, 177
American Soybean Association, 70
American system, 53
Amurthavalli, tea picker, 9–11, 27
Angell, Norman, 216–17
apartheid *see* inequality, vaccines and

APIs *see* active pharmaceutical ingredients
Aquinas, Thomas *see* God, self-sufficiency of
Argentina, 1, 38, 57, 59, 62, 71
artificial intelligence (AI), 118
Arusha Declaration, 44
Asia, 2, 5, 7, 16, 69, 124, 130, 133, 204, 208–9; *see also* China; Japan; South Korea
ASML *see* Advanced Semiconductor Materials Lithography
AstraZeneca, 191–3, 195
ATAS *see* Academic Technology Approval Scheme
autarchism
   libertarianism and, 47–9
   neo-*sakoku* and, 54–6
   totalitarian autarky, 49–52
autarky *see* self-sufficiency
Autor, David, 171

Baldwin, Richard, 223
Banerjee, Abhijit, 157
Bannon, Steve, 172
batteries, 5, 31, 96, 103–4, 106, 108, 111, 114, 176, 220
Beard, Mary, 36

INDEX

Beasley, David, 58
Bell Labs, 119–20
Bessant, Scott, 29
Bessemer, Henry, 165, 182
Biden administration, 21, 29, 109, 121, 129, 184, 192, 221
Biden, Joe, 7, 28, 54
   imposing tariffs on Chinese EVs, 108
   and mask demand, 191
   and nanotechnology, 121–2
   objective of the Biden administration, 121
   and Solyndra, 90
   and US Steel, 165
   and US gasoline prices, 88
BioNTech, 140, 144
Blinken, Antony, 85
blood, poisoning *See* people, exile economics and
Bohr, Niels, 144
Bolle, Monica de, 197
Bollmann, Hermann, 67
Borjas, George, 155
Boston Consulting Group, 129
Bourla, Albert, 207
Brazil, 2, 19, 23, 33, 61, 71–2, 74, 79, 92, 97–8, 103, 113, 167, 181, 183, 185, 194, 212–14
Britain, 1, 27, 58, 66, 76, 213, 216
   academic exchange, 148–51
   and closed country policy, 40–2
   and energy self-sufficiency, 83, 86, 93, 112
   existential threat to British steel industry, 169–70
   food self-sufficiency, ratio of, 61
   Great British Energy, 87
   historical head start in industrialisation, 181–2
   increasing exports and imports, 29
   infant industries, 52–4
   and Marielonomics, 156
   national energy self-sufficiency, 86–9
   numbers of immigration, 159
   'one country, two systems' agreement with, 215
   steel industry, Port Talbot, 168–70,
   steel recycling economy, 181–3 and 'tiny gardens of Eden', 43–4
Brown, Gordon, 15, 17
Brown, Sherrod, 97
Brundtland, Gro Harlem, 209
Buenos Aires, G20 meeting in, 15
Build Your Dreams (BYD), 96–7, 113
Buncombe, Andrew, 171
'Buy British', problem with, 74–6
BYD *see* Build Your Dreams

Canada, immigration numbers in, 159–60
carbon border adjustment mechanism (CBAM), 223–4
Card, David, 155–6
Carnegie, Andrew, 163, 171, 172
Caryle, Thomas, 38
Castro, Fidel, 154
CATL *see* Contemporary Amperex Technology Co. Limited
CBAM *see* carbon border adjustment mechanism

INDEX

CCSI International, 117
CDC *see* Communicable Disease Center
CEPI *see* Coalition for Epidemic Preparedness Innovations
cereal, 59, 61–2, 64, 76, 79–80
Chamberlain, Joseph, 53–4
Chamberlain, Neville, 3
Chang, Ha-Joon, 167
Chang, Morris, 130, 145–8
chemurgy, objective, 68 9
Chiang Kai-shek, 65
Chile, 62, 100–1, 185
China
    and academic exchange, 148–53
    alternative to protectionism in era of EVs, 112–15
    building out renewable electricity, 107
    China shock, 170–2
    chip choke on, 72–4
    and closed country policy, 40–2
    collapse of exports of masks, 206
    and critical minerals, 98–103
    and electric vehicles (EVs), 95–8
    and face mask shortage, 202–7
    future of steelmaking, 183–7
    Great Firewall of, 222–3
    investment in clean energy, 104–8
    meat and, 76–7
    and modern weapon systems, 118–21
    and Morris Chang, 145–8
    and nanotechnology, 121–4
    and overcapacity, 104–11
    and overproduction problem, 32–4
    and perfect storm, 22–6
    pharmaceutical nationalism, 195–200
    remaining problem of, 215–19
    and totalitarian autarky, 49–52
    sanctioning Skydio, 31
    science graduates in, 152–3
    and self-sufficiency in steel, 178–83
    semiconductor nationalism, 131–4
    shipping soy to, 69–72
    solar energy in, 89–92
    soybean production in, 65–6
    Spruce Pine quartz and, 126–7, 129
    and steel overproduction, 177–8
    and wind energy, 92–5
China shock, presence of, 16–17; *see also* steel, exile economics and
Chinese Communist Party, 73
Chinese Students and Scholars Associations (CSSAs), 149
chip choke, 72–4, 122–3
chip production, reshoring, 131–14
Chip Wars (Miller), 120
chipageddon, 117–18, 136, 137; *see also* silicon chips, exile economics and
chipmaking *see* silicon chips, exile economics and
CHIPS Act *see* Creating Helpful Incentives to Produce Semiconductors Act

Chu, Steven, 90, 151
clean energy, investment in, 104–8; *see also* energy, exile economics and
Clinton, Hillary, 24, 171
Closed Commercial State, The (Fichte), 39
closed country, policy, 40–2
Coalition for Epidemic Preparedness Innovations (CEPI), 195
Cold War, 11, 19, 21, 70, 85, 153, 208–9, 219
'Columbian exchange', 66
Communicable Disease Center (CDC), 208
consumer electronics sector, chipageddon and, 117–18
Contemporary Amperex Technology Co. Limited (CATL), 96
Conway, Ed, 126, 173–4
cooperation, downgrading of *see* exile economics
corn, exports/imports of, 58–62
COVAX *see* Covid-19 Vaccines Global Access
Covid-19, 139–41, 189–91
  face mask shortage, 202–7
  nationalistic grandstanding during pandemic, 207
  and pharmaceutical nationalism, 195–200
  and shark liver oil, 193–5
  and vaccine inequality, 200–2
  and vaccine nationalism, 191–3
Covid-19 Vaccines Global Access (COVAX), 200–2

Creating Helpful Incentives to Produce Semiconductors Act, 119–20, 129, 133–4, 152
critical minerals, 98–103
cross-border trade measures, 221
crude steelmaking, global capacity of, 175
crypto-Communism, 48
CSSAs *see* Chinese Students and Scholars Associations
Cuba *see* Marielonomics

Davies, Mark, 168–9
de-risking, framing, 17–21
Declaration of Dependence upon the Soil and the Right of Self-Maintenance', 69
Defense Production Act, 190–1
deglobalisation *see* self-sufficiency
Democratic Republic of the Congo
  cobalt in, 100–1
  share of staple foods, 59–60
developed countries, steelworkers in, 186–8
Devi, Sakunthala, tea picker, 9–11
digital insecurity, 7
Diogenes, 35–6
discrimination, avoiding, 112–15
dog-wash systems, chipageddon and, 117–18
domestic renewables production, protection boosting, 110
Dorn, David, 171
Dragon's Jaw, importance of silicon chips and, 118–21
Dranger, Teresa Jay, 189
Duflo, Esther, 157

INDEX

Egypt, 57, 215
electric vehicles (EVs), 95–9
   alternative to protectionism in era of, 112–15
   difficulty in accepting, 108–9
   fears of national security, 110–11
   speeding up global rollout of, 109
employment creation, immigration and, 145–8
energy, exile economics and
   alternative to protectionism, 112–15
   critical minerals, 98–103
   electric vehicles (EVs), 95–8
   national energy self-sufficiency, 86–9
   Nord Stream pipeline, 83–6
   overcapacity, 104–11
   solar energy, 89–92
   wind energy, 92–5
Erdoğan, Recep Tayyip, 97–8
Europe, 3, 7, 9
   breadbasket of *see* Ukraine
   building out renewable electricity, 107
   decline of globalisation, 9–34
   energy, 83–115
   far right in, 2
   food and, 57–82
   and future, 211–25
   and logic of exile economics, 15–22
   medicine, 189–209
   national energy self-sufficiency, 86–9
   objections to warnings of exile economics, 28–32
   and PPE stockpile shortage, 202–7
   silicon chips, 117–38
   solar energy consumer, 92
   steel and, 163–88
   steel recycling economy, 181–3
   and wind energy, 92–5
European Chips Act, 124
European Commission, 28–9, 86
European Union, 34, 40, 76
   future of steelmaking, 185–6
   imposing tariffs, 91, 97, 110
   introducing carbon border adjustment mechanism (CBAM), 223–4
   and vaccine nationalism, 191–3
EVs *see* electric vehicles
exile economics
   decline of globalisation, 9–34
   energy, 83–115
   fertilizer as example of, 9–11
   food and, 57–82
   and future, 211–25
   logic of, 15–22
   medicine, 189–209
   objections to warnings, 28–32
   origins of, 35–56
   overview of, 1–8
   people and, 139–62
   silicon chips, 117–38
   steel, 163–88

face masks, shortage of, 202–7; *see also* Covid-19
FAO *see* Food and Agriculture Organization
Ferguson, Niall, 70
Fermi, Enrico, 143–4, 151, 154–5

INDEX

fertiliser imports, loss of, 9–11
Fetterman John, 164
Fichte, Johann, 39–40
financial system, breakdown of, 13–15
Food and Agriculture Organization (FAO), 59
food, exile economics and
   American soy production, 68–9
   'Buy British' problem, 74–6
   chip choke, 72–4
   exporters of food, 60
   global usage of lecithin, 66–8
   importers of food, 60
   'made in China' label, 65–6
   measuring degree of food self-sufficiency, 58–62
   meat, 76–7
   national consumption, 58–62
   overview, 57–8
   security of, 77–82
   shipping soy to China, 69–72
   soybeans case study, 62–4
Ford, Henry, 68
Fourier, Charles, 45–7
France, 1, 11, 27, 32, 50, 62, 66, 107, 193, 195, 213, 217
   droit de sol, 141
   mask production in, 190–1, 205
   numbers of migrants in, 157
   rising restrictionist mood in, 142
   steel in, 170, 178
Francia, Gaspar Rodriguez de, 38–9
Frank, Andre Gunder, 56
Frederiksen, Mette, 95
Freedom School *see* Lefevre, Robert

future, exile economics and
   cross-border corporate data flows, 222–3
   globalisation changing shape, 222
   overview, 211–15
   problem of China, 215–19
   trade finding way, 219–22

Gadsden, Amy, 150
gallium, 102
Gallup, 157
Gandhi, Mahatma, 43
Gazprom, 83; *see also* Nord Stream pipeline
Gelsinger, Pat, 128
geography, food self-sufficiency and, 58–62
Gericke, Carla, 48–9
germanium, 102
Germany, 1, 11, 17
   and energy, 83–6, 91, 97, 107, 113–14
   and future, 213, 216–18
   and medicine, 193–4, 197
   national diet of, 60
   overproduction problem, 32
   and people, 139–44, 148, 157, 161
   searching for new forms of protein and oils, 66
   share of vegetarianism in, 77
   and silicon, 121, 132
   and soybeans, 68–9
   and steel, 170, 173, 177, 181
   and tariff reform, 53
   and totalitarian autarky, 49–50
Global Capability Centre services, 222

INDEX

global trade, major fragmentation of, 27
Global Wind Energy Council, 108–9
globalisation, decline of
   breakdown of globalised financial system, 13–15
   diagnosis of, 211–15
   future of globalisation, 222–5
   hyper-globalisation, 29, 221
   kicking away ladder, 26–8
   logic of exile economics, 15–22
   marking end of era, 15–22
   objections to warnings, 28–32
   perfect storm, 22–6
   retreat from *see* exile economics
   self-sufficiency, 11–13
   Sri Lankan fertiliser imports, 9–11
globalised financial system, breakdown of, 13–15
God, self-sufficiency of, 36–40
Goldman Sachs, 17–18
Great Britain *see* Britain
Great Depression, 2, 14, 50, 69
Great Illusion, The (Angell), 216–17
Great Leap Forward, 50–1
Gwangyang, 176

Habeck, Robert, 86, 89
Hamilton, Alexander, 52–3
Hanson, Gordon, 171
Hawley, Josh, 164–5, 196
Hawley, Willis, 3
Henderson, Donald, 208
Hill, Tony, 131
Hitler, Adolf, 49–50, 217–18
Hobbes, Thomas, 38

Hoover, Herbert, 3-4, 7
Huang, Jensen, 145–8
Human Rights Watch, 150
Hungary, 57, 113, 148
hyper-globalisation, 29, 221

IEA *see* International Energy Agency
IMEC *see* Interuniversity Microelectronics Centre
immigration
   academic exchange, 148–53
   employment creation born from, 145–8
   integration of Marielitos into workforce, 154–7
   migrant numbers, 157–61
   negative reception towards, 160
   negative sentiments on, 141–3
   scientific contributions, 143–4
import taxes, 1
independence, energy, 86–9
Independent, 13–14, 171
India, 1, 11, 23, 33, 41, 181
   and China crisis, 195–8
   and chip industry, 134
   and future of globalisation, 222–3
   imposing tariffs, 110, 185
   iron ore in, 183
   'Make In India' initiative, 29
   moving in same direction as Europe and America, 88
   national energy self-sufficiency, 86–9
   and overcapacity, 104
   politics of self-sufficiency in, 30
   response to Russian grain blockade, 57

India (*cont.*)
  shark liver oil in, 194–5
  steel production in, 177–8
  and 'tiny gardens of Eden', 43–4
  vegetarianism in, 77
  wheat production in, 61
  'world system' of trade beginning in, 56
inequality, vaccines and, 200–2
infant industries, 52–4
Inflation Reduction Act, 88, 107
infrastructure, digital connectivity of, 118–21
intermediate goods, 24
International Energy Agency (IEA), 94, 103
  examination of steel numbers, 172–4
  and overcapacity, 108–9
International Food Policy Research Institute, 59, 80
International Monetary Fund, 27, 34, 82, 177
international summits, failure of, 2
Interuniversity Microelectronics Centre (IMEC), 125
Ipsos, 142
Iran, 23, 183
isolationism, inclination to *see* exile economics

J.P. Morgan, 163
Jacob, Ian, 144
Japan, 1–2, 32, 65–6, 68, 92, 97, 132, 167, 181, 187, 214, 217–18, 220–1
  automotive might of, 112
  and closed country policy, 40–2
  critical minerals and, 98
  and food self-sufficiency, 60–1, 78
  melting of processed silicon in, 127
  Nippon Steel in, 164–5
  and 'photoresists', 125
  rice self-sufficiency, 60–1
  security of, 78
  semiconductor nationalism, 131–4
  semi-processed rare earths from, 99, 102
  and shark liver oil, 193–5
  solar panels in, 91
  and soy, 68–70
  and steel overproduction, 177–8
  Tōhoku earthquake, 134–8
Jingye Steel, 169
JIT *see* just-in-time model
Jones, Peter, 36
just-in-time model (JIT), 134–8

K-Chips Act, 124
Kabalkin, Roman, 66
Kant, Immanuel, 39
Karikó, Katalin, 144, 207
Kavanagh, Ben, 198
Keenan, Margaret, 139–40
Kenya, agricultural produce in, 80
Key West, Florida *see* Marielitos, workforce integration of
Keynes, John Maynard, 45
Kindleberger, Charles, 4
Koch, Charles, 48

ladder, kicking away, 26–8
Latin America, 7, 16, 40, 103, 114
Le Pen, Marine, 141

League of Nations, 230n9
Lebensraum, 218
lecithin *see* soybeans
Lefevre, Robert, 47–9
legacy chips, 136
Lehman Brothers, 13, 89
Leviathan (Hobbes), 38
Lewis, Arthur, 7–8
Leyen, Ursula von der, 28–9, 86
Li Daokui, 195–6
libertarianism, 48
Liebreich, Michael, 108
Liese, Peter, 191–2
Lighthizer, Robert, 212
List, Friedrich, 53
local manufacturing, encouraging, 112–15

McCallum, Ken, 149
McGuinness, Mairead, 110
McKinsey Global Institute, 214
Macri, Mauricio, 15
Macron, Emmanuel, 29, 58, 190
Malaysia, 19, 21, 26, 92, 220
Manningham-Buller, Eliza, 58
Mao Zedong, 50–1, 65, 70, 215
Mariel boatlift *see* Marielitos, workforce integration of
Marielitos, workforce integration of, 154–7
Marielonomics *see* Marielitos, workforce integration of
masks, demand for, 189–91
Material Economics, 182
Material World (Conway), 126
Mauritius, food insecurity in, 26, 82
May, Theresa, 40

meat, national food self-sufficiency and, 76–7
medicine, exile economics and
 global public goods, 207–9
 overview, 189–91
 pharmaceutical nationalism, 195–200
 PPE stockpile shortage, 202–7
 shark liver oil, 193–5
 vaccine apartheid, 200–2
 vaccine nationalism, 191–3
Mein Kampf (Hitler), 49
messenger RNA (mRNA), 140, 194, 199–200
Mexico, 1, 15, 21, 33–4, 71, 104, 113, 141, 160, 167, 185, 187, 191
Middle East, 57–9, 80, 213, 220
military-civil fusion, alarm of, 119–20
Miller, Chris, 120
Mimerel, Auguste, 39
Modi, Narendra, 29–30
Moldbug, Mencius *see* Yarvin, Curtis
mRNA *see* messenger RNA
multilateralism, rejection of *see* exile economics
Musk, Elon, 163

NAFTA *see* North American Free Trade Agreement
nanotechnology, 121–4
national agricultural production, 58, 79
National Biotechnology and Biomanufacturing Initiative, 193

national power, gauge of, 166–8; *see also* steel, exile economics and
National Semiconductor Strategy, 131–2
NATO *see* North Atlantic Treaty Organization
'natural experiments', 155; *see also* Marielitos, workforce integration of
neo-*sakoku*, 54–6
net zero energy target, 94
net zero migration, 141
New Hampshire Free State Project, 48–9
'new oil', chips as, 128–30
Nippon Steel, 164–5
Nissan Bluebird 2.0 GTX, 112
Nixon, Richard, 70
Nord Stream pipeline, 83–6
North American Free Trade Agreement (NAFTA), 171
North Atlantic Treaty Organization (NATO), 84–5
North Korea, self-sufficiency in, 51–2
Northern Ireland Protocol, 192
Norway, 142, 174, 180
Nvidia, 164
Nyerere, Julius, 44

Obama, Barack, 90
OECD *see* Organisation for Economic Co-operation and Development
offshoring, 113–14, 222
Ohno, Taiichi, 135
Okonjo-Iweala, Ngozi, 224
onshoring, 6, 11, 133–4, 203–4
Operation Warp Speed, 192–3
Orbán, Viktor, 141
Organisation for Economic Co-operation and Development (OECD), 28, 142, 147, 148, 157, 160, 176, 178
    global mask demand, 189–9
    steel overcapacity doom loop, 181
Organized Crime and Corruption Reporting Project, 203
origins of exile economics
    autarchism, 47–9
    closed country policy, 40–2
    infant industries, 52–4
    neo-*sakoku*, 54–6
    overview, 35–6
    phalanstery influence, 45–7
    recommending self-sufficiency as trade policy, 36–40
    religious strain, 36–40
    romantic strain, 36–40
    'tiny gardens of Eden', 43–5
    totalitarian autarky, 49–52
overcapacity
    China and, 104, 108–11
    self-sufficiency and steel, 181–2
    steel and potential for, 174–8, 185–6

Paraguay, 38, 71
Park, Chung Hee, 166–8
PCR *see* polymerase chain reaction (PCR)
peace, globalisation and guarantee of, 215–19

INDEX

Peloponnesian Wars, 36
people-to-people exchange, 150–1; see also academic exchange
people, exile economics and
   academic exchange, 148–53
   anti-immigrant sentiments, 141–3
   employment creation, 145–8
   immigrant contribution to science, 143–4
   integration of Marielitos into workforce, 154–7
   migrant numbers, 157–61
   overview, 139–41
perfect storm, potential for, 22–6
Pericles, 225
Perry, Matthew, 68
phalanstery, influence of, 45–7
pharmaceutical nationalism, 195–200
Phillips-Davies, Alistair, 92
Pittsburgh, Pennsylvania, 171–2, 187–8
Pohang Iron and Steel Company (POSCO), 166–7
political communication, challenge of, 224
polymerase chain reaction tests (PCR), 205–7
polysilicon, 111; see also solar energy
Port Talbot, steelworks, 16, 168–70
POSCO see Pohang Iron and Steel Company
Posen, Adam, 151
potatoes, 59, 66
PPE stockpile shortage, 202–7

Prentice, Deborah, 151
Pritchett, Lant, 157–8
protectionism, 1, 7, 11, 14–15, 17, 23–4, 33, 45, 53, 73, 80, 109–10, 112, 115, 133, 184–5, 220, 222–3; see also exile economics; self-sufficiency
pure-play foundry, chip manufacturing, 145
Putin, Vladimir, 57–8, 85, 219

quartz, chipmaking and, 125–7, 129

Rabi, Isidor, 144
Raimondo, Gina, 95–6
Rajapaksa, Gotabaya, 10, 12–13
rare earths see critical minerals
Reagan, Ronald, 84, 170, 219
Reciprocal Trade Agreements Act, 224
recycling, steel, 181–3
Reeves, Rachel, 29
reglobalisation, 221
REPowerEU, 86, 107
resource nationalism see critical minerals
rice, exports/imports of, 58–62
Robinson, Joan, 3
Rodrik, Dani, 221
Rogers, Richard, 131
Roosevelt, Franklin Delano, 4, 48, 224
Rousseau, Jean-Jacques, 37–9, 56
Rubio, Marco, 149, 164–5
Russia, 11, 148, 215, 218–20
   cereal crop in, 61

INDEX

Russia (*cont.*)
   as food exporter, 62
   gas and oil fields, 83–4, 92, 95, 107
   invasion of Ukraine, 10, 17, 57–8, 79, 87, 127, 142
   and medicine, 207–7, 214
   and Nord Stream pipeline, 83–6
   and steel, 177, 183
   Western sanctions imposed on, 30

Şahin, Uğur, 14, 139–41, 161, 207
sakoku see closed country, policy
Sanyustiz, Hector, 154
Schularik, Moritz, 70
Schwarzenegger, Arnold, 90
science, immigrant contribution to, 143–4
science, technology, engineering and maths (STEM), 147
Second World War, 7–8, 11–12, 15, 142, 145, 164, 167, 212, 217, 221
   compensation row, 132
   immigrant contribution to science, 143–4
   meat production during, 70
   protectionism during, 14
   soybean production during, 69
   vegetable oil imports from Asia in, 69
security, food, 77–82
Segre, Emilio, 144
self-sufficiency, 11–13
   and closed country policy, 40–2
   national energy self-sufficiency, 86–9
   as personal virtue, 35–6

autarchism, 47–9
   measuring in terms of food, 58–62
   of God, 36–8
   phalanstery and, 45–7
   recommending as trade policy, 38–40
   steel and, 178–83
   striving for *see* exile economics
   'tiny gardens of Eden', 43–5
   totalitarian autarky, 49–52
Semiconductor Industry Association, 129, 152
semiconductors, 5, 22, 29, 95, 102, 119–22, 126, 131–4, 136, 144, 153, 195, 220–1
shark liver oil, 193–5; *see also* Covid-19
Sheffield Forgemasters, 169
Shipworth, Michelle, 148
silicon chips, exile economics and
   chipageddon, 117–18
   chips as 'new oil', 128–30
   geographical diversity, 124–5
   just-in-time model, 134–8
   modern weapon systems, 118–21
   nanotechnology, 121–4
   raw materials, 125–7
   reshoring chip production, 131–4
   semiconductor nationalism, 131–4
Singapore, 51, 174, 180, 212
Singh-Watson, Guy, 74–6
Skydio, sanctioning, 31
Smoot–Hawley Tariff Act, 3
Smoot, Reed, 3

INDEX

solar energy, 111
Solyndra product, 89–92
   investment in clean energy, 104–8
Solyndra, 89–92
Soriot, Pascal, 191
South Korea, 15, 17, 26, 28, 32, 77, 122, 125, 127, 21, 221
   and future of steelmaking, 183–7
   and self-sufficient steel, 178, 181, 183
   and steel as gauge of national strength, 166–8
Soviet Union, 11, 50, 70, 84–5, 157, 219
soybeans
   American soy production, 68–9
   and 'made in China' label, 65–6
   and chip choke potential, 72–4
   and global use of lecithin, 66–8
   importance of, 62–4
   introducing to Brazil, 71–2
   shipping soy to China, 69–72
   trans-Pacific rotation of soybean production, 71–2
Spain, 1, 27, 38, 41, 107, 113, 170, 194
Spanish Armada, 40–1
Spruce Pine, North Carolina, quartz in, 126–7, 129
squalene *see* shark liver oil
Sri Lanka, fertiliser plight of, 9–11
Stalin, Joseph, 50
Steel City *see* Pittsburgh, Pennsylvania
steel, exile economics and
   exporter-importer statistics, 179
   future of steelmaking, 183–7

   gauges of national power, 166–8
   global capacity of crude steelmaking, 175
   looking at numbers, 172–4
   overcapacity, 174–8
   overview, 163–5
   Port Talbot steelworks, 168–70
   protection implementation, 170–2
   recycling, 181–3
   self-sufficiency, 178–83
   specialness of steel, 165–6
   steelworkers in developed countries, 187–8
STEM *see* science, technology, engineering and maths
Suez Canal, *Ever Given* container ship in, 31
Sullivan, Jake, 54, 121, 122, 205
Sunak, Rishi, 75–6
supply chains; *see also* energy, exile economics and; food, exile economics and
   critical, 152, 165, 213
   global, 22, 31, 130, 191, 205, 220, 247n40
   weaponisation of, 102–3
Swadeshi, 43–5
Szilard, Leo, 144

Taiwan, 21–3, 26, 65, 72, 102, 125, 127, 137, 145–6, 190, 212–13
   and chips as new oil, 128–30
   grasping importance of Silicon chips, 119–21
   reshoring chip production, 131–4

INDEX

Taiwan Semiconductor Manufacturing Company (TSMC), 121–2, 129, 145–6
Taiwan Strait, 21–2
Tanzania, self-sufficiency in, 44, 57
tariffs
   on Chinese imports, 74, 97, 108, 110, 113, 185, 220
   import tariffs, 34, 60, 61, 97, 180
   imposing, 1–2, 34, 43, 110, 113, 185
   new tariffs, 1–2, 33, 53, 113, 133, 185
   and perfect storm, 24–6
   on soybeans, 65–6
   steel tariffs, 166, 170, 183
   tariff war, 4, 7, 214
Tata Steel, 168–70
Tax Foundation, 183
Taylor, Andrea, 200
Teller, Edward, 144
Texas Instruments (TI), 118–21, 145
TI *see* Texas Instruments
'tiny gardens of Eden', 43–5
Tohoku earthquake, 134–8
Tokyo Electron, 125
Tooze, Adam, 33
Toyota, 134–8
Toyota Production System (TPS), 135–6
TPS *see* Toyota Production System
Trump, Donald, 3, 5, 7, 12, 110, 159, 171
   aspirations of economic 'decoupling', 21
   chip choke on China, 72–4
   and foreign college graduates, 161
   inaugural speech of, 16–17
   June 2015 speech, 156–7
   launching 'China Initiative', 149
   and mask demands, 190–1
   and neo-*sakoku*, 54–6
   Nippon Steel and, 165
   pulling United States out of WHO, 208
   reducing dependence on foreign manufacturers, 196
   and steel as national strength, 166–8
   steel tariffs of, 183–7
   and tariff retaliation, 33–4
   tariffs diverting trade rather than stopping trade, 220
   2024 trade election manifesto of, 23–6
   vindicating economic approach of, 170–2
Trumpf and Zeiss, 122, 125, 129
Truss, Liz, 87
TSMC *see* Taiwan Semiconductor Manufacturing Company
turbines *see* wind energy
Turkey, EVs and, 97–8

U.S. Steel *see* United States Steel Corporation
Ujamaa movement, 44
Ukraine, 6, 17, 30, 50, 84–5, 183, 215, 218–19
   invasion of Ukraine, 10, 17, 57–9, 79, 87, 142
   as major grain producer, 79
   refugees from, 142

INDEX

Russian grain blockade, 57–8
supplier of neon, 127
Uniper, 83; *see also* Nord Stream pipeline
United Kingdom, 11, 14, 17, 28, 32, 80, 87, 112, 117, 125
  and academic exchange, 148–53
  'Buy British' problem, 74–6
  food exports of, 60
  government, 14, 76, 106, 131, 149, 156, 182, 203
  and meat, 76–7
  migrant arrivals in, 156, 159–60
  Port Talbot, 168–70
  PPE stockpile shortage, 202–7
  reshoring chip production, 131–4
  and rhetoric of 'poisoning the blood', 141–3
  and self-sufficiency in steel, 178–83
  semiconductor nationalism, 131–4
  UK Independence Party, 159
  and vaccine nationalism, 191–3
United Nations, 10, 30, 57–9, 94, 157, 174, 208, 214, 216
United States
  and academic exchange, 148–53
  alternative to protectionism in era of EVs, 112–15
  building out renewable electricity, 107
  and chip choke on China, 72–4
  and critical minerals, 98–103
  and electric vehicles (EVs), 95–8
  future of steelmaking, 183–7
  implementing protections for steel industry, 170–2
  integration of Marielitos into workforce, 154–7
  and modern weapon systems, 118–21
  and nanotechnology, 121–4
  national energy self-sufficiency, 86–9
  pharmaceutical nationalism, 195–200
  and PPE stockpile shortage, 202–7
  public's estimate of first-generation migrants, 157
  and self-sufficiency in steel, 178–83
  semiconductor nationalism, 131–4
  solar energy in, 89–92
  Spruce Pine quartz and, 126–7, 129
  and steel overproduction, 174–8
  steel recycling economy, 181–3
  and vaccine nationalism, 191–3
United States Steel Corporation (U.S. Steel), 163–6, 171–2, 187
US National Academies of Sciences, Engineering, and Medicine, 156
US-China Economic and Security Review Commission, 196

vaccines; *see also* Covid-19; medicine, exile economics and nationalism and, 191–3
production of, 193–5

Vance, J.D., 164–5
Venediktov, Dimitri, 208
Venezuela, 23, 62
Vestager, Margrethe, 93–4
Vietnam, 26, 62, 92, 118, 185, 212–13, 220

Wall Street, 13–14, 117, 163
Wandel durch Handel maxim, 85
Wang, Seaver, 101
Washington, George, 52
Weirton, West Virginia, 171–2
WFP *see* World Food Programme
wheat, exports/imports of, 58–62
WHO *see* World Health Organization
Widodo, Joko, 101
Wilders, Geert, 142
Williamson, Gavin, 207
wind energy
   investment in clean energy, 104–8
   turbines for, 92–5

World Bank, 12, 167
World Economic Conference, 4
World Food Programme (WFP), 57–8, 79
World Health Organization (WHO), 202, 208–9
World Steel Association, 181
world trade collapse, 14
World Trade Organization, 15–16, 19, 23, 32, 34, 65–6, 215–16, 221, 223–4

Xi Jinping, 21, 33, 73, 82, 153, 199, 215–16

Yarvin, Curtis, 54–5
Yellen, Janet, 104, 164–5
Yemen, 57, 59
Yu Hua, 218–19

Zambia, food insecurity in, 80–2
Zheng He, 40–1